The Late Dramatic Works of Arthur Schnitzler

American University Studies

Series I
Germanic Languages and Literatures

Vol. 10

PETER LANG
New York · Berne · Frankfort on the Main

Brigitte L. Schneider-Halvorson

The Late Dramatic Works of Arthur Schnitzler

PETER LANG
New York · Berne · Frankfort on the Main

Library of Congress Catalog Card Number:
83-48139
ISBN 0-8204-0009-2

© Peter Lang Publishing Inc., New York 1983

All rights reserved.
Reprint or reproduction, even partially, in all forms such
as microfilm, xerography, microfiche, microcard, offset prohibited.

Printed by Lang Druck Inc., Liebefeld/Berne (Switzerland)

Meinem Bruder, Dr. Joachim Schneider, und den Angehörigen
meines Familien- und Freundeskreises gewidmet

TABLE OF CONTENTS

INTRODUCTION 9

CHAPTER   I: DIE SCHWESTERN ODER CASANOVA IN SPA 15

CHAPTER II: KOMÖDIE DER VERFÜHRUNG 45

CHAPTER III: DER GANG ZUM WEIHER 83

CHAPTER IV: IM SPIEL DER SOMMERLÜFTE 113

SUMMARY AND CONCLUSION 137

NOTES 141

SELECTED BIBLIOGRAPHY 161

INDEX 171

INDEX OF REFERENCES TO WORKS BY SCHNITZLER 174

INTRODUCTION

The more creative the artist, the more original the thinker, the greater the genius, the less can his achievements be subsumed under universal principles or general rules. If anything, he is the source of new rules...[1]

In spite of an increased interest in evaluating and appreciating the literary and intellectual development of Arthur Schnitzler, progress in this direction which would demonstrate a fundamental change of attitude toward the author's late dramatic works on the part of literary historians and Germanisten has been slow. The observation Lonergran presents in general about the creative artist and original thinker pertains to Schnitzler in particular, because in his late dramatic writings he departs from traditions and conventions generally accepted in the genre.

Richard Alewyn, one of the modern critics who in the past two decades also contributed to the growing reputation of Schnitzler as a writer, observed keenly: "In Deutschland...[zählten] die Pathetiker immer mehr als die Ironiker, die Lyriker mehr als die Prosaisten, die Tragiker mehr als die Komiker, die Philosophen mehr als die Psychologen."[2] This traditional view is one of the reasons, according to Alewyn, for reluctantly admitting, "[...] dass wir in ihm [Schnitzler] einen Dichter von überzeitlichem Range besessen haben. Er ist uns unentbehrlich aus dem gleichen Grund, aus dem er es schwerer haben wird als andere, uns davon zu überzeugen."[3]

Among important present-day scholars who share Alewyn's convictions and who themselves contributed to a greater appreciation of Schnitzler's literary excellence and intellectual complexity in his writings, are: Gerhart Baumann, Françoise Derré, Michael Imboden, Klaus Kilian, Ernst L. Offermanns, Herbert W. Reichert, William H. Rey, Hartmut Scheible, Martin Swales, Reinhard Urbach, and Robert O. Weiss.[4] They all agree that Schnitzler's artistic contribution to literature is unique because of his talent for handling with stylistic ease problems of the human mind and heart in their utmost complexity. Alewyn calls him "einen unserer wenigen Meister des Gesprächs, des witzigen Dialogs sowohl wie der zwanglosen Plauderei."[5] This unusually supple and evocative style serves to intensify the author's message. It is "[...] das Medium Schnitzlers [...] des Seelenzergliederers und Sittenschilderers, des Gesellschaftskritikers und Wahrheitsfanatikers, als der er berühmt zu werden verdient."[6] Reinhard Urbach suggests that Schnitzler research should begin to turn to details of the author's writings. He points out:

> Die Figur ist umrissen, das Werk bekannt — nun müsste ihre Eigenart durch Einzelheiten belegt und gestützt werden. Jenseits der Bewertungen des gesamten und einzelner Werke ArthurSchnitzlers, die meist den Sinn von Aufwertungen haben, muss festgestellt werden, dass es nur wenige Analysen und kaum Versuche kritischer Textuntersuchungen gibt.[7]

The purpose of this present study, therefore, is to concentrate through detailed analyses on the late dramatic works of Arthur Schnitzler in an attempt to show evidence that Schnitzler in his late productions is a better dramatist than critics have been willing to admit. This discussion will focus upon *Die Schwestern oder Casanova in Spa* (1919), *Komödie der Verführung* (1924), *Der Gang zum Weiher* (1926), and *Im Spiel der Sommerlüfte* (1930).[8] I decided to concentrate on these plays written in the period after the

European Conflict of 1914-1918 for the following reasons:

1. To disprove the notion that his late dramatic works have added little or nothing to his dramatic excellence.
2. To show that Schnitzler's range of theme, discussed in general terms by Frederick J. Beharriell,[9] truly goes beyond that of life and death: Schnitzler is concerned with social injustice, addresses himself to the problem of dueling and the double standard in man-woman relationships, deals with the currents of his time, when man is no longer at home in the religious, social, moral, and existential certainties of past ages.
3. To examine Schnitzler's works with regard to his penetrating analysis of human nature, which can scarcely be labeled "frivolous," "out of date," "superficial," "trivial" — as some critics have claimed. As a psychologizing author, Schnitzler is deeply interested in problems such as isolation and loneliness of man, quest for personal freedom and why man tends to shy away from true commitment and responsibilities, the dynamics of human conduct, the psychology of death, the problems related to a changing environment and philosophic outlook.
4. To demonstrate the difficulty of chronological order in Schnitzler's works because most of his later plays as well as prose works were originally conceived much earlier under working titles (many plays were developed from earlier prose sketches).

In these last four plays, the author has moved away "from impassioned youthful cynicism to a greater reflective maturity."[10] This maturity includes a revaluation of the author's ethical and philosophical views. Josef Körner made the statement that Schnitzler's later work is almost void of any metaphysical or ethical problems of a higher order at a time when German literature is again filled with philosophic content:

> Denn immer noch, auch in den gedanklich schwerst befrachteten Spätwerken, bleibt für ihn das diesseitige Leben der höchste, der unbedingte Wert und der physische Tod die absolute Entwertung; es fehlt jede über das Diesseits, über das Individuum, über das gelebte Nun hinausweisende Idee —, die Dichtung ist ohne Wort Gottes.[11]

A more realistic view is advanced by William H. Rey, who recognizes Schnitzler's ability of finding unity in polarity as a fundamental religious experience.

> Wenn das Staunen vor dem grossen Mysterium eine religiöse Grunderfahrung ist, dann erweist sich Schnitzler gerade darin als religiöser Dichter. Aber er ist es auch in einem anderen Sinne: Das Ineinanderfliessen des Gegensätzlichen, das er so oft behandelt, setzt ja eine Einheit voraus, in der die Widersprüche aufgehoben sind, die also Leben und Tod, Wachen und Traum, Ernst und Spiel als gleichberechtigte Komponenten umfasst. Angesichts dieser Einheit ist die Problematik von Schein und Sein von sekundärer Bedeutung. Die höchste religiöse Forderung wäre die Bejahung des Ganzen in seiner Widersprüchlichkeit.[12]

The idea of seeing unity in the various opposites recurs in all four dramas in the form of "Leitgestalten" and "Leitmotive." These are discussed to demonstrate Schnitzler's process of maturation. The author explored a variety of themes related to human actions and interactions and employed highly skilled techniques in adding increased complexity to the dramas. In this way he accomplished what Urbach summarizes as Schnitzler's artistic intent:

Immer ging es [...] in seinem Werk darum, den Menschen seiner Selbst bewusst zu machen und ihn durch Erkenntnis zu heilen [...]. Nur den einzelnen Menschen hat Schnitzler gestaltet. Es gibt in seinem Werk keine Masse, in seinen Dramen keinen Chor.[13]

But the characters of his late dramatic works take on greater complexity in direct proportion to their political, social, and economic involvement in society. Schnitzler himself was sensitive to the fluctuations of society which is reflected in his late dramas. In an interview with George Sylvester Viereck he tells us: "I must write of life as I see it. If I see it crowded with characters I cannot banish them from my play or from my story."[14] The plethora of themes in these late dramatic works follows the same reasoning: important issues of life require attention.

Not all critics recognize Schnitzler's viewpoint as valid. Beharriell observes "that the longer plays lose in unity through a tendency to break up into a series of 'Einakter'."[15] Although Martin Swales in his *Critical Study* of Schnitzler has contributed much to the so-called Schnitzler Renaissance, he seems to go not far enough. He still considers the one-act play "on the whole more satisfactory than his five-act dramas," which, he believes, are in line with "Schnitzler's mastery [...] in focusing on a brief period of time [...]."[16] Rey formulated his assessment of Schnitzler's works in a similar way: "Schnitzlers schöpferische Leistungen liegen auf dem Gebiet des Dramatischen und Epischen. In beiden Gattungen zeigt er eine Neigung zur kleinen Form, d. h., zu Einakter oder Szenenfolge und zur Erzählung," which leads Rey to the conclusion that "der Gipfel seines dramatischen Schaffens [...] in den Jahren vor dem ersten Weltkrieg [liegt]."[17]

In my present study I disagree with this point, because the complexity of Schnitzler's late dramatic works must be seen in conjunction with his theoretical writings: *Buch der Sprüche und Bedenken* (1927)[18] and "Der Geist im Wort und der Geist in der Tat. Vorläufige Bemerkungen zu zwei Diagrammen" (1927),[19] which are considered in this discussion.

Similar differences of opinion among critics exist in the area of organization. In previous Schnitzler research several attempts have been made to arrange the author's works into creative periods. Josef Körner speaks of three periods. He closes the first period with 1897, because "wirklich ist in den Theaterstücken und Erzählungen [...] die Welt einzig aus der Lebemannsschau gesehen."[20] An exception in this first period is Paracelsus (1899), because it is "tiefer und zukunftsträchtig; er eröffnet die Aussicht in eine zweite Periode Schnitzlers, die männliche; sie reicht bis ans Jahr 1913 heran."[21] A third period starts with 1915, called "die Altersperiode" which "hat noch nicht genügend zahlreiche und noch nicht so bezeichnende Werke hervorgebracht, dass man sie ohne Gefahr eines künftigen Desaveus heute schon zu charakterisieren vermöchte."[22] Richard Allen in his introductory survey observes that "many critics have designated the publication of *Der einsame Weg* in 1904 as the beginning of the author's second period [...]. With the publication of *Professor Bernhardi* in 1912 the second period draws to a close."[23] Consequently, the publication *Komödie der Worte* in 1915 would start the third period.

The most recent publication by Urbach divides the work into five categories:

(1) From 1886-1889, beginning of first occasional publications.

(2) From 1890-1893, visits of Schnitzler's to Café Griensteidl, first literary contacts with his later friends Beer-Hofmann, Salten, and Hofmannsthal, premiere of *Märchen*.

(3) From 1893-1895, struggle for literary recognition, success of *Liebelei*, first

publication of *Sterben* by S. Fischer in Berlin.

(4) From 1896-1914, recognition and considerable theater success.

(5) From 1918-1931, scandals, protests, hostility from critics, rejections, but also new success with prose works and film versions of his writings.[24]

My definition of Schnitzler's late dramatic works does not follow any of the above categories. I selected the author's latest four dramas because they display coherence not only in theme but also in the sense of a stricter ethical and philosophical standpoint. As will be shown subsequently, the "scandals" and "protests" which Urbach mentions in Schnitzler's last creative period are, for the most part, not directed toward the dramas discussed in this study. It will also become apparent that the "hostility from critics" and "rejections" in general accompanied Schnitzler's entire career; they are not merely restricted to his last years of creative activity. Schnitzler himself was concerned with the problem of journalistic criticism and its far-reaching influence upon public opinion and, consequently, on the fate of any particular work. The section entitled "Werk und Widerhall" in *Buch der Sprüche und Bedenken* (1927) reflects in numerous ways his discontent with critics: "Des Kritikers erste Frage müsste sein: Was hast du mir zu sagen, Werk —? Aber das kümmert ihn im allgemeinen wenig. Seine erste Regung ist vielmehr: Nun, Werk, gib Acht [sic], was ich dir zu sagen habe."[25] Among his posthumous papers can be found a notation which states: "Schon als Achtzehnjähriger begann ich einen Essay zu schreiben über die 'Grenzen der Kritik,' also schon damals, zu einer Zeit, da ich noch keinerlei persönlicher Erfahrungen gemacht hatte, fiel mir auf, dass es hier eine Frage zu behandeln gebe."[26]

When Urbach commented: "[...] sämtliche Werke sind ungenügend kommentiert," [27] I found this aspect true of the author's latest dramas, which in many cases have been refused the solid respect accorded to Schnitzler's early plays. Such views as those of Josef Körner in his article "Arthur Schnitzlers Spätwerk"[28] are no longer acceptable and urgently in need of revision. His introductory remarks read as follows:

> Ein heimlicher Märchendichter war Schnitzler schon immer, nur hatte er sein Wesen verhüllt mit dem Scheine zeitgerechter Wirklichkeitspoesie [...]. Arthur Schnitzlers Werk [...] bleibt bestehen als ein schwermütiges Märchen von der unnennbaren Süsse, der unbegreiflichen Not menschlicher Liebesbeziehungen.[29]

Sol Liptzin assesses this aspect in Schnitzler's work differently, because he recognizes that "as Schnitzler grows older, his characters mature with him [...] he becomes interested to an ever greater extent in the relations between husband and wife [...]."[30]

This realm of man-woman relationships is of importance in Schnitzler's latest dramas as a basis for increased psychological complexity. The concept of polarity, as will be shown, goes beyond the arrangement of characters to include polar ideas in the realm of ethics and philosophy. In addition, this study demonstrates that major conflicts in the four dramas arise, when Schnitzler applies the concept of triangularity to his character portrayal in order to show the scope of human interrelationships as they exist in a complex society. This concept of constellations is not unique to the late dramatic works, although Urbach seems to emphasize that point when he states: "Das Formprinzip seiner Jugend hat er in seinen späten Dramen auf die Durchführung einer Dreiergruppe reduziert."[31]

Brigitte Anne DeLay in her recent study shows, however, that the theme of triangularity occurs throughout Schnitzler's writings.[32] The intent and purpose of her dissertation is to show "all of the possible ramifications of such a constellation" (p. 3) in selected prose works, whereas the present study is devoted to an analysis of Schnitzler's late dramatic works. DeLay's work stresses the female characters in these triangular configurations; my study demonstrates that the pattern of triangularity not only involves the various characters, but also applies to concepts of thought and values. The two dissertations, therefore, are considerably different from one another.

To allow for better organization, each of the following four chapters uses these subdivisions: (1) Background of the play and statement of purpose; (2) Outline of the play; (3) Review of criticism; (4) Analysis of the drama; (5) Comparison with other late dramatic works discussed in the study. (Chapter I, of course, omits the point of comparison until the other three dramas have been analyzed). Each chapter closes with a brief summary.

Chapter I — *Die Schwestern oder Casanova in Spa*: There are three reasons for beginning this study with an analysis of this play: (1) As the first drama Schnitzler published after World War I, it contains key ideas which he pursued in subsequent dramatic productions in more detail and with greater consequences for his characters. These ideas include the complexity of human nature, especially with regard to his women characters; the question of fidelity in terms of "Heimkehr" or "Wiederkehr;" the acceptance of free will and individual responsibility. (2) As a "Gestaltendrama," a term suggested by Urbach,[33] it contains the constellations of polarity and triangularity which will also serve as a basis for the interpretation of *Komödie der Verführung, Der Gang zum Weiher*, and *Im Spiel der Sommerlüfte*. (3) The shift from the outer to the inner world of man, where life is truly lived, is emphasized in this drama and provides an important key for a better understanding of the author's late dramatic works. Rey's observation, "dass Schnitzler sich nicht auf eine Formel bringen lässt [...],"[34] applies also to his late dramatic work. It should not be permitted in the future, suggests Rey, to speak any longer of "Schnitzlers Gestalten" and with it mean exclusively the chain of egoists from Anatol, Julian Fichtner, Friedrich Hofreiter to the Casanova figure, because Schnitzler groups his figures in polar constellations. "Den Treulosen stehen die Treuen, den Selbstsüchtigen die Opferbereiten gegenüber. Dies verleiht seinem Werk die innere Spannkraft, die die gegensätzlichen Aspekte des Menschlichen umfasst."[35] This polar arrangement also applies to certain themes. The theme of the duel, for example, runs almost like a leitmotif through his mature writings. It is present in each of the four dramas, but in contrast to his earlier works, "it is no longer used to express Schnitzler's abhorrence of petrified social customs," points out Heinz Politzer.[36] "Much rather it is shown as an elementary constellation of human destinies, man fighting man for the possession of woman, age fighting youth because it refuses to abdicate."[37]

Chapter II — *Komödie der Verführung*: The constellation of Eros-Krieg-Märchen/Imagination is the dominating theme in this drama. It involves all characters and the various motives for their actions. This drama represents a process of moral revaluation which for two of Schnitzler's characters is a tragic one. The play conveys the message that one cannot experiment morally with a human being without fundamentally changing that person. The joint suicide of Falkenir and Aurelie is the result of their moral dilemma, as Martin Swales calls it,

> a dilemma which envelops them not because they are indifferent to moral values, but rather because the very intensity of their moral sensibilities leads them to misunderstand what is involved in morality, to sacrifice their spontaneous feelings to general principles.[38]

The war issue raised in the drama necessitates a discussion of Schnitzler's essays

Über Krieg und Frieden [39] and "Aufzeichnungen aus der Kriegszeit" [40] to show that Schnitzler took an active part in important issues of his time. He has often been criticized for not writing anything that deals with conditions and people of the postwar period. This kind of criticism generally assumes that he could not face the new times and therefore took flight into the past. "Certainly society as a whole and the social scene had changed dramtically," points out Robert O. Weiss, but more importantly he reminds his readers that "people as individual human beings had not turned into a different species. Their psychological makeup, their constitutive all-too-human faults had remained the same [...]." [41] I agree with Weiss, who considers the external changes after World War I "immaterial" to Schnitzler's work because the author's main purpose was not "to depict or protest objectionable political and social conditions." [42]

In addition, the discussion focuses on polarities such as Jugend-Alter, Lüge-Wahrheit, Träumen-Wachen, Leben-Kunst, Heimat-Ferne, Traum-Wirklichkeit to provide added insight into the drama. [43]

Chapter III — *Der Gang zum Weiher*: This drama adds another view to Schnitzler's already established reputation as a realist. The wealth of symbolism in the work shows that Schnitzler was interested in examining surrealistic aspects of symbols such as water and vision. The author's contemporaneity in this drama rests on his assumption for his characters that no guilt attaches to any behavior so long as one accepts the responsibility for one's actions and decisions. With regard to his women characters Schnitzler establishes the position that "women share with men not only the need to express their sexuality but also the desire to determine for themselves what course of action their lives will take [...]." [44]

In Sylvester Thorn we meet again an "Augenblicksmenschen," a character so predominant in Schnitzler's work. Because Sylvester reduces time to an abstract moment, he does not believe in memories; neither is he able to realize his freedom of choice. At the end of the play he removes himself from time permanently through the act of suicide. [45] This study disagrees with the one-sided interpretation of death as "the inescapable pinnacle of utmost, unspeakable loneliness" [46] by pointing to Schnitzler's polarity concept of death. [47]

Chapter IV — *Im Spiel der Sommerlüfte*: The drama deals with the peculiar relationship of skepticism and belief, doubt and trust and again shows the author's dialectic mode of thought. There is partial truth in every thesis and antithesis. When these polar opposites are recognized, a higher level of cognition may be found as synthesis. This dialectic way of thinking allows Schnitzler to view that which is chaotic as a justified part of life without hindering him to perceive reverently the cosmic order of the universe. As Rey observes: "Die Andacht vor dem Rätsel alles Seienden, die Beglückung durch die wunderbare Tatsache der Existenz — das sind Leitmotive von Schnitzlers Religiosität." [48]

The characters portrayed in this play are again modern individuals who live in a complex society. However, Schnitzler shows here, how society at times threatens their feelings of human worth and self-respect, which in turn pushes them periodically into passive patterns of living. The symbolism of the weather is related to emotional patterns such as jealousy, doubt, guilt, despair.

It is not the intent of this study to relate the themes found here to earlier works. That would be the task of a comparative study. Therefore, limited reference is made to works outside of the four dramas.

The main purpose in the discussion of each drama is to show evidence that — contrary to common assumptions — Schnitzler's late dramatic works continue to demonstrate his importance as a dramatist.

CHAPTER I

DIE SCHWESTERN ODER CASANOVA IN SPA
— Ein Lustspiel in Versen. Drei Akte in einem —

Background of the play and statement of purpose

The drama *Die Schwestern oder Casavona in Spa*[1] was published in 1919 by S. Fischer Verlag and produced a year later with some success at the Burgtheater on March 26, 1920. It is one of the rare productions which the author designated as "Lustspiel." He seems to have reached here the ability to create such "wundervolle Heiterkeit" which was a necessary condition, "um das wahre Lustspiel hervorzubringen."[2] Schnitzler himself confesses his fondness for the work in a letter to Hofmannsthal: "[. . .] mir selbst ist selten was von mir so lieb gewesen."[3]

Whenever a date of completion is mentioned for a work by Schnitzler, it must be remembered that it is really only a "date." Most of his works took years to grow into their final form, and since he was usually engaged in several pieces of writing at the same time, it is generally possible to find specific links between the emotional content of a given piece and the course of his life at the time of its composition. *Casanovas Heimfahrt*[4] and *Die Schwestern*, for instance, date from roughly the same years. According to Reinhard Urbach, Schnitzler had his first inspiration on March 28, 1908, at which time the working title reads *Eifersucht*. It was conceived as a one-act play.[5] After Schnitzler's perusal of the Casanova Memoirs in 1914 he changed the title to *Spion*, and by summer of 1916 he had decided to mold the text into a three-act play which he now called *Die Wiederkehr*. Only after that year did the play receive its present title. His prose writing *Casanovas Heimfahrt* progressed parallel with the play, and both works were finished by 1917.

A letter to Georg Brandes explains how he became interested in Casanova: "Meine beiden Casanova-Sachen, das Lustspiel 'Die Schwestern' und die Novelle 'Casanovas Heimfahrt' sind so entstanden, dass mir zwei Stoffe, die schon geraume Zeit unter meinen Papieren lagen durch die Lectüre [sic] der Casanova Memoiren plötzlich lebendig geworden sind."[6] Here is proof that Schnitzler chose to reconstitute faithfully a fragment of history because of his desire to illustrate a theme, and to study a psychological problem interesting to him.[7] These two productions stand outside Schnitzler's "popular" works and therefore are customarily neglected. Josef Körner, who in his study of Schnitzler's "Spätwerk", for example, does not hesitate to lay the comedy aside because it seems to him of "little importance,"[8] shows the Novelle not much more respect in his monograph of 1921.[9]

The purpose of this analysis is to demonstrate that this play has been underestimated until now and to prove that Schnitzler is better as a dramatist than critics have given him credit for. All major characters in the drama are interpreted in their relationships, problems and challenges. Recurring "Leitmotive" and "Leitgestalten" are discussed to show how they gain in complexity and depth, thus demonstrating a process of maturation and thereby a distinct positive development in Schnitzler's late dramatic works. "Ich empfand es als meinen Beruf," says the author in a letter to the Austrian historian Richard Charmatz, "Menschen zu gestalten und habe nichts zu beweisen, als die Vielfältigkeit der

Welt. Eine Handlung so zu führen, dass jede an ihr beteiligte oder nur an sie anstreifende Figur ihr innerstes Wesen preiszugeben genötigt wird, darin liegt am Ende das Geheimnis aller dramatischen Energie."[10] Indeed, the "Vielfältigkeit der Welt" is a key idea for a better appreciation of the author's late dramatic work. In it he depicts many life styles and also shows the consequences as a result of selecting one over the other; however, he neither condones nor condemns any of his characters for whatever choice they made, because each one represents an aspect of his soul.[11] "Every play is produced in the soul of the dramatist before it is staged in a theater," he tells George Sylvester Viereck in an interview, and continues: "A play is a conversation of the dramatist with himself. In portraying dramatic conflicts the dramatist wrestles with his soul."[12]

Outline of the play

All conditions are provided in the play to create a staging favorable to the unfolding of frivolous and joyous incidents. The scene is set in an elegant inn in the health resort town of Spa, on a lovely summer day. The characters are nearly all young, beautiful and charming. As age begins to touch them (a case in point is Herr von Gudar, who is over sixty) they make up for their lack of physical attraction by their polished manners and complacent philosophy of life. The less important characters are all "types" and include a nobleman, a rich widow from Amsterdam, eager to find a new husband, and a mother and daughter from Lyon, who are rivals in false prudery. They are all attracted by the preparations for an excursion into the countryside, preceded by a sumptuous outdoor banquet which is given by the false baron named Santis. He is eager to retrieve the cost of the dinner by inviting his guests to a gambling party afterwards. His wife Flaminia is young and sexy and just as scheming as her jealous husband, whom she deceives in order to further her own style of business. Then there is the famous dancer Teresa, who travels through Europe from one theater and lover to the next; and finally Tito, the hotel page, bold and hardworking in the duties of lover as well as servant. All, dominated by the legendary figure of Casanova, surround Andrea and Anina, the central couple, a wealthy young man of Ferrara and a young woman from the same city, with whom he has eloped and whom he counts on marrying very soon.

The play in its time sequence is limited to a few hours; it starts about mid-morning and ends before the feast has taken place. Act I of the comedy serves to disclose Anina's changed attitude toward the question of faithfulness. On the preceding night she received a visit from Casanova and yielded to his advances. Her confession provokes Andrea to outrage and, subsequently, a change of marriage plans at the moment when he discovers by chance conversation with his rival that Casanova, deceived by darkness and the location of their rooms, believed he was visiting Flaminia. Andrea, thus comforted, would be willing to pardon Anina, but she resents the motives which led to his change of mind. When Flaminia learns of Casanova's confusion of the previous night, she reasserts her rights over the man she considers as her conquest.

In Act II Andrea casts the existing quarrel into a fable. Santis and later Casanova himself are invited to bring a solution to the enigma that is posed. The question which justifies the entire play is this: "What does true fidelity consist of?" or, as Schnitzler formulated it: "Welcher Mann hat mehr Berechtigung, eifersüchtig zu sein: der, dem seine Frau gesteht, sie möchte gern einem anderen angehören, oder der, dessen Frau bewusstlos von einem anderen besessen ward?"[13]

In Act III all of the main characters — the two women, Santis, Andrea, Casanova — discern that what they took for a theoretical debate, the invention of a strict moralist, represents in fact a hurt which each one feels in his or her own vanity. The men conclude by drawing their swords to defend their injured honor at the cost of their lives. At this point, outside intervention is necessary to keep the tenor of the comedy. The dancer Teresa, introduced by Gudar, arrives on the scene just in time to restore peace among the rivals. She returns to Casanova with new plans for their future, thus reclaiming him for herself alone. This scene then brings reconciliation for all concerned, but only on the basis of an anti-social understanding of the term "fidelity." All except Andrea go off to enjoy the pleasures of the outdoor dinner and thus drown their disappointments and heartaches in the excitement of the evening. Andrea is lost in thought; he learns from Casanova the moral from the standpoint of an adventurer, who considers Teresa the most faithful of all, for "sie kehrte mir zurück. Nur das ist Treue" (733). [14]

Review of criticism

Ernst L. Offermanns is the only recent critic who analyzes the drama *Die Schwestern oder Casanova in Spa* in any detail.[15] Part of his title for the chapter reads: "Die erborgte Idylle des 'Lustspiels' " (110), referring to the designation which Schnitzler himself gave to the play. Offermanns recognizes the special position which this drama occupies within the context of the author's entire dramatic work. The carefully chosen term "erborgte Idylle" acknowleges the fact that Schnitzler's experience in writing a "Lustspiel" remained an isolated attempt to work with this genre, "dessen 'Spielheiterkeit' und Anmut nicht darüber hinwegtäuschen können, dass jenseits des Festes das Chaos und hinter der Göttermaske das Nicht-mehr-Menschliche lauern. Die nächste Komödie," Offermanns points out, "impliziert denn auch den Widerruf oder die Zurücknahme des 'Lustspiels'."[16] He refers to *Komödie der Verführung*, where the three women characters — Aurelie, Judith, and Seraphine — are not inclined to embrace each other. Max in his rather passive role as "Casanova" reports in the end for military service. "Die für eine Weile erborgte Idylle," concludes Offermanns, "musste zerbrechen." [17]

In theme as well as in terms of motives Offermanns considers this play a continuation of previous comedies, because the phenomenon of "impressionistischen Weltverhaltens" is associated with the Casanova-figure. To see this drama as a continuation of previous comedies is debatable, especially in light of the women characters who have gained in complexity, as this analysis will demonstrate. "Es wird auch, wie zuvor, eine Reihe von Konflikten vorgeführt," adds Offermanns, "die sich aus dem Gegensatz einer kontinuierlichen und einer auf den Augenblick gestellten Lebensform ergeben."[18] This polarity principle, however, received more attention in this play, as well as in subsequent dramatic works, than in earlier writings. The polar constellation of characters — Offermanns discusses in this respect Anina-Andrea, Anina-Flaminia, Casanova-Andrea — can be amplified by similar arrangements of incidents as well.

Klaus Kilian, on the other hand, does not examine any details of the play. His book, published in 1972 under the title *Die Komödien Arthur Schnitzlers. Sozialer Rollenzwang und kritische Ethik*, includes only a brief chapter devoted to "Schnitzlers 'erstes' Lustspiel."[19] His discussion focuses primarily on the adventurous role Casanova chooses to play which in his later years leads to complete isolation, rejection, and death. Kilian formulates the result of his considerations of the "role"-concept in modern sociology as well as of the range of meaning of the word "comedy" — as Schnitzler used it — in his central thesis as follows:

"Komödien als Bauform" — und zwar im Drama wie in der Erzählung — entsteht bei Schnitzler immer dann, wenn "Komödie als Verhaltensweise des Menschen" thematisch und in entlarvender oder vermittelnder Tendenz problematisch und programmatisch für das soziale Verhalten des Menschen wird.[20]

Earlier than Offermanns, Kilian considers *Die Schwestern oder Casanova in Spa* "am Endpunkt einer geistigen Entwicklung," and states: "Im Rahmen der Komödienproblematik bietet dieses Werk nichts eigentlich Neues, das nicht latent schon in der Thematik früherer Dramen und Erzählungen angelegt gewesen wäre."[21] Kilian does not find an unequivocal and final answer to the question,

ob Schnitzler hier tatsächlich zu einer echten Vermittlung der Ebenen von Realität und Rolle gelangte, oder ob diese Vermittlung nicht vielmehr erst durch die Aufgabe der Aktualität, eine resignierte Flucht in die Distanz der Historie, erkauft wurde [...].[22]

In line with the explanations Schnitzler provides for his diagram "Der Geist im Wort und der Geist in der Tat,"[23] Kilian points out the negative realm of the adventurer who is not bound by social roles and comedies of society."[24]

Similarly, Friedbert Aspetsberger in his article "Drei Akte in einem" addresses himself to the "Formtyp von Schnitzlers Drama"[25] and concentrates on the character of Casanova. Because of the double title of the drama, he considers *Die Schwestern oder Casanova in Spa*

eine Exempeldichtung; Träger des Geschehens ist hier die Casanova zugedachte Geisteshaltung, der Sinnzusammenhang ihr sich stets wiederholendes Handelnsschema, das 'Funktionieren,' mit dem er immer wieder die eigene Wahrheit ins Licht rückt.[26]

He points out correctly: "Die bedeutendste der Bedingungen für den reibungslosen Ablauf der 'Drei Akte in einem' ist der Verzicht auf die Zeit als Bestimmung des Lebens."[27] However, I disagree with his conviction that Anina and Andrea serve merely as background for the unfoldment of Casanova. As the analysis will show, the lack of development within Casanova is caused by his self-imposed isolation from society, whereas Anina and Andrea emerge as more mature human beings by the end of the drama.

Mme Derré by virtue of her all-inclusive study of Schnitzler's works provides excellent explanations for the 18th-century atmosphere chosen for the play.[28] Her outline of the play contains some commentary on nearly all characters, with most of her attention directed toward Casanova.[29]

Richard Alewyn in his article "Casanova"[30] provides the most detailed background information with regard to the historical figure of Casanova. He portrays him not only as adventurer and eroticist, but also as "Renaissancemensch" because of the diversity of his talents and interests.[31] Alewyn concludes with a valuable discussion of the Baroque and Rococo heritage which is evidenced in *Die Schwestern oder Casanova in Spa*.

Several scholarly studies recently published include a discussion of this drama with an emphasis on the women characters. They are important for the present study, because in his late dramatic works Schnitzler provides for more complexity of his women portrayals, no longer presenting them as mere types. Among these doctoral dissertations which deal specifically with women in Schnitzler's works, is the most recent thesis, submitted to the University of Wisconsin in 1973 by Willa Elizabeth Schmidt. It carries the title "The Changing Role of Women in the Works of Arthur Schnitzler," correcting some areas of neglect by scholars in their research and criticism. She points out that the most significant deficiency [...] is a unanimous failure to take into account the development which occurred in Schnitzler's attitude as he matured as a human being and as an artist. He has generally been judged, especially where his female figures are concerned, on the basis of his early writings, although even these are often seen in too superficial a light. [32]

She goes on to criticize "observers such as Boner, Derré, Rey and Körner, who are aware that the later works are different" and yet "do not offer detailed evidence of the effects of the change [...] but rather tend to persist in their original assessment of the women as all belonging to one or several static types." [33]

Schmidt's last chapter, entitled "Woman in Her Own Right," is still concerned with earlier types such as wives, fiancées and mistresses, but in the late dramatic works these characters have for better or for worse changed their roles, becoming more comprehensive, differentiated individual expressions of being. This chapter includes a brief discussion of the female characters analyzed in my study.[34] Schmidt "detects in the author an increasing tendency toward reflection and character analysis" in his late dramatic works which she finds "apparently better served by the prose medium, where he had time to study and dwell on psychological detail."[35] This leads her to agree with William H. Rey "that in the final period of his writing Schnitzler's narrative works are superior in quality to the dramas."[36] I disagree with this notion on the grounds that Schmidt herself overlooks some of the complexities encountered in Schnitzler's late dramatic production.

Another dissertation, submitted in 1949 at the University of Vienna by Susanne M. Polsterer, is entitled "Die Darstellung der Frau in Arthur Schnitzlers Dramen." Although the title indicates only a study of the dramatic works, the prose writings seem to receive as much attention as the dramas. She depicts Schnitzler as a threat to Austria and Austrian womanhood, accusing him of fabricating women characters in his mind in order to work off his own psychological problems: "Keinesfalls können diese Frauen als typische Wienerinnen aufgefasst werden."[37] She recommends Schnitzler's type of writing only for mature and stable people, and sees the work less fit for youth and for foreigners, because "die Jugendlichen müssen zu unrichtigen Vorstellungen über die Geschlechtsbeziehungen gelangen und die Ausländer zu unrichtigen Vorstellungen über die Österreicher."[38] Her work, therefore, appears to be an attempt to protect the national image of Austria in general and its charming Viennese women in particular rather than to recognize the reasons behind Schnitzler's concerns. As I see Schnitzler, his concern was a search for truth which he pursued with total honesty not only toward himself but also toward facing the prevailing conditions in his country. Such an endeavor most certainly attracts enemies, and Schnitzler, indeed, had plenty of experiences during his lifetime in this respect. Numerous articles have been written on behalf of Schnitzler to correct deliberate and inadvertently damaging criticism. Among those authors are Heinrich Schnitzler, Robert A. Kann, and Rena R. Schlein, to name a few.[39] One finds the slightness of such a study as Polsterer's even more striking when one looks at her interpretation of statistics compiled in an effort to justify her own moral and ethical prejudices. I concur with Schmidt's conclusion which states: "[...] her [Polsterer's] study cannot be taken seriously. It is a prime example of poor scholarship [...]."[40]

A third dissertation, submitted in 1930 by Georgette Boner at the University of Basel, entitled *Arthur Schnitzlers Frauengestalten* is mentioned here mainly for its significance in reflecting a welcome change in critical attitudes toward Schnitzler's women characters.[41] Her goal is, "das Besondere von Schnitzlers Frauengestalten im Gegensatz zu seinen Männerfiguren hervorzuheben."[42] A priori, she assumes, "dass Schnitzler durch die Frauen seiner gedichteten Welt ein positives Element beizufügen trachtet."[43] Although the author states at the beginning of her work that she will address herself mainly to the dramatic works, "[...] weil in diesen die Konflikte meistens akuter, die Entscheide dringender sind als in den epischen Werken [...],"[44] she seems to cite for her discussion almost as many examples from the narrative works as from the plays. A chapter entitled "Schwestern" discusses the polarity of negative and positive members within the male and female categories, which is based on Schnitzler's theoretical essay "Der Geist im Wort und der Geist in der Tat" (1927).[45] It also includes a discussion of the play *Die Schwestern*. Although Boner develops some excellent insights into Schnitzler's treatment of women in his works, she fails to see in his later dramatic production any changes in the nature of these women who, in their quest for emancipation, exert personal freedom and choice in such matters as love and marriage. Furthermore, she overlooks the complexity which the author realizes for his female characters in the later works.[46]

Analysis of the drama

The title: The first part of the title *Die Schwestern* [...] places the emphasis upon the three female characters in the play: Anina, Flaminia, and Teresa. They are, however, not related to each other by family ties, nor do they share other common interests on the basis of education, life style, personality traits, or family background. What allows them, nevertheless, to move into such a close relationship is revealed in the second part of the title [...] *oder Casanova in Spa*.[47] Casanova is the character who combines all three acts into one because through him the three women become "sisters of fate." He is the sophisticated adventurer, placed in the setting of the Rococo period around the middle of the 18th century, whose travels on a lovely summer day lead him to Spa, a plush health resort city in Belgium, at precisely the right time for another round of passionate relationships.[48] He encounters these three women who are united solely by their common ability to give themselves completely to a moment of pure sensuality. They are light-hearted, carefree people, as are most other characters in the play, without too much thought spent on the consequences of their moments of passion.

The Rococo theme: These characters help in bringing alive the Rococo period of the 18th century — Johannes Jahn calls it the end phase of the Baroque tradition —[49] which is characterized by fanciful, frivolous and light-hearted modes. Even though the psychological problem in this play was perhaps most interesting to the author, he carried the Rococo theme through the entire play. Because the style of literature in the first half of the 18th century was typified by light-hearted, playful lyric pieces, often with erotic hints, this comedy is written in verse. The tone of the play, as Mme Derré points out, "is livelier, the rhythm often breathless, the phrasing broken up by exclamation points and marks of hesitation; the vocabulary and syntax are adapted to the violent and perverse 18th century."[50]

The setting, with its alcove to the right of the stage, further emphasizes this period. Preparations for the evening dinner are made in the garden and not in the banquet hall of a Baroque palace. Most important, however, are the characters in the play, each of whom contributes to the Rococo atmosphere already prevailing. As Richard Alewyn points out:

> Das Rokoko ist der Erbe des Barock [...]. Man lebt hastiger und gieriger [...] man misst auch das eigene Leben nicht mehr nach den Massen der Stände oder der Geschlechter, die man repräsentiert, sondern man lebt sein persönliches Leben, das mit dem Tod unweigerlich ein Ende hat, ja schon vor dem Tod mit dem Alter. Man hat keine Zeit zu verlieren und will sich des Augenblicks bemächtigen, ehe er zerrinnt.[51]

In Act I, Herr von Gudar, a retired Dutch officer in his sixties, leads this kind of life. In his conversation with Anina he points out that aging people do not sleep: "Uns Greisen frommt kein Schlaf. Zu töricht wär' es, / Dem Wuchrer Tod, der bald des Daseins Schuld / Im ganzen holt, allnächtlich Vorschuss zahlen" (652). He does not find Anina very receptive to his "Lebensweisheit"; as a result of her youth, she is only seventeen, she connects the key words "Schuld" and "Vorschuss zahlen" with gambling. This leads her to believe that Gudar might have lost the game last night to Andrea, her fiancé, who returned with many gold pieces. But Gudar does not care whether he wins or loses, for to him gambling is fate, which he battles every time anew (653). To satisfy Anina's curiosity, he tells her that not he but Herr Casanova lost, thus introducing Casanova to the audience early in the play.

Twice more, to nourish his inspiration, Schnitzler had recourse to an actual personage of petty history, Casanova, attributing invented circumstances to the exploits of the celebrated seducer whom he used in this drama as well as in his Novelle. Thus, Schnitzler continues his treatment of the adventurer, a "Leitgestalt" appearing throughout his work from Anatol to Casanova. In his late work, however, he has reworked the adventurer figure to a greater complexity.[52]

Polarity: With the introduction of Casanova through Gudar, a polarity between age and youth is provided. Although polarity and inner tension are basic forms of all Baroque thought, of Baroque world experience and art expression,[53] Schnitzler carries them over into this play with its Rococo setting as well. This polarity principle appears to be the key to an overall understanding of the message which the poet conveys to us through his entire work. It relates such seeming opposites as youth and age, truth and falsity, dream and reality, gaiety and solitude, love and hate, reason and emotion, skepticism and belief, tragedy and comedy, life and death, fate and chance as equally justified components. Schnitzler says about fate and chance: "In logischem Sinne sind also Schicksal und Zufall niemals Gegensätze, sondern durchaus das Gleiche und um so unwidersprechlicher identisch, von je höherem Standpunkt aus wir ein Ereignis betrachten."[54]

This explains in part why Gudar looks upon his gambling activity not in terms of chance but of fate. The world around him may see in gambling nothing but chance; for Gudar, however, it is an important part of his life style. It provides him with pleasant memories of younger years, whether he thinks of his courage in combat or of his amorous adventures in Casanova-style. Gudar has been acquainted with Casanova for more than ten years, long before he "unter dem berühmten Bleidach / Freigeisterei und leicht're Sünden büsste [...]" (654). He knows him as part of himself and therefore does not seem to be worried about Casanova's credibility as an honest debtor, but Anina certainly doubts that Casanova can be considered a man of honor (654). Nevertheless, later she calls him a "nobleman." Now it is Gudar's opportunity to correct the picture in her mind, by saying that Casanova is a nobleman "wie Santis ein Baron, wie ich ein Fürst, / Und wie Flaminia etwa Nonne wäre —" (655).

Another aspect of polarity, that of "Schein" and "Wirklichkeit," — comes into play at this point, and involves each character. Gudar, as was seen, speaks not only for himself but also for Casanova, Santis, and Flaminia, when he describes the false roles each one of them is playing. Even Anina is not free of falsity. She pretends that she has only heard of Casanova's name; yet the audience sees her write a letter which she has the page boy Tito deliver to Casanova (657). Later on, in the scene with Andrea, she confesses to him her intimate relationship with Casanova the night before, which has changed her concept of faithfulness.

Although Gudar appears only twice on stage, at the beginning of the first and toward the end of the third act, the author has given him the major task of casting the proper light upon nearly all of the main characters, not only in negative, but also in positive ways as in the case of Andrea. When Gudar finds out from Anina that Andrea is not her husband — though twice before she did not correct him regarding her relationship — (653) Gudar pictures him as a respectable "Bürger" who will no doubt settle down to marriage. Later in the play, Casanova has the same opinion about Andrea. He sees himself bring "Ehrbiet'gen Gruss dem edlen Paare" for Andrea's goal "heisst Frieden, Ordnung und Gesetz / Wie Heimkehr Ihrer Wand'rung letzter Sinn" (681). As Gudar describes Casanova to Anina in his various roles as "Exzellenz," "Dieb," "Handelsmann," "Dichter," "Polizeiagent," "Millionär," "Bettler," "Bürger," "Falschspieler," "Lügner," "Gauner," "Ehrenmann," "Frauenheld" (656), he speaks actually of himself just as Casanova later discusses Gudar's life only to reveal the various stations in his own life (681). Thus, Schnitzler expands his polarity concept of age and youth to include a relationship between the two characters on the social as well as the intellectual level.

The concept of risk is for Casanova what "fate" is for Gudar. Alewyn points out:

> Ein Gewinn ohne Risiko erscheint ihm schlechterdings als unmoralisch. Er ist eine Spielnatur, jederzeit bereit, alles auf eine Karte zu setzen, und jederzeit gefasst, seinen ganzen Einsatz zu verlieren. Das Risiko ist es überhaupt erst, was dem Gewinn seinen Wert verleiht.[55]

Even though Casanova had spent his money, he continued his game on borrowed gold from Gudar. But he does not want to stay long indebted to Gudar. In order to return the money to his friend who is not a rich man, according to Casanova (679), we see him appear before Andrea to whom he had lost the night before, offering him an unsecured thirty-day promissory note. Among "men of honor," he considers his signature enough of a guarantee for return of the money. He reasons that Andrea is rich and, in addition, had won so much the night before. Besides, Casanova might return the money sooner, for he plans to travel with Gudar when he leaves town and hopes to win the money back at that time: "Ein Spielchen — auf der Fahrt, im ersten Posthaus; — / Und lächelt mir das Glück wie gestern ihm — / Und die Wahrscheinlichkeit spricht sehr dafür —, / So hab' vor Abend ich mein Gold zurück" (680). So we see Casanova scheming and manipulating, always taking advantage of the opportune moment, thus living up to the description Gudar gave of him earlier.

However, the real specialty for which Casanova is noted in European history is of course his adventurous love life: "Er sucht weder den Kauf noch den Raub, sondern das Geschenk," observes Alewyn and explains:

> Zu diesem Zweck gab es nur einen Weg: die Verführung, eine Kunst und ein Spiel, dem das Rokoko verfallen war und dem es in Bildern und Büchern gehuldigt hat wie kein zweites Zeitalter, von dem wir wissen. Ohne die Herstellung des seligen Einvernehmens, ohne die völlige Verschmelzung der Wünsche mit denen der Geliebten gibt es für Casanova keine Liebe.[56]

Andreas's suspicion that Casanova may have gained entrance to their bedroom and to Anina by force (672-673) is not confirmed, because Anina was at the open window expecting Andrea after a long night of waiting, and instead attracted Casanova, as she tells him:

> Er war's. Und eh' die Lippen mir
> Zu einem Schrei sich auftun, hat er über
> Die Brüstung ins Gemach sich frech geschwungen,
> Ist mir so nah, dass über meine Lider
> Sein Atem weht, dass seiner Pulse Beben

> Den meinen sich gesellt; — in seinem Hauch —
> Der kühl und heiss zugleich — kein Kuss, viel eher
> Ein Flüstern ohne Wort, ein Fleh'n, ein Bann —
> Doch endlich, ach, von meinem Mund ersehnt,
> Zum Kusse wird — löst all mein Sein sich auf,
> Und auf den Traumeswellen dieser Stunde,
> Vergangner nicht, zukünft'ger nicht bewusst,
> Treibt es, wie von sich selbst befreit, dahin. (673)

This moment in time, "der Augenblick," turns to an interval outside of time without effect or fear of consequences. Life was for the moment discontinued for Anina in favor of a dreamlike state of being, from which she awakens

> So reulos wie aus Kinderschlaf erwacht?!
> Unfassbar gestern noch — und heut erlebt?!
> Und fühle mich die gleiche, die ich war,
> So unverwandelt und so unverwirrt
> Und deiner Zärtlichkeit so wert.... (674)

Casanova, after shocking Anina mildly at first, thus achieves total harmony with her. He surrenders to her, and his devotion for the moment in time is reciprocated by Anina and remains lovingly in her memory: "In der Tat übertrifft Casanova alle seine Vorgänger in Schnitzler's Werk durch den Reichtum seiner Natur," comments William Rey.

> Er trägt, wie sie, impressionistische Züge, da ja sein Leben aus einer scheinbar endlosen Folge erotischer Episoden besteht. Aber es wäre doch falsch, ihn deswegen als einen flachen Genüssling zu bezeichnen. Im Grunde sucht er nicht so sehr das eigene Glück, als vielmehr die Beglückung seiner Liebespartnerinnen.[57]

The adventurer, then, is a frequent character in Schnitzler's work and is present not only in *Die Schwestern*, but also in other parts of the late dramatic works, where he belongs to nobody and nobody belongs to him. In his diagramm accompanying the essay, "Der Geist im Wort und der Geist in der Tat" (1927), Schnitzler himself relegates the figure of the adventurer to the lower triangle, thus indicating that the adventurer as a state of mind ("Geistesverfassung") belongs to the negative type. Schnitzler comments: "Das Verhältnis der negativen zu den positiven Typen im Diagramm 'Der Geist in der Tat' entspricht völlig den Verhältnissen im Diagramm 'Der Geist im Wort'."[58] In Casanova, the author created one of those significant personalities which, according to him, can also exist in the negative realm of the lower triangle; really great human beings, however, only occur in the positive area (*AuB*, 141). The author admits: "Erregend, belebend, öfter freilich noch beunruhigend, nicht nur durch seine Leistungen, sondern schon durch sein Dasein, wirkt manchmal der Repräsentant des negativen Typus in höherem Masse als der positive; wahrhaft fördernd nur dieser" (*AuB*, 141).

This description fits Casanova, for he evokes excitement wherever he is present, but his philosophy is based on anti-social premises. In his desire for unlimited freedom, he shies away from any responsibility or commitment. Schnitzler remarks in his *Buch der Sprüche und Bedenken*: "Das muss schon ein Mensch von hoher Art sein, dem die Sehnsucht nach Freiheit etwas Anderes [sic] bedeutete als die Begier nach Verantwortungslosigkeit."[59] By the author's own definition Casanova does not rank with a "hoher Mann." He lives only one day at a time:

> Der negative Typus lebt ohne das Gefühl von Zusammenhängen; das Gestern ist tot für ihn, das

> Morgen unvorstellbar, nur im Raum vermag er sich auszubreiten, er hat im wahren Sinn des Wortes 'keine Zeit'; daher seine Ungeduld, seine Unruhe und seine Unbedenklichkeit in der Wahl seiner Mittel. (AuB, 142)

The adventurer, therefore, follows an impressionistic life style.[60] He knows only the present, which consists for him of a sequence of isolated moments. Schnitzler deplores this kind of life, for "Wer aber nur die Gegenwart hat, der hat nur den Augenblick, somit eigentlich nichts" (AuB, 149).[61]

This restlessness which Casanova demonstrates by his quick change of travel plans, for instance, is a hopeless flight from his nothingness. To be sure, he is the "life of the party" wherever he goes; everybody remembers him and yet one may never penetrate the wall that is built around him, may never know anything beyond that which Casanova is willing to share. He is sociable but isolated, as the author defines the negative type (AuB, 142). Casanova only seems to stand in the stream of life; in reality he is rather distant from it. Gudar, Casanova's polarity, has even less to look forward to. The cardgame appears to be the only pleasure at his age, a means to fight, even though fate seems the only battle left for him, an old retired officer.

In his conversation with Anina, Gudar does not reveal much personal detail about Casanova beyond his amorous proclivity, which was already common knowledge in European resorts. Anina is eager to find out more; her encounter with Flaminia adds much to complete her picture of Casanova. Flaminia does not believe his story of escape from Venice, and therefore calls him a "liar"; his gambling habits are those of a "fraud"; his "age" makes him less desirable to women — just three days ago the famous dancer Teresa "walzed away from him"; and finally, with her last breath of disappointment and jealousy perhaps, Flaminia labels him "Trauerweide," "Schatten," "Narr," "Geck" (661, 666).

Anina, the polar opposite to Flaminia, does not seem to believe much of her talk; in fact, Anina realizes that Flaminia was driven to Anina's room by curiosity. Flaminia sees in Anina her younger sister in "trade" as well as personality, even the innkeeper considered them to be sisters (662). She is eager to share with Anina her own experiences and "tricks of the trade." We find Flaminia identifying so much with Anina that she ignores completely the latter's feelings and her efforts to set the record straight regarding her own reputation as well as the integrity of Andrea.

> Flaminia: Wie lange schon reisen Sie mit ihm umher?
> Anina: Drei Wochen, — *rasch* und wir werden uns vermählen. (662)

Much to Anina's dismay, she hears Flaminia speak of "providence" that the four had to share a carriage before they reached the town of Spa, and Santis, we hear from Flaminia, was already calculating:

> Wenn zwei Paare sich
> Wie ich und du, und Bassi mit der Seinen
> Zu Arbeit und Vergnügen klug gesellten —
> Zum grössten Vorteil schlüg's uns allen aus.
> Denn dieser Bassi — Santis' Worte sind's —
> Als meinen Meister muss ich ihn erkennen. (662)

Anina has not been able to stop Flaminia's double-mindedness, for neither did Andrea ever gamble before, nor is he a "Meister" — "in anderen Dingen" (663). She takes every possible opportunity to let Flaminia know that they have nothing in common, that their lives and affairs are miles apart. Her explanation as to why they eloped is cut short by Flaminia's answer:

> So fängt es eben an. Aus Flucht wird Reise,
> Aus notgedrungener Reise heitere Fahrt,
> Leicht wird der Sinn, und in der Fremde lernt sich,
> Was uns der Heimat Enge vorenthielt,
> Meist nur allmählich, — manchmal über Nacht. (663)

Flaminia even tells Anina how funny it is when she and Santis share their adventurous love affairs, "Denn, ach, die Welt ist dumm. / Zumal die Männer —" (663).

Flaminia seems to consider herself rather superior, and yet her "intelligence" is nothing more than natural calculation and cunning. She has attached herself to Santis who is nearly twice her age, mainly for reasons of social advantage, security, and protection — as a matter of convenience. When Santis had won heavily in his gambling activities, she seized upon the opportunity of acquiring a precious string of pearls. Now she assumes that Anina likewise is receiving pearls this morning from Andrea which, as she conjectures, must be the reason for his absence. Since this is not the case, she immediately judges him to be stingy (661). However, it is Anina who emerges as the intelligent woman from this dialog with Flaminia. With wit and humor she is able to counteract every one of Flaminia's exaggerated stories, whether they depict Casanova, Teresa, and Santis, or attempt to fasten upon Andrea's reputation. She easily sees through all façades and has already proven herself in this respect during her conversation with Gudar. She shows it again with Santis, who at this point enters the scene, boasting about the supper he will give in honor of twelve important wealthy people, while at the same time discrediting Andrea in the eyes of Anina as he blames him for wearing the mask of a philosopher (665-66). It is interesting to note that Flaminia used the same term earlier in the play (661). Thus, she and Santis display the same mentality in their thinking and reactions. They establish a polarity to Andrea and Anina.

In Act II, Anina continues to control her relationship with Flaminia by means of humor, but now it is used as a weapon of defense in her own behalf. She no longer protects Andrea and his reputation by the kind of love, concern and respect we saw her employ before. Her argument with Andrea over the night she spent with Casanova and the ensuing changes in Andrea after his conference with Casanova have left her with heartache and disappointment. She is ready to break her relationship and leave him without delay. This provides a humorous incident when Andrea opens the door to part with Anina just at the moment that Flaminia has come to the door inviting them to the table for the festive evening meal (695-96). She seems to be familiar with marital quarreling, which she calls "Liebeszank." Probably her own experience of having been beaten by the husband is recalled, as she projects it into this situation. Her advice to Anina is simple: "Man hat gezankt — / Man söhnt sich wieder aus. So ist's der Brauch" (696). Two more reasons for reconciliation are of a practical nature to her: a thunderstorm may break out at any moment and, furthermore, as no carriages are available in Spa this afternoon, walking in such weather is not the thing to do (696).

As soon as the spotlight falls on Flaminia and her disappointing "night in waiting for Casanova," and Andrea creates suspense in releasing the real reason for Anina's sudden departure, the "older sister" is no longer interested in repairing discrepancies and disharmonies between Andrea and Anina. She turns instead in self-pity to her own misery, throwing insults at them at every opportunity. Her dramatization develops along the lines of polarity:

>   Ins Leere durstig breitet sich mein Arm —
>   Indessen schlingt der ihre sich um ihn? ! —
>   Die Nachtluft trink' ich, seine Küsse die — (697)

Flaminia's eyes are red from crying, staring sleepless into the gray dawn; Anina's are slumbering blissfully, dreaming happily into the sweet morning. Another polarity with a double twist refers to their bedrooms. Flaminia is waiting passionately in her "chaste" bedside, whereas Anina knows how to lure Casanova into her "voluptuous" bed (697-98). Apparently, Flaminia regards herself as virginal before each new sexual encounter but considers a rival as innately wanton if the same man is the object of desire.

The insults increase in intensity as she questions Anina's origin and relegates her to a "Mädchenkammer, Freudenhaus" (698), where Andrea must have bought her from a procuress. Flaminia considers herself a good-natured fool to have given them a ride in her husband's carriage to Spa, treating Anina as a "girl friend and sister" in the face of this deception. Her earlier arrogance about "die Welt ist dumm — zumal die Männer" is taking its toll on Flaminia because now "die Welt is dumm — zumal die Frauen" fits Flaminia's situation much better in more than one way. When one compares the two women in their distress, Anina behaves in a more dignified manner, whereas Flaminia shows a rather vulgar personality. Another polarity occurs with regard to the women's intentions. At the beginning of the encounter it was Anina who was rushing after Casanova, according to Andrea; now, it is Flaminia who discloses her desire to forgo the dinner gladly and "fly after Casanova" (699).

Clearly, it is Flaminia who has lost her temper in this mutual rivalry, which has the opposite effect upon Anina. She perceives keenly in Flaminia a reflection of her own fate, and this helps her to gain distance. She is able to adopt an attitude of humorous observation which turns Flaminia to greater outrage, hatred, and bitterness. The stage directions read: "Anina hat zuerst starr, dann immer gelöster und heiterer den Worten der Flaminia gelauscht. Der Ausdruck ihres Antlitzes zeigt, dass sie den Humor der Sachlage zu erfassen beginnt und immer bereiter wird, sich ihm selbst anzupassen" (699). In Anina's reply to Flaminia she repeats the same words of advice given to her earlier about the stormy weather and the shortage of carriages. Flaminia finally resorts to cunning in hopes of winning out over Anina, who insists just as stubbornly now on her right to Casanova as does Flaminia. The dispute in its polar situation becomes a serious psychological problem for both:

Flamina:	Was kommt dich Böse an,
	Dass du mir nehmen willst, mir vorenthalten,
	Was Rechtens mein? ! Du Unersättliche! —
	Dass du, sei's nun durch Zufall oder Lust,
	Doch unverdient gewiss, die Seine warst,
	Ist das nicht Glücks genug? Willst du noch mehr?
Anina:	Ich war die Seine nicht.
Flaminia:	Wer denn als du?
Anina:	Viel eher du.
Flaminia:	Für ihn, doch nicht für mich.
Anina:	Er weiss nicht, dass ich's war, so war ich's nicht.
Flaminia:	Ich war's nicht, denn ich weiss, dass ich's nicht war.
Anina:	So hätten beide wir ein Recht an ihn. (701)

Both women suffer in their vanity because only a portion of their love has been fulfilled. Anina is longing for Casanova's individual affection, since he only desired her because he thought she was Flaminia; and the latter is longing for the physical consummation of love with Casanova which he gave to Anina. The inner disturbance and disappointment present in both women finds opposite relief. Rage and anger in Flaminia intensify to an open attack against Anina: "Und da die finst're Nacht dir hold gesinnt, / Sei ewig sie um dich. Mit dieser Nadel —" (703). The attempt of blinding Anina with the hairpin fails, but it shows clearly the pinnacle of Flaminia's jealousy, grudging her any daytime encounter with Casanova, just as Anina is too jealous to allow Flaminia a night with Casanova. This day and night polarity finds also a parallel in the behavior of both women. Anina, although she is just as insistent and stubborn as Flaminia, handles the entire encounter from beginning to end with humor, even though the humor is aimed at Flaminia as a challenge. Flaminia, on the other hand, is unable to recognize this maneuver which places her out of control entirely; her only responses are insults.

However, at the moment of greatest danger, Andrea comes to the rescue of Anina by stepping between the women and taking each by the hand. Forgetting his own trouble for the time being, he assumes the role of mediator and tries to handle with reason and objectivity a situation which cannot be resolved in the presence of flaring emotions. He objectifies the happenings by lifting them out of the highly charged personal realm and dressing them in a parable about two sisters, one of whom is to be married soon but finds herself in the arms of her sister's lover before her own wedding has yet taken place. With the consent of Flaminia and Anina, the controversial question from the parable is to be answered by Santis who, "etwas betrunken, noch in der Tür" (703), is urging Flaminia to get ready for the celebration. It is ironic that Santis is considered qualified for the job of arbiter on the supposition that he is facing this question "unverwirrten Sinns" (709). But Santis, by reason of his intelligence and, mainly his physical condition, is unable to tell the end of the story. He suggests instead that Casanova fulfill the task because

> ... was Erfahrung anbetrifft, so findet
> Zu so verzwickter Rätsel Lösung sich
> Wohl mancher, der in Liebeslanden weiter
> Als ich gereist und mehr sich umgetan. (709)

Nevertheless, Andrea handled this situation with more elegance than he had managed his own quarrel with Anina. This time he succeeded in lifting the circumstances from the sphere of mere passion into the proposition of a mathematical problem (718), and even succeeded in having both women agree with his story in their identification as "sisters" (705), a phrase which translates more accurately into "sisters of fate." Thus, Andrea in his role as mediator finds his polar counterpart in Casanova.

The name "Casanova," and Santis' assurance that he is safely back in town as an invited guest to the evening dinner, has an electrifying effect upon Anina and Flaminia. At the end of Act II, they seem to have forgotten their quarrel and are now impatiently waiting for him.

> Flaminia: Wo bleibt er denn?
> Anina: Warum lässt er uns warten?
> [...]
> Flaminia: Er ist es!
> [...]
> Anina: Er! *Anina und Flaminia öffnen das Fenster.* (712-13)

But why had Casanova left town in the first place? Returning to the first Act, we find Andrea and Anina in an argument over a letter to Casanova. Andrea knows that

Anina wrote this letter, but he is even more humiliated that she employed Tito, the lad of the inn, to deliver it. Andrea's reproach grows stronger with every new idea he expresses. He suspects that Anina in her vanity has inquired more in detail about the lace from Brussels which Casanova had promised to buy from a friend at more favorable prices. Andrea had overheard the conversation between them the night before. Anina could have left Andrea in his belief, but faithful to her promise "Du weisst, dass ich nicht lügen will, noch kann" (668), she tells him the truth: her letter contained a request "Dass er noch in dieser Stunde / Die Stadt verlasse" (669). This knowledge creates even more anxiety within Andrea, because his pride and vanity are hurt. "[...] ihm verfallen —? Und ich bin nichts [...]?" (669). He continues with ideas very close to Schnitzler's own heart.

> [...] Als wäre Sehnsucht nicht
> Um Tausendfaches schlimmer als Erfüllung,
> Weil sie fortwühlend in der Seele Gründen
> Den reinen Lauf ihr bis zur Quelle trübt —! (670).

Andrea gives here the answer to a problem which Schnitzler pondered in his aphorisms:

> Ist der berechtigter zur Eifersucht, dessen Frau früher einen Geliebten hatte, mit dem sie nun völlig fertig ist, oder einer, dessen Frau als Mädchen geliebt hat, ohne den Geliebten zu besitzen, so dass sie noch immer voll Begehrens ist? [62]

Since Andrea senses in Anina a longing for Casanova, not realizing as yet that she has been fulfilled, he has an impulse to leave the place immediately, thus breaking his relationship with Anina. He considers her confession a joke, and is disappointed that she would become so friendly with those adventurous people as to follow through with a type of trick that must have been suggested to her. The fact that she really had spent the night with Casanova and has demanded his departure in return does not register with Andrea at this point. However, he at least recognizes that neither Anina nor he himself fits into this kind of company. He also regrets the gambling activity he engaged in the night before, because he realizes the risk in leaving Anina alone for so many hours. This town, as he sees it, is a potential danger and a source of confusion for them; so he is ready to leave together with Anina at the same hour. This presents a comic situation for the audience, because all negatives have already befallen the couple and they will, in fact, sharpen in focus as the scene goes on into the next act.

Anina's statement "Ob wir uns trennen müssen, steht bei dir" (672) places the proof of true love and continued trust upon Andrea. The thought of searching her own conscience does not enter her mind at all. She explains that all came about because she felt neglected by Andrea, longing and waiting all night for him. She considers her experience with Casanova an involuntary dream state which has passed as quickly as it came upon her, never to return again and not having any consequences "weil nichts geschah" (674). But Andrea needs to go full circle before he is able to gain a similar conviction.

The thought "Weil nichts geschah" would never mean anything to the opposite couple, Santis and Flaminia. They are set up in the play as polarities to Andrea and Anina. We have already heard Flaminia's motives for marrying Santis, who himself is not necessarily a faithful husband. His main purpose in life is to attract money by whatever means available. He speaks about this freely with Flaminia; indeed, she helps him in her own way to reach this goal. Whenever they spend time together, they seem to speak freely about their individual activities, looking upon the world and mankind as an open field to play their cunning game. Andrea and Anina, on the other hand, come from an honest and sincere background; they find themselves temporarily out of place in this company and this resort town.

Andrea regrets his weak moment in accepting a place at the gambling table. However, he does not make any allowance, nor shoulder part of the blame, for what happened to Anina during his absence. He is unable to grasp that moment in time which Anina spent with Casanova as a discovery of her own identity. Neither does he comprehend that in her confession she is releasing the secret of that moment and thereby relegating it to her past.[63] No real communication has taken place between the two of them because they cannot see beyond the circle of their personal involvement; thus no understanding is reached.

At present Andrea sees only a prostitute in Anina and considers the money he won from Casanova as ransom which Casanova paid to gain her favors; therefore, he wants to dispose of this "Teufelsgold," as he calls it, by giving it to Anina as whore money:

> Hier ist das Teufelsgold, du wirst es brauchen —
> Fürs erste jedenfalls, bis von Flaminia
> Das weit're du gelernt. (675)

As Martin Swales points out:

> The prostitute is often seen as the female counterpart of the adventurer in that she surrenders over and over again to erotic experience, but without ever being totally committed to the actuality of each relationship.[64]

Therefore, Flaminia and Teresa fall into this category, for they really are attached to their "counterpart of the adventurer" in this non-committed way. Andrea, however, is never portrayed as an adventurer at any point in the play. By placing Anina in this category, Andrea indeed degrades himself to the role of whoremaster. In addition, he demonstrates a considerable lack of sensitivity in listening to Anina's story as she reveals her thoughts, her feelings, and the circumstances which led her into this experience. But she emerged from it still totally committed to Andrea. His uncontrolled reaction now leads to new difficulties.

Not only has Anina's individuality been damaged, but also his own, for he sadly recognizes that his relationship with her was not so unique after all: he could be replaced, exchanged. We see here that Andrea struggles with the egotism and vanity of which he had accused Anina earlier in their dispute. His motivation to leave her has its foundation in this inner conflict. After this dark hour of personal insult, Anina too, sees no basis for any future companionship. "Das Band ist zerrissen" (677), she exclaims, just as Andrea had said earlier. When Casanova's visit is announced by Tito, she seems to seal their separation with these words: "[. . .] merke: Kein Bräutigam, nicht meiner Ehre Anwalt — / Du bist ein fremder Mann für mich — wie er" (677). This second Act ends in the disagreement between them. Apparently, Anina felt no obligation to her honor and Andrea's to resist Casanova, who she knew was not Andrea, although he was deceived as to her identity. She is not an inexperienced woman and therefore would be expected to have sufficient loyalty to her prospective husband to handle the advances of a deluded visitor such as Casanova. On the contrary, she thoroughly enjoys the experience and on awakening the next morning feels herself in a state of innocent bliss, for her excessive vanity tells her that no guilt attaches to one who has not sought out a sexual experience outside the stable relationship which she already enjoys with Andrea.

As the discussion shows, it is possible in this argument to take sides for and against Andrea and Anina at the same time. What Schnitzler is demonstrating here is the complexity of the issue which involves the polarity of honor and vanity. Honor in men requires dignity, integrity and especially excellence of character which Andrea did not demonstrate entirely, as shown by the weakness for gambling, thus leaving Anina alone and unprotected. Honor in women involves chastity in light of a marriage commitment, to which she felt not obligated in the loneliness of the night. Both, therefore, were carried off on the wings of vanity.

This polarity of honor and vanity is shown in other characters as well. At this point, Casanova is just as uninformed about events as Andrea was earlier, and as Santis will be later. The purpose of Casanova's visit is to borrow money from Andrea in order to repay Gudar. This desire to honor his debt, however, is not really motivated by genuine principles of honesty and integrity. Instead, Casanova intends to gamble with Gudar during their forthcoming mutual journey and win the money again from him, so that he can repay Andrea, hopefully sooner than within thirty days. This activity of losing and winning is set up here by the author in a polar sequence, and he works with this polarity principle, as has already been shown, throughout the play. Not only are the characters in polar position to each other, but incidents as well.

It can be seen at this point in the "open window." The night before, Casanova was attracted by it; presently, during his visit with Andrea and before he has started any conversation, he is repelled by it and asks that it be closed. Another polarity occurs within Andrea himself. At first, he is very reserved toward Casanova because he feels uncomfortable in his role as cuckold. Later on, as he regains his bearings when Casanova tells his story, thus revealing that he really does not know whom he seduced the night before, Andrea is more outgoing. He no longer is interested in securing Casanova's promissory note by asking questions about his sources of income; he gathers the gold rather quickly to hand it to him. He is also able to recover from Casanova the letter Anina sent him. Thus, Andrea wipes away all traces of any proof to the contrary, for Casanova assumes that Flaminia sent him this note to warn him of her jealous husband, who already looked for him in the morning. Andrea is now changing his mind about Anina considerably. To make certain that Anina would not fall into another temptation, Andrea suggests to Casanova that he might seek a safer refuge in Holland or England instead of Belgium; at any rate, further away from them. — What is one man's loss is another's gain!

The polarities between Andrea and Anina change in the ensuing scene. Whereas Andrea is ready for reconciliation, Anina wants to be left alone so that she can pack her suitcase. "Neu fängt mein Leben an" (693), she proclaims. The letter which started the original dispute between them is now again the cause of disagreement — this time in the opposite direction. Anina believes it was bought back with gambling money which Andrea had in the drawer and which has now disappeared. "Dafür das Gold — ein Handel? — Schmach und Torheit!" (692). Anina sees in this bargain nothing more than a reduction of human relations and problems, whereas for Andrea it is a reinstatement of his integrity as well as Anina's. When she asks him how he came into possession of this letter he replies by repeating her own words: "Neu fängt dein Leben an" (694); therefore, it should not matter. As she insists on hearing about it, Andrea tells her that Casanova assumes this letter has come from Flaminia to warn him of her jealous husband and his revenge. Andrea admits that he gladly left Casanova in this belief, for he considers this circumstance a special act of fate, thus providing a new level of consciousness upon which to rebuild their relationship. In the measure of forgiveness he sees a first step on their new path. As Anina questions this "big" word of forgiving, he reduces it to mean understanding and forgetting, but Anina at this point is not ready to forget all the insults, mental abuse, and hatred that have been heaped upon her. She repeats the same words Andrea originally said to her:

> Nimmt er nicht die Erinn'rung jener Stunde,
> Den Duft von meinem Leib, von meinen Küssen
> Den Nachgeschmack, der Seufzer Wonnehauch
> Für ewig mit — ? (694)

thus setting again herself and Andrea in opposition to one another. He thinks he is ready for reconciliation, while she is still trying to cope with the mental damage suffered as a result of these strong accusations and is at the same time questioning the motives behind his sudden change of mood. As she grabs her coat and gets ready to leave, she rightfully poses this question to Andrea:

> Genest, weil Eitelkeit des Stachels ledig,
> Ein Herz so rasch, das todverwundet schien?
> Nun erst verlor ich dich! — Fahr hin! (694-95)

Schnitzler himself has a dim view of this subject, for he maintains that understanding and forgiving rarely stem from goodness, but from indifference and lack of love. In a series of aphorisms, he explains his standpoint on this matter quite distinctly: "Alles verstehen heisst alles verzeihen; — das wäre sehr edel gedacht und gesagt. Nur schade, dass das Verzeihen neunundneunzig Mal unter hundert aus Bequemlichkeit und höchstens einmal aus Güte geschieht [. . .]."[65] In another instance, he observes that these mental processes of "Verstehen," "Verzeihen," and "Vergessen" are almost too great for human nature to handle: "Du hast verstanden? Du hast verziehen? Du hast vergessen? Welch ein Missverständnis! Du hast nur aufgehört zu lieben."[66]

Andrea's "Eitelkeit" (694), as Anina calls his vanity, is suddenly no longer in distress, only because the fear of being ridiculed as a cuckold has been dissolved, so that his honor has been rescued. On a psychological level Andrea's willingness to forget may translate into suppression, but the more human aspect of Andrea's change of mind can be seen in his explanation to Anina that Casanova did not carry away her "Bild" (694), because her countenance was not recognized by him as Anina, nor was it the face he had expected that night. Since she was taken for somebody else "[. . .] so ist es nie gescheh'n" (694).

Although different ways of thinking were involved, Andrea arrives at the same evaluation of the situation as did Anina earlier, when she said "Weil nichts geschah" (674). But she no longer has this conviction. Because Casanova has loved her as Flaminia and not as Anina, she has a strong urge from wounded vanity to repair her individuality and integrity. By this revelation of her personality, Schnitzler neatly convicts her of excessive vanity and of delinquency in the most vital area of a woman's honor. "Jetzt lieb' ich ihn . . . und nun erst wird es Glück" (695) represents a renewed commitment to Casanova, and she held firm on that position during her encounter with Flaminia, as has been seen. The only concession both women have made is to put this dilemma into a fable and present it as a problem to Casanova, who is asked to find the solution.

In Act III, Casanova joins the two couples on stage; his stage directions read: "Er springt über die Brüstung ins Zimmer" (714), which is the same way he entered the night before. Thus Casanova arouses negative emotions and memories immediately in all players with the exception of Santis, whose remark "Er ist's gewohnt" (714) comes ironically close to the truth of which he is not aware at this point. Santis' eyes are geared only to material things; immediately he discovers the emerald on Casanova's snuff box. Casanova generously parts with this jewel box and gives it to Santis, thus paying the husband for the pleasures he thought he had had with his wife. This is another subtle polarity to the scene before, when Andrea considered his gambling money in a similar way. On the surface, of course, Casanova finds another reason for this generosity. He considers Santis his "savior" who through interference in his flight plans "saved" him from running after another "unfaithful woman" and probably into "death" (712).

Because Santis had the original idea of involving Casanova in this affair, he is supposed to tell the story about the two sisters and let Casanova find the proper ending. Throughout the drama Santis has been playing with the terms "Philosoph" and "Dichter" because he saw these qualities in Andrea. Now he has the opportunity to imitate Andrea by telling the story. He enjoys this new role so much that he pays no attention to proper sequence; in fact, Andrea impatiently labels it "Unsinn" (717) and helps out with a short summary. Casanova's answer, which seems to catch everyone by surprise, singles out the young man as being the one who is most deceived of all because he is the victim of a twofold cheat in that he actually possessed neither one of the women (719).

Before Casanova can justify his decision, they are interrupted by considerable noise from the garden, where the guests are complaining about the fact that they have received neither drinks nor food. Tito appears to collect advance payment from Santis before anything can be served. Santis is outraged: "Ein Arzt herbei, der Wirt ist krank! Ich zahle, / Wenn ich vom Mahle aufsteh', nicht vorher!" (720). But Tito stands firm: "Und meine Bestellung lautet: Kein Bissen auf / die Teller, kein Tropfen in die Becher, ehe die Rechnung / beglichen ist" (720). Santis calls the bill "Betrug," "Erpressung," "Gaunerei," but is willing to pay half of it in advance and give him securities for the other half in the form of jewelry. Finally, Casanova saves Santis from any further embarrassment by paying the entire bill: "Wo Casanova man zu Gaste lud, dort muss der Wirt nicht für die Zeche zittern" (721). In addition, he is still in a position to repay Andrea the gold which he had borrowed from him earlier.

Although Casanova and Santis are both adventurer types, Schnitzler has set them up as polar opposites. In Casanova we see the carefree, self-centered but generous person who does not pretend to be anything other than an adventurer. Santis, on the other hand, has an elevated social consciousness; hence, his title "Baron" as well as his conformity to social customs such as marriage, however open such marriage may be. His self-centeredness is carried to a further extreme by the combination of cunning and of deliberate deception of other people for his own benefit. In contrast to Casanova, he is not a generous person; part of his personality is his suffering from unsatisfied greed. Instead of paying the bill, he first tries to reduce the amount; then to pay half now and the rest at an indefinite later time; then to secure the remaining amount as if at a pawn shop. He even wanted to take away the pearls from Flaminia, but probably had not reckoned with her own crafty skill, for she had had the clasp soldered in wise anticipation. Nor does he measure up to Casanova in terms of intelligence and education. In Schnitzler's diagram Santis would certainly occupy a lower position than Casanova in this triangular arrangement of types and states of mind.

Casanova, through his generosity in paying the dinner bill, has now switched places with Santis in becoming the host of the evening. In that capacity he invites everyone to the garden banquet: "Und nun, es blinkt der Wein, die Schüsseln dampfen. / Ich denk' es wäre Zeit, zu Tisch zu geh'n" (722). But he must first find an end to the unfinished story; so he has the following solution:

> Betrogen alle drei: Der Jüngling zweifach,
> Einfach die Frau'n auf ihre Weise jede.
> So glich sich alles aus, und ich erkläre:
> Ungültig war das ganze Abenteuer. (722)

Andrea sees the problem as solved, but not yet the "Novelle," because the women still have the daggers in their hands and have only agreed to a temporary armistice. What has happened cannot be erased from memory — especially since neither of the women wants to relinquish her claim nor share with the other (722). Santis, with his new suggestion in that matter, is setting himself up as a cuckold, for this time it will be Flaminia who will realize the pleasure with Casanova, while he is dreaming of Anina. Although Santis is still ignorant with regard to the women involved, Casanova is catching on; stage instructions for him read: "[. . .] hat bei diesen Worten in sinngemässer Weise bald auf Flaminia, bald auf Anina geblickt" (723). He may also remember that he did not feel the string of pearls the night before. Besides, Andrea's drawing his sword gives him the final perception. But Casanova, who has watched the delicious food being served at the table is asking for "zwei Bissen und ein Schluck, nachher der Tod!" (723). This request complies with his impressionistic life style of enjoying always the present moment. Andrea insists that only one of the two will be physically able to go to the table. Santis now surmises that it must have been more than simply "ein Problem" and immediately suspects Flaminia, so that the audience now sees two swords pointing against one.

At this point some outside intervention is necessary because the play is no longer moving along the lines of a comedy. In connection with several earlier experiences during theater visits, Schnitzler speaks in his autobiography "vom Ineinanderfliessen von Ernst und Spiel, Leben und Komödie, Wahrheit und Lüge," which stirred and occupied him "immer wieder, auch jenseits alles Theaters und aller Theaterei, ja über alle Kunst hinaus" and considers it a "Grundmotiv" in his thinking and in his entire works.[67] Indeed, the realms of seriousness and playfulness have moved dangerously close together; not just two but three swords are involved.

Gudar interrupts the duel by bringing in Teresa, who has just arrived to claim her lover and take him along to Vienna, where her next engagement as a dancer is scheduled. With her appearance Schnitzler creates a polar opposite to Casanova, because both characters experience each aspect of their life just for the moment. Teresa had broken her relationship with Casanova only three days ago, as we heard earlier from Flaminia (660); yet, her new sexual adventure has cooled off already. She answers Casanova's curious question: "Liegt er im Grab? " with these words: "Viel tiefer! In Vergessenheit. [. . .] " (726). Death, contrasted here with oblivion instead of life, creates an unusual polarity. However, when this is seen in the context of time and space, oblivion does appear at the opposite end of the scale. A person who has sunk into oblivion in the mind of another has truly ceased to exist for that individual. If, on the other hand, a person had departed through death, he may still be kept alive in the memories of those he left behind.

Teresa, who exists only in and for the moment, and so uses life's opportunities always to her greatest benefit and enjoyment regardless of responsibility and commitment to another person, drops each of her experiences into the sea of oblivion, as soon as it is over. She handles another situation in a similar way later in the play. Tito reports the arrival of two guests at almost the same time, each asking for Teresa. He locked each of them into a room because they acted rather irritated, and is awaiting instructions now. But Teresa is brief: "Ich kenn' sie nicht, man jage sie zum Teufel," later adding: "Ich kenne sie nicht mehr" (730).

Given the standards which she sets for herself, it can be argued that she lives in harmony with her nature: she exists only in the present moment. According to Schnitzler's diagram she would rank as a negative type: "Der negative Typ lebt ohne das Gefühl von Zusammenhängen; das Gestern ist tot für ihn, das Morgen unvorstellbar [...]."[68] Quite noticeably, Schnitzler here mentions this loss of the sense of time so characteristic of the negative types, a deficiency which is also the cause of their irresponsibility in the choice of their means. As soon as Teresa finds Casanova again, she becomes very possessive, almost aggressive, past happenings notwithstanding. When she sensed his involvement with the two women, Flaminia and Anina, she could have become jealous, but quickly changed her attitude: "Doch tu' ich's nicht. / Ich hab' dich wieder, so ist alles gut" (727). However, she urges him to pack immediately because they must soon be on their way. Casanova pretends to have other plans, and of course, at present, he still has the duel on his mind. But Santis is swift in extending his hand for peace; whereupon Andrea follows grudgingly: "Wer kann wem was wehren?" (728).

The three women form a polar opposite to the men. Earlier Teresa had embraced Flaminia and called her "teu're Freundin" (725). Now, she turns to Anina with these words, in a sense emphasizing the double meaning: "Auch Sie, mein schönes Kind? Nun ja, wer kann / Ihm widerstehn" (728). These episodes are over; she alone lays claim to Casanova now: "Ewig bin ich dein" (730). Not one of his plans has been acknowledged by Teresa, who in this way shows her insensitivity to any other person outside her own frame of reference. She is certain that they will travel together and has even made arrangements to take along Tito as their servant, since he has proven himself to be rather clever. Casanova's insistence on having dinner first is finally granted under one condition, that she will eat with him with the two other women on her side. Teresa thus becomes the peacemaker in this inevitable encounter between Casanova and the two couples. In this activity she functions like Casanova, who earlier had a similar task as mediator between Flaminia and Anina. Now they have gone hand in hand into the garden in sisterly harmony; it appears so, at least on the surface.

All but Andrea seem to have overcome their injured vanity so as to join the other guests at the evening meal, and nobody but Casanova appears to have noticed Andrea's difficulty in overcoming his inner conflict. "Ich bin Ihr Freund" (731), are the opening remarks which eventually lead to a deeper understanding between the two men on the subject of faithfulness. Andrea at first rejects this offer of friendship, but the gesture is seen correctly as "Knabentrotz" (732) in Casanova's estimation. If Andrea's heart is closed to Casanova, at least it should not remain so toward Anina, the woman he loves. Passionately, Andrea explains that he cannot marry an unfaithful woman, nor is he able to understand Casanova, who seems to have selected the most unfaithful woman of them all as his companion. But Casanova looks at fidelity from a completely different angle:

> Ich frage Sie, mein Freund, gibt's bess're Treue,
> Gibt's, frag' ich klarer noch, gibt's eine and're
> Auf Erden zwischen Mann und Weib, Andrea,
> Als die Teresa eben mir bewies?
> Sie kehrte mir zurück. Nur das ist Treue,
> Die einz'ge, die mit Fug so heissen darf.
> Denn was uns sonst Gewähr der Treue gilt,
> Das hält nicht stand vor philosoph'scher Prüfung. (733)

The point of return represents for Casanova the highest level of fidelity, for it demonstrates to him a renewed desire for a certain companionship as a result of inner growth toward maturity. What other proof can there be, he asks: "Sexual closeness after a long struggle? A holy oath? To shoulder some danger? To kill herself and hopefully conquer all doubts in the partner?" (733).[69] For each of these questions Casanova has his own defeating answer such as the one for the first question: "Wer weiss, von wem sie träumt in Ihrem Arm!" (733).

Recurrently in his work, Schnitzler has pondered over the degree of commitment between two people; in his *Buch der Sprüche und Bedenken* he gives the following advice:

> Nicht früher darfst du dich von einer Frau geliebt glauben, ehe du nicht sicher bist ihre ganze erotische Sehnsucht auf dich allein vereinigt und alle andren Möglichkeiten ihres Wesens, auch die ungeahntesten, zur Wirklichkeit erlöst zu haben. [70]

Andrea is not convinced by Casanova's argument and creates a polarity to the concept of "Wiederkehr": "Ja, wenn sie Heimkehr wäre, dann vielleicht" (733). If the woman were coming home, then he might be better able to accept her. The degree of frequency with which one steps outside a relationship becomes the focal point here. "Heimkehr" relates to a close relationship such as a marriage. After previous longings for variety in sexual experiences are satisfied, the partner comes home because of a desire for order and stability, and for a deeper sense of sharing and caring. "Wiederkehr, von wo es immer sei" (733), on the other hand, carries a degree of uncertainty to the point of chaos in the relationship, because it would include maximum freedom for the individual to come and go and as such create a disruptive element. It certainly describes Casanova's life style, for he lives in and for the moment and does not belong anywhere. It might also leave him free of jealousy and anxiety, because he does not feel possessive about any partner.

Jealousy, responsibility, freedom, fidelity are key issues, not only for Andrea and Casanova, but throughout the entire play. These are the points of polarity between "vanity" and "honor," that is, honor in its basic connotation as "personal integrity." Schnitzler himself has formulated the difficulty in his *Buch der Sprüche und Bedenken*:

> Dass wir uns gebunden fühlen mit der steten Sehnsucht nach Freiheit — und dass wir zu binden versuchen, ohne die Überzeugung unseres Rechts dazu, das ist es, was jede Liebesbeziehung so problematisch macht. [71]

Andrea feels obligated to a serious relationship; yet, at the beginning of the play he also struggled with the freedom to gamble and drink and take exception to his commitment to Anina for one night — at least his suggestions to Santis regarding the excursion for that evening seems to indicate his secret desire:

> Wenn sich die Nacht senkt, werden schleierlos
> Von Busch zu Busch des Waldes Nymphen schweben
> Und ihre Gunst an Sterbliche verschwenden —
> Weh dem, der sie am Morgen wieder kennt —
> Und — rat' ich recht? — anstatt des grünen Tuchs
> Wird uns ein leuchtend weisser Frauenleib —
> Das Los entscheidet welcher — Spieltisch sein,
> Darauf das Glück in gold'nen Wellen rollt —
> Und wer verliert — der sei der Hauptgewinner. (667) [72]

Still, Andrea acts extremely jealous and hurt in his vanity that Anina did just that: take leave for one night from her otherwise solid commitment to him.

There are discrepancies in Anina's behavior as well. If she was serious in turning the page on her experience with Casanova by sending him the letter, she should have followed through with this decision. The love relationship between Santis and Flaminia, on the other hand, does not seem problematic at all in the sense Schnitzler formulated it, because they do not take their commitment to each other seriously, nor do they restrict each other in their freedom. Casanova and Teresa are so independent that their companionship does not reach any problematic state, either. Thus, Schnitzler shows here a variety of possible relationships and allows the audience to see their merits and deficiencies.

"Aus einem bestimmten Anlass betrügen, heisst beinahe schon treu sein"[73] is another statement Schnitzler gave us in his *Buch der Sprüche und Bedenken*, which is rather all-inclusive in its application. The key words are "distinct occasion" for being unfaithful. This stipulation would fit the situation of each of the main characters. Their independence would be without restrictions; thus, true fidelity could not exist.

This independence is perhaps the reason for Casanova's total rejection of Andrea's concept of "Heimkehr," as he expresses himself in this way:

> Heimkehr? — O Wahn! Als wenn ein Mensch dem andern
> Heimat zu sein sich jemals schmeicheln dürfte.
> Ist Wand'rung nicht der Seele ew'ger Ruf?
> Was gestern noch als fremd uns angefröstelt,
> Umfängt's uns heute nicht vertraut und warm?
> Und was uns Heimat hiess, war's jemals mehr
> Als Rast am Weg, so kurz, so lang sie währte?
> Heimat und Fremde — Worte tauben Klangs
> Von Vorurteil, verschüchtert vom Gesetz
> Und feig verstrickt im Wirrsal des Gewissens,
> Sich Ordnung lügt ins Chaos seiner Brust,
> Der aufgetanen Sinns und freier Seele —
> Gleich unsereinem aus dem Stegreif lebt. (733-34)

This last one of Casanova's long dialogs (which seem like monologs) touches upon another polarity which was expressed at the beginning of their first encounter; it is the opposition "Bürger" and "Abenteurer." The life style which a "Bürger" like Andrea leads, according to Casanova, is hampered by prejudice, adherence to law, fears from one's conscience, and determination to see order where disorder truly reigns (733). Yet, it must be remembered that Casanova used the term "Heimkehr" earlier in the play in a rather positive way. He observed during his conversation with Andrea: "Ihr Ziel heisst Frieden, Ordnung und Gesetz / Wie Heimkehr Ihrer Wand'rung letzter Sinn" — and almost enviously he added: "Ein frühgeschloss'nes ist das stärkste Band, / Weh dem, der ewig sucht; wohl dem, der fand" (691). Andrea, who did not believe his ears, asks: "Ein solcher Spruch aus Casanovas Mund?" He is reassured by Casanova: "Bewahren Sie ihn sorglich im Gemüte, / Noch keinem gab ich höh're Weisheit kund" (691).

A further seeming paradox regarding the adventurer who travels "aufgetanen Sinns und freier Seele" and lives "aus dem Stegreif" (734) appears in contrast to what Casanova had said earlier. To sleep in strange beds, eat in all kinds of inns, and travel in the company of all sorts of people (691) is void of excitement and color; as if Casanova — had he the choice to start his life all over — would this time settle down early with a young woman, "schön wie Anina, klug und tugendhaft" (691). Thus, Casanova has gained certain insights, and he seems to give Andrea the key as to what their conduct in marriage should be. Andrea will have to be Anina's conscience. Casanova seems to feel that women do not have a conscience, and this is one of his reasons for ranking Teresa superior because she has come back to him who is her substitute for conscience. Regret, envy, and a certain weariness seem to emanate from Casanova's words to Andrea, an indication that "Wahrheit" and "Lüge" are polarities equally present within Casanova. For a split second he is able to glance into the future and foresee his later years, which Schnitzler describes to his readers brilliantly in his Novelle *Casanovas Heimfahrt* (EW II, 231-323).[74]

Andrea whose objections to Casanova become progressively shorter in this last scene, calls him a "Sophist" and does not recognize him as a "Philosoph." Casanova seems to accept when he replies: "Mag sein. Daher ist's mir bestimmt, zu irren" (734). The word "irren" in its twofold meaning of making a mistake and of roaming applies ironically in each respect to Casanova, thus pointing to his fate in later years as a result of earlier mistakes. Davis interprets this passage quite differently, when he observes: "Casanova, the ebullient egoist, is proud of his deviation from the bourgeois norm. He can find no connection between himself and another person except for the fortuitous crossing of their paths or meeting of their desires."[75] However, when seen in context with the thoughts Casanova expressed earlier, he does not appear so "proud of his deviation."

Significantly enough, the play ends with the focus on the three "sisters" who are seen in the garden arm-in-arm, chatting, smiling and laughing, completely reconciled. They have forgotten and forgiven each other, a task which Andrea was not able to accomplish with Anina. "Wie schwesterlich vereint," remarks Casanova, "[. . .] — Und könnten Männer je / So Brüder sein wie alle Frauen Schwestern" (735). This expressed desire may not work for all men, but Casanova at least puts it into action for himself and Andrea as he walks arm-in-arm with him into the garden, seeing in him the "Bruder meiner Wahl!" (737).

Boner in her dissertation offers the following interpretation of the term "sisters": "Es ist die Fähigkeit des Selbstvergessens in Momenten höchster Daseinsintensität, die ein Band schwesterlicher Ähnlichkeit um Schnitzlers Frauen schlingt."[76] This ability is possible for them, because "Sie alle kennen uneingeschränkte Ergriffenheit und Hingabe. Sie alle vermögen das Reflektieren auszulöschen. Sie alle stehen jenseits des Postulates der Rechtfertigung durch Wort oder Tat."[77] Men, on the other hand, function differently. Boner concludes: "Diejenigen Männer dagegen, die in ihrem Geiste das Leben begreifen und durch eine Leistung rechtfertigen wollen, errichten um sich einen Wall."[78] Casanova seems to be aware of this rampart around him which prompts him to imitate the women by holding on to Andrea's arm. Besides, the invitation to join is there. The women have already called the men's names; Anina has called Andrea twice.

It is a happy note upon which the drama ends, demonstrating the perplexity and complexity of human nature. Man is uncertain of himself and uncertain of his relationship with others, a problem which Schnitzler handled throughout his works, and especially with greater detail and seriousness in his late dramatic works. The question of fidelity which the author posed time and time again must also be understood in this context. "Human acts and human emotions are the result of many shifting and interlocked causes that may reach back even beyond the birth of consciousness," ponders Liptzin. "Hence, none are guilty. All live as they must."[79] He continues to remind us: "Let us, therefore, not judge, Schnitzler would emphasize; and, above all, let us hesitate to condemn."[80]

Körner seems to be "guilty" of both judging and condemning. He finds, "[. . .] dass in jeden Weibes Seele ein Dämon schlummert, den nicht zu wecken höchste Weisheit ist." [81] He sees this "demon" lurking in all of Schnitzler's women characters and upon closer scrutiny considers them "allesamt als Dionysias Schwestern."[82] It is obvious that Körner's assessment represents a gross generalization and does not take into consideration the complexity of the female characters in later works, such as *Die Schwestern*. Certainly, Boner in her evaluation of the three women characters shows more sensitivity in this respect.

Definite evidence toward a change can already been seen in Schnitzler's selection of the title. The focus is on the women as they present themselves in their various predicaments. They are no longer reflected through the eyes of their male counterparts, as they were in the Anatol-cycle, for example. These women display much more personality and individuality as compared to the women of earlier works. Most dominant is their emancipation in matters of companionship, courtship, and marriage.[83]

Although only one of the four dramas considered here carries the title *Komödie der Verführung*, it became apparent that *Die Schwestern* is also a comedy of seduction. The emphasis, however, is placed upon human relationships rather than a mere act of seduction. In this play, as well as in the other three late dramatic works, "[. . .] die Bedeutung der Schnitzlerschen Gestalten liegt nicht in 'ihrem Schicksal,' sondern in 'ihrem Wesen'."[84] Solutions to the various problems in the play are achieved on psychological rather than moral grounds. As we know from his *Buch der Sprüche und Bedenken*, Schnitzler distrusted any dogmatic system, be it religious, philosophical, political or social laws of morality. Yet Schnitzler was by no means immoral. "Our chief moral fault lies in our not listening to the infallible measuring instrument in our souls," which Liptzin calls "a moral seismograph that registers every minute deviation from the right path."[85] Because we do not understand ourselves, Liptzin points out:

> All moral confusion results from the fact that but few people know their own true nature, and that only a very small minority of these have the courage to act in accordance with it. Yet these alone are on the road to freedom.[86]

In challenging conventional thought, Schnitzler himself traveled the road to inner freedom, as his diversified writings demonstrate. He realized that there is no absolute knowledge with regard to human nature and the world as a whole. What is true for one person may not be so for another, for each one is unique in his own expression and sees the world according to his level of consciousness and understanding. Schnitzler's literary production shows how he as a humanist has collected these observations from the realm of everyday experience, in protest against old established systems of thought and ancient prejudices. This seems to be the reason for his satisfaction with "Weltbetrachtung" instead of "Weltanschauung". " 'Dies ist's, woran's vor allem dir gebricht: / Die tief're Weltanschauung hast du nicht.' / Nun, lächelnd Eurer zünftigen Verachtung, / Bescheid ich mich in Weltbetrachtung."[87] "Weltanschauung" would indicate to him an authoritative evaluation of the world in its entirety, without leaving room for the ever-expanding, ever-questioning mind.[88] It would also mark for him a narrower point of view instead of openness and receptiveness.

This suggests distinctly a shift in emphasis from the outer world to the complexity of the inner world of man, which is part of the maturing process in Schnitzler's late dramatic work. In an interview with Viereck, he discusses the relationship between his early works and his later production as follows:

> I think the critics are sometimes disposed to overestimate some of my earlier works at the expense of my more mature production. Every talent has a countenance of its own. It took me some time to find myself — to discover my own face so to speak.[89]

Schnitzler's lifelong struggle for truth is related to these words of the interview, for as he realized the many facets of truth, he also discovered that human action and interaction relates to truth in complex ways. Körner points out that "Arthur Schnitzler vom sittlichen Relativismus, ja Amoralismus seiner Frühwerke sachte aber stetig zu immer strengerer sittlicher Bewertung vorgeschritten [sei]."[90] In *Die Schwestern*, and with each new work, he either revises earlier conceptions or adds another dimension to his literary and philosophical development. This change in adopting a stricter ethical and moral standpoint is the key to a better understanding of his late dramatic works. "Wer diesen Wandel des Standpunktes nicht beachtet," admonishes Körner, "mag leicht den irrigen Eindruck empfangen, der Dichter wiederhole sich, habe sich ausgeschrieben, wisse nichts Neues mehr zu sagen. In Wahrheit sind diese Wiederholungen Widerlegungen und sinnvolle Absicht."[91]

The acceptance of free will and individual responsibility represents a relatively late stage in his work. Asked about free will by Viereck, Schnitzler remarks:

> I believe in Free Will. Man is responsible for his actions. He could not live in a world without responsibility [...]. In the moral sphere as well as in the sphere of space, conduct is self-determined. Man is the master of his soul, even if his freedom of choice is limited by circumstances and hampered by heredity.[92]

How did Schnitzler know that the will is free? He gives an answer to Viereck in these words:

> If you ask me to prove that the will is free, I must confess my inability. Certain things cannot be argued. One must rely on intuition. One knows that they are so [...]. Intuition is an invaluable guide in art, in politics, in business, in love. Even our friendships are largely determined by 'hunches'.[93]

The conditions under which any will is able to function are, according to Schnitzler, "Selbstüberwindung, Erkenntnisdrang und Opfermut."[94]

In overcoming his ego as the center of attention, man is free to direct his interest toward the world around him and to be of service to his fellow men. As we have seen in *Die Schwestern*, this noble concept could not easily be carried out; it required great struggle both within and without, for most egos were still self-centered. Some characters such as Santis, Flaminia, and Teresa only exerted free will, but assumed no responsibility. Gudar, Casanova, Andrea, and Anina had usually more desire to express free will than to show responsibility, but exercised occasional responsibility. Gudar interfered in the duel which was about to start; Casanova paid the bill for the banquet when Santis had reached the pinnacle of irresponsibility; Andrea saved Anina from losing her eyesight when Flaminia attacked her with a hairpin; and Anina wrote the letter to Casanova to prevent more serious consequences from happening in her relationship with Andrea.

Working with the concept of individual responsibility in this drama, Schnitzler again placed it on the scale of polarity. Some characters can handle responsibility to a certain degree; others are not as yet aware of it. The principle of polarity, therefore, becomes an important key in understanding the play *Die Schwestern* and Schnitzler's work as a whole. This idea is based on Urbach's suggestion regarding the method of interpretation: "Die Gestalten müssen zueinander in Beziehung gesetzt werden, aus ihnen und nicht aus Hypothesen oder Ideen entwickelt sich das dramatische Geschehen. Einzig durch Konfigurationen lassen sich Schnitzlers Stücke begreifen."[95] Not only are Schnitzler's "Leitgestalten" used in polar arrangement such as "Bürger" and "Abenteurer", respectable woman and "Dirne," but each part of a polarity can give rise to a new polarity within the sphere of "Leitmotive." Casanova, the youthful adventurer, for example, has his counterpart in Gudar, the aging adventurer. "Letzten Endes also umfasst das Dasein für Schnitzler [...] alle Gegensätze," Rey observes, "[...] und verbindet sie zu einer Ganzheit, deren Wesen zwar geahnt, aber nicht mehr definiert werden kann."[96]

Within a single character Schnitzler also develops polarities such as truth and falsity (Casanova), dream and reality (Anina), gaiety and solitude (Casanova), love and hate (Flaminia), reason and emotion (Andrea). Although all characters have these qualities, some seem to become more aware of the polar opposites within them and their synthesis on a different plane; Andrea, for example, remarks that "Irrtum und Wahrheit sich wunderbar verschlingen" (722). On the other hand, we see Santis who recognizes: "Die Rollen sind vertauscht [. . .]" (723), but he is not aware that his statement rings true on different levels, for he only considers the change in hosts for the banquet. His idea of "zweifach glücklich [. . .] zweifach betrogen" (723) does not grasp the whole truth, either.

Boner in her chapter entitled "Vom gelebten Leben" observes this polarity in terms of "Sehnsucht" and "Wollen" which creates suffering in Schnitzler's characters:

> Schnitzlers Gestalten bewegt zweifache Sehnsucht, diejenige nach dem Fernen und Unbekannten, diejenige nach Rückkehr und Geborgenheit. Da sind Gestalten, die nur eine, da sind Gestalten, die nur die andere Sehnsucht kennen; aber die meisten haben zwei Seelen in ihrer Brust, und wenn sie der einen leben, sehnt sich die andere nach Verwirklichung.[97]

This polarity principle, of course, represents an important part of Baroque thought. Austria has a strong Baroque heritage, which significantly influences modern Austrian thought to this day, and which had an impact upon the author's production. Swales summarizes best the Baroque aspect of Austria, when he says:

> Many of the themes from Baroque literature are restated in a way that gives them a peculiarly modern resonance. The notion of the 'theatrum mundi,' of man as a player on the stage of life, the juxtaposition of 'Schein' and 'Sein,' of 'dream' and 'reality,' these and many other legacies from the Baroque assert themselves in one form or another in much of the literature of the 'Jahrhundertwende'.[98]

This modern resonance of earlier Baroque themes which Swales mentions is demonstrated in *Die Schwestern* not only by the lightness of tone in the drama but also by the carefree attitudes of its characters. The Rococo flavor already discussed earlier in this analysis is prevailing on every level: setting, plot, characters. Alewyn's assessment of Rococo serves to highlight the play again:

> Das Rokoko ist eine durch und durch ephemere und vordergründige Welt, ohne die barocken Spannungen zwischen Vernunft und Leidenschaft, aber auch ohne die unheilbare Diskrepanz zwischen Wunsch und Wirklichkeit [. . .] eine Welt ohne Tiefe, ohne Dunkel, ohne Geheimnis, ohne Vergangenheit und ohne Zukunft — die Entdeckungen der Romantik. Seine Menschen sind jeden Augenblick durchaus identisch mit sich selbst, freilich um den Preis, dass ihr Selbst von heute selten dem Selbst von gestern gleicht. Man will lieber zu leichtfertig erscheinen als zu schwerfällig.[99]

Indeed, the concept of "Augenblick" was very important in *Die Schwestern*; all significant turns in the play were prompted by a momentary action, beginning with Casanova's jump through the wrong window. The "Augenblick" is an important leitmotif in Schnitzler's entire work, one which increases in significance with each new drama in his late period. In *Die Schwestern* it was used to create this carefree attitude among nearly all characters in the play; it served also to highlight opposite situations, those rare moments in time when a certain understanding or realization was reached within a particular character.

To see in the Rococo aspects of the play merely an escape of Schnitzler's from the political and social realities of the time, constitutes a rather one-sided view.[100] Schnitzler indeed was interested in the events of his time in so far as they did not involve revolutionary movements of post-war Europe. Such activities met with his utter disapproval and disdain. The following aphorism most closely expresses his thinking:

> Der Pedantismus missverstand die Menschenliebe; — das Resultat ist als Marxismus bekannt. Das Ressentiment missverstand den Marxismus, da wurde der Bolschewismus daraus. Das Literatentum missverstand den Bolschewismus, da galt er wieder als Menschenliebe; — aber nun sah sie auch darnach aus. [101]

Schnitzler was not a politician by profession who would step on the platform and proclaim the necessity of certain measures for social change. As a writer he certainly gave an accurate "portrait of the intellectual climate of his times" in describing "the kind of psychological situation which individual participation in that society produces." [102] Even though the play takes place in the Belgian resort town of Spa and portrays the summer guests of various European countries, it easily parallels the Viennese society of Schnitzler's time. When once questioned about his country of post-World War I, Schnitzler answered with these words: "Das wird unsere Generation nicht mehr übersehen und schon gar nicht mehr gestalten können." [103]

This may be one reason why *Die Schwestern* remained the only play which Schnitzler designated as "Lustspiel." He could justify ending it on a happy note in the Rococo atmosphere of light-heartedness and frivolity among the characters. Brandes' admiration is cast into the following words: "Ich finde das Stück sehr fein, sehr unterhaltend und echt, bin leise erstaunt, dass Sie in so trauriger Zeit sich den Muth und die Spannkraft bewahrt haben, ein Lustspiel zu schreiben." [104] Jakob Wassermann in his remembrance of Arthur Schnitzler goes one step further with enthusiasm:

> Einer, der das Diktum prägt: mehr Haltung und weniger Geist! muss viel Geist besitzen, um es zu rechtfertigen. Nach meiner Meinung, die ich ihm nie verhehlte, war er der geborene Lustspieldichter. Er hat es bewiesen, er hatte die Leichtigkeit, er hatte Welt, sein Witz war sublim und traf stets in den Mittelpunkt einer Schwäche oder Lächerlichkeit, aber in späteren Jahren hat er diesen Bezirk seines Talents brachgelegt, kaum begreiflich, warum. [105]

The answer, however, can be found in the psychological depth and complexity which Schnitzler creates for his main characters and in the principle of polarity which involves dynamic action within each character, either to evolve and grow or at least to recognize the limitations imposed upon himself by the nature of his own thinking.

In *Die Schwestern,* to be sure, we have only witnessed the meager beginnings of greater complexity in characters and psychological insight, which develops even further in the subsequent dramas, as will be seen. Rey in his study *Die späte Prosa* denies any such development, at least in so far as the person of Casanova in *Die Schwestern* is concerned. He only observes, "[. . .] dass Schnitzlers Darstellung des alternden Casanova höheres Gewicht und höheren Rang besitzt. Denn das Lustspiel kennt weder die Schwere des Lebens, noch den Ernst der ethischen Problematik." [106]

It is true that the nature of a "Lustspiel" does not detail the difficulties of life; "ethische Problematik," however, was handled in such characters as Andrea and Anina, and even Casanova saw glimpses in the discrepancies of his own life style. The audience of *Die Schwestern* certainly had emotions similar to those which Rey experienced when reading the Novelle: "Wir fühlen Bewunderung, Abscheu, Mitleid zur gleichen Zeit — ein Anzeichen dafür, dass es Schnitzler gelungen ist, aus dem Abenteurertyp eine Gestalt von überraschender Komplexität zu entwickeln." [107]

Casanova's diminishing attraction to women in the Novelle has very natural physical and physiological reasons and does not constitute greater complexity, only a different range of clientele to be expected. "Erst in seinen späteren Jahren lichtet sich der Reigen der weiblichen Gestalten," Alewyn points out, "der durch sein Leben zieht: Herzoginnen und Näherinnen, betagte Matronen und halbwüchsige Mädchen, Nonnen und Kurtisanen."[108] To identify the aging Casanova with Schnitzler's own predicament of aging is not true to the facts, either. Even at age sixty-three, Schnitzler considers himself by no means old; instead, he only speaks about "Grenzjahre," those borderline years which follow the prime of man's life. This is revealed in a letter to Brandes in which Schnitzler also states that he has no reason to complain, "[. . .] weil ich mich in meiner Schaffenslust eher noch wachsen als abnehmen fühle. Auch an äusseren Erfolgen fehlt es nicht [. . .]. [109]

Rey's study concentrates on five of the later Novellen; he bases his study on the following assumption:

> Da die dramatische Produktion im letzten Lebensjahrzehnt des Dichters an Bedeutung verliert, darf in der späten Prosa die Krönung seines Schaffens gesehen werden. Dass auch hier Qualitätsunterschiede festzustellen sind, versteht sich von selbst.[110]

Schmidt concurs with Rey, "that in the final period of his writing Schnitzler's narrative works are superior in quality to the dramas."[111] One of her reasons mentioned is the author's tendency to reflect on psychological detail. Yet, the trend in modern drama seems to move in this direction.[112]

It is not the purpose of this study to argue that Schnitzler is a better dramatist than prose writer; instead, I want to show that his late dramatic work is more significant than has been recognized heretofore. Nevertheless, in order to place Schnitzler in proper context as a dramatist, one needs to be reminded that the author's talent for both genres was exceptionally strong, and many dramas started out as prose works. In this respect, it is perhaps useful to draw upon the characterization Hofmannsthal gave Schnitzler in his Wiener Brief of April 1922, written with the authority of a close friend and contemporary:

> Arzt und Sohn eines Arztes, also Beobachter und Skeptiker von Beruf, ein Kind der obern Bourgeoisie und des endenden 19. Jahrhunderts, einer skeptischen, beobachtenden und 'historischen' Epoche, nicht ohne innere Affinitäten mit französischem Wesen und der Kultur des 18. Jahrhunderts, wäre es fast ein Wunder, wenn dieser grosse erfolgreiche Theaterautor nicht auch ein bedeutender Novellist wäre; denn in der Tat sind sich nie zwei Kunstformen näher gestanden als das psychologische Theater und die psychologische Novelle der letzten Generation.[113]

In Hofmannsthal's view, therefore, Schnitzler is a "great and successful playwright." He is also a "significant prose writer" because of the literary proximity of the two art forms, the psychological theater and the psychological Novelle. Even Schnitzler's narrative works show certain characteristics of the drama which Rey in his interpretation of *Casanovas Heimfahrt* recognized keenly. "Das Geheimnis der Form," according to Rey, "besteht in dem meisterhaft bewahrten Gleichgewicht von epischen und dramatischen Elementen."[114] Further on we read: "Seine Gestaltungskraft zeigt sich darin, dass er die formsprengenden Kontraste des Seelendramas einzuordnen vermag in die geschlossene Form des pseudohistorischen Berichts."[115] Earlier Rey wrote about "dramatische Spannung," "die dramatischen Höhepunkte," "die Erzählung zerfällt in fünf Akte," "die Dramatik der inneren Bewegung," "nach den dramatischen Erschütterungen," "Akt der Selbstverleugnung," "die Bühne ist vorbereitet," "in ihrem dramatischen Kontrast," "in der ganzen Szene."[116] These details are merely mentioned to show that Schnitzler's preoccupation appears to be that of a dramatist, even when he was writing prose.

In his concluding remarks Rey admitted "die Typenhaftigkeit der Darstellung [...] bei den weiblichen Hauptgestalten [...]" and contrasts "die Differenzierung der männlichen Charaktere ist viel stärker entwickelt. Hier stehen Abenteurer und Wahnsinniger als Gegensätze gegenüber."[117] "Typenhaftigkeit," however, points to Schnitzler's earlier works. If this aspect is still present in his late prose works, then they do not seem to qualify as the high point of Schnitzler's artistic achievement.[118]

His late dramatic works, on the other hand, show distinctly a process of maturation, especially with regard to the women characters. The author's characters in the late dramatic works begin to assume command of their own lives. They no longer are victims of moral and conventional customs which earlier would have hindered their individual expression and freedom of choice. They gain control over their lives and affairs and try to take advantage of social and economic situations to fulfill their inner desires, good or bad. In most cases, Schnitzler's characters show a sense of self-acceptance and self-authority. They authorize their own decisions and deeds, and take responsibility for the consequences, whatever the result may be. Because the emphasis in this drama is placed on the unfoldment of the women characters, I consider this drama — contrary to Offermanns' view, a departure from previous comedies in spite of Casanova's "impressionistischen Weltverhaltens."[119] *Die Schwestern oder Casanova in Spa* represents the beginning not the "Endpunkt einer geistigen Entwicklung"[120] for indeed Schnitzler's women characters take the lead in his late dramatic productions. This point will be developed more convincingly through the analyses of the subsequent dramas.

The key issues raised in the drama *Die Schwestern oder Casanova in Spa,* namely the principle of polarity exhibited in both the characters and the incidents in their lives, the complexity of human nature especially with regard to women characters, the question of fidelity in terms of "Heimkehr" or "Wiederkehr," the acceptance of free will and individual responsibility, also occur in the drama *Komödie der Verführung* (1924). However, new aspects added to each issue create even more complexity, as the large number of characters in the play demonstrates. The principle of triangularity receives more attention in *Komödie der Verführung.* In *Die Schwestern oder Casanova in Spa* triangular constellations occurred only among characters as for example the triangle of Flaminia-Anina-Teresa, Flaminia-Santis-Casanova, Anina-Andrea-Casanova. The triangularity in *Komödie der Verführung* not only includes the relationship of characters, but also important political and social themes in addition to psychological issues.

CHAPTER II

KOMÖDIE DER VERFÜHRUNG

Background of the play and statement of purpose

The play *Komödie der Verführung*,[1] first performed at the Burgtheater in Vienna on 11 October 1924 and published by S. Fischer Verlag the same year, picks up the key ideas such as the question of fidelity, the acceptance of free will and individual responsibility, polarities and triangularities from the previous drama *Die Schwestern oder Casanova in Spa* (1919), and carries them to greater complexity in terms of characterization and plot. The first performance of the play received a very sketchy and superficial review by Robert F. Arnold which was typical of the kind of criticism Schnitzler drew in general from the press. Arnold, who had had nothing good to say about *Die Schwestern*,[2] seems to have changed his mind as he now discusses *Komödie der Verführung:* "[...] einen neuen Zug zum Bilde des Dichters steuert sie nicht bei, und fast will es scheinen, als gebräche es diesmal an der alten, zuletzt in den 'Schwestern' bewährten Meisterschaft, eine kreuz und quer verliebte Menschenschar mit sicherer Hand auseinander- und zusammenzuhalten."[3] His judgment completely ignores the significance of this play in comparison to Schnitzler's earlier works.[4] Neither does he consider the importance of the title, when he states:

> Mindestens aber sucht der Titel einen Ring um all dies Haschen und Danebengreifen und Fahrenlassen und Zugreifen, um diese österreichischen Don Juans und Casanovas und ihre Partnerinnen zu legen, indem er die Liebesredoute des Lebens unter dem Gesichtswinkel der Komik nimmt, einer erhabenen Komik, die durch Doppelselbstmord eines der Augenblickspaare so wenig gestört wird wie durch das Wetterleuchten und den ersten fernen Donner des Weltkrieges.[5]

It is true, the idyllic atmosphere prevailing at the end of *Die Schwestern,* which made possible a reunion of the major characters taking part in the celebration, breaks apart in *Komödie der Verführung.* By no means, however, is this breakup subject to comic treatment in the play.

Sol Liptzin provides an informative genesis of the play.[6] He points out that Falkenir and Aurelie in *Komödie der Verführung* reveal a remarkable similarity to the main characters Erasmus and Dionysia in *Die Hirtenflöte* (1911), and a detailed study of Schnitzler's manuscripts helped Liptzin to discover that both dramas were begun in 1908. Thus there is a parallel to the genesis of *Die Schwestern oder Casanova in Spa,* for Schnitzler also worked simultaneously on a drama and prose version of similar themes. In addition, Reinhard Urbach points out that Schnitzler already in 1904 had worked on a new version of the old Novelle *Verführung,* and a year later was also influenced by the *Friedmann*-Novelle which later turned into the drama *Das weite Land* (1911).[7] Both works in their final version preceded *Komödie der Verführung* by more than twelve years. This indicates that only after several attempts did Schnitzler master to his satisfaction the complexity he intended for the new play. According to Urbach, the drama went through several versions during the First World War.[8]

Indeed, the complexity of the drama begins with the very selection of the title. Schnitzler employs rather cleverly the triple definition of the word "Verführung" to show that he designed it to mean not only "seduction" but at the same time "enticement" and "temptation," so that it includes the various plots in the play. "Verführung," Urbach observes correctly, "ist der Weg im Drama, nicht sein Ziel."[9] As the meaning of the word "Verführung" is expanded, it involves nearly all characters of the play in different ways. The deep-rooted relationship between the erotic and the political part of the drama becomes significant as the key to an in-depth interpretation of the drama. Love, the most powerful and irresistible power in human relationships, and war, the most destructive and dangerous threat to peaceful co-existence among nations, serve as a new combination in Schnitzler's late dramatic production to allow a panoramic view of society, thus adding intellectual complexity to the drama. But the play also shows that some members of society prefer to take flight into a fairytale-like atmosphere of an imaginary world. They use this escape mechanism on the one hand to cover up their inner inadequacies with regard to a meaningful love expression; and on the other hand to allow their reasoning power to engage in destructive activities. This aspect of triangular configuration is important in my study, for "einzig durch Konfigurationen lassen sich Schnitzlers Stücke begreifen," according to Urbach.[10]

The constellation *Eros-Krieg-Märchen/Imagination,* therefore, becomes the focal point of this analysis; leading up to it are the various triangular combinations which form around the aspect of Eros. Hartmut Scheible points out: "Die Absicht des Autors ist offenkundig: die erotischen Verstrickungen sollen in enger Verflechtung mit der politischen Katastrophe vorgeführt werden."[11] Ernst L. Offermanns calls this new type of drama a "universale Gegenwartskomödie" because it uncovers "die Wechselwirkung," containing the themes of Eros and war.[12] The third angle in this constellation can be observed in the first and third act which have a deeper significance than Körner is willing to admit.[13]

Other focal points of the discussion include details such as communication, the question of fidelity, the acceptance of free will and individual responsibility, and polarities such as "Jugend-Alter," "Lüge-Wahrheit," "Träumen-Wachen," "Leben-Kunst," "Heimat-Ferne," "Traum-Wirklichkeit," as well as symbols and motifs. In addition, a comparison with the previous play shows how Schnitzler as a dramatist deepens continuously his insight into human nature.

In my critical comments I will reflect upon evaluative judgments made by other critics in an effort to correct inaccurate assessments and to demonstrate how the play has been underestimated by showing that Schnitzler's artistic development as a playwright defies critical commentary. As early as 1913 Schnitzler pointed out in his own defense that the main objective of his dramatic activity is to create human beings as they act and interact in a multiplicity of ways to cope with life and the world around them.[14]

In his late dramatic works the female characters receive more emphasis than in his early works, for they no longer function as certain stereotypes, nor are they depicted only from a man's point of view. Instead, they are portrayed in various degrees of independence and maturity. This process began in *Die Schwestern oder Casanova in Spa* and continues to be significant in the drama *Komödie der Verführung.*

Outline of the play

Komödie der Verführung is set in the three-month period prior to the outbreak of World War I. The events on the political front are deliberately ignored by some characters, while others take advantage of the situation by negotiating personal gains. Westerhaus, who is president of a large banking institution, is gambling on the outbreak of war to increase his profits. The disdainful yet charitable great lady, Franziska Fürstin von Degenbach, on the other hand, arranges a spring festival evening in anticipation of "eine Rieseneinnahme für den wohltätigen Zweck" (848). She raises this money prior to undertaking a three-week cure in the spa at Karlsruhe, as was traditionally her custom. We also learn that she spends the summer on her estates at the Russian-Polish frontier, totally ignoring the dangerous political situation and its consequences for her in the event of war.

The play is divided into three acts. Act I depicts the garden party on May 1, 1914, "ein nächtliches Frühlingsfest" (847) in the park and castle of Prinz Arduin von Perosa, which he opens for the first time to the public as his contribution to charity. All of the characters are introduced, except for the minor ones necessary for the background in Act III. Besides exposing the social environment of his time, Schnitzler develops the various personal and interpersonal as well as political episodes in this first act. The three concurrent plots revolve around the three major female characters. First is Aurelie, who has promised to choose her husband from a group of three suitors on this particular night of the ball. Second is Judith, who is in love with Westerhaus, the discontented banker husband of her nymphomaniac sister Julia. Judith has plans to study voice in London and later accept an engagement in Dresden. The third plot concerns Seraphine, a young violinist, who is scheduled to go on concert tour with her father, a retired opera singer.

Another episode develops marriage problems between Westerhaus and his wife Julia, who in turn is interested in Prinz Arduin as well as in a scheme with Braunigl, the public prosecutor, against her husband. Gysar, the artist, uses his peculiarly erotic talent in adventurous ways in that he paints both the bodies and the portraits of ladies of high society. Before Act I is over, Gysar expresses in no uncertain terms his desire to paint Judith (849) as well as Aurelie (885). Another episode involves Seraphine's sister Elisabeth who is deeply in love with Leutnant Leindorf.

The political theme concentrates upon the possibility of war and its consequences. Westerhaus, Braunigl and Franziska, who are involved in this discussion, either nurture vague ideas about war and an ignorance of its devastating consequences, or, like Westerhaus, they are intensely interested for reasons of profit-taking. Another aspect of the political part of the play involves Prinz Arduin, who is appointed to various diplomatic missions with the duty of averting the outbreak of the war. He uses Ambros Doehl's talent as a writer for his political needs. In general, Ambros plays a more sympathetic role than most writers in Schnitzler's earlier works.[15]

Both Arduin and Ambros are suitors to Aurelie, awaiting her decision that particular night in the park — Aurelie has mysteriously determined the hour of midnight. The third suitor, and one of the main characters in the play, is Ulrich Freiherr von Falkenir, who appears rather late on stage, thus paralleling the late stage appearance of Aurelie. When he joins Ambros and Arduin shortly before midnight, each one expresses his doubts about Aurelie's promise to meet them at that time, since she has not been seen during the entire evening. It is Ambros, who reminds Arduin that it is "kein Faschingsspass, sondern ein Märchen, und das Märchen hat seine Gesetze wie die Wirklichkeit. Sie heissen Pünktlichkeit, Geduld und Glaube" (868). At this very instant, Aurelie appears on the scene; her choice is Falkenir, who is also a friend of the family. Conscious of his age, Falkenir withdraws his proposal, for he feels himself at an advantage over the other two suitors, since he also was Aurelie's guardian after she lost her parents. Moreover, he is afraid that Aurelie may be confusing friendship with love. She is young and should experience life to the fullest. Against her will, Falkenir sends her dancing and as he watches her flexible body turn and twist, he cuts any last emotional ties between himself and her; in the end he forces her to follow her impulses. Act I ends as Aurelie, bewildered, leaves with Max for a ride into the countryside on this early spring morning (890).

Act II occurs six weeks later in mid-June.[16] It is divided into three scenes, each one representing a turning point in the lives of the major female characters. Aurelie leaves Max to accept Gysar's offer to paint her portrait. Gysar does not succeed in this task when he is in Aurelie's home, "dem kleinen Merkensteinschen Palais in der Salesianergasse" (891). Instead, he finally is able to lure her into his garden with the high walls, to paint her there and to seek a closer relationship with her. The portrait repels and fascinates Aurelie because she discovers her sensuous desires caught in it. The horror she feels at this vision of her hidden nature affects her mind. In Act III she not only hears "die ewigen Ströme" (964-65), she lets herself glide into them. Falkenir, who has learned a lesson in responsibility and commitment toward others and who desires now to marry Aurelie and offer her security, shelter, and his name (951), comes too late. He joins Aurelie and both sink into the sea with a kiss on their lips and a smile of bliss in their eyes. They have cleansed themselves symbolically to deserve one another in a new world beyond.

The turning point for Judith occurs in Scene 2 of Act II. The political manipulations and intrigues unfold around Westerhaus which lead to his committing suicide. Judith, previously a part of the Westerhaus household, is determined to be the new, emancipated woman. Dismayed by the flagrant affairs of her sister, disappointed by the brutality of Westerhaus whom she unrequitedly loved, she will be more honest than others, as she explains to Max, and bind herself to no one. When she finds herself, nevertheless, responding to Max's tenderness, she draws away from him, for intellectually she knows that she must explore the whole of life to find out whether the night she spent weeping over Westerhaus' corpse was all that life could offer, or whether perhaps it was directing her into the future. Scene 3 of Act II leads to the house of Kammersänger Eligius Fenz, where the wedding of his daughter Elisabeth is celebrated. After everyone has left, his second daughter Seraphine practices her music for the concert tour; she is accompanied by Max. She is a most unusual character, a woman who fulfills her destiny and is happy. An uncomplicated nature, she has transferred any longings for a lover to longings for a child, the highest possible fulfillment for a woman in Schnitzler's works. In Act III, she is perfectly content to achieve motherhood without a marriage partner, since Max, the father of her child, is not sufficiently mature to enter such a relationship.

Act III takes place on August 1, 1914, at the Danish coast in the sea resort town of Gilleleije.[17] After the official announcement of the declaration of war each one is making plans to leave: Arduin with Judith on his pleasure trip; Ambros to catch the last train across the border. Max, who was the instrument by which each of the three women won her particular future, finds himself alone as he prepares to report to his regiment. Seraphine decides to stay with her father in Denmark. Falkenir and Aurelie have ended their lives. The old Fenz, accompanied by Gilda, the youngest character in the play, files away the tragedy that has just happened with these words: "Und haben nicht gewusst, dass das Leben köstlicher wird, je weniger davon übrig bleibt" (974).

Review of criticism

Josef Körner in his evaluation of Schnitzler's "Spätwerk" does not seem to be aware of the new complexity in female characters. He continues to maintain the standpoint held since 1921: "[...] statt das Wesen der Frau schlechthin zu suchen, ihre menschliche Würde, erfasst er sie nur als Geschlechtswesen und fährt dergestalt an dem wichtigsten und brennendsten Problem unserer Tage eben doch nur vorbei. Er sieht die neue, die freie

Frau, aber über den schrecksam begriffenen Nöten ihrer Freiheit, über der Wirklichkeit ihrer sexuellen Gefährdung übersieht er die Möglichkeit ihres Aufstiegs zur autonomen Persönlichkeit."[18]

In a similar way, Körner overlooks completely the significance between the erotic and the political part of the drama and criticizes the author rather harshly with these words: "Mit einem erstaunlichen Mangel an Stilgefühl hat Arthur Schnitzler neben die pathetische und düsterstrenge Tragödie von Aureliens und Falkenirs verhängnisvoller Prüfung den unbeschwerten Leichtsinn und die seelenlose Heiterkeit eines [. . .] moralisch 'bewusstlosen' Libertins gefügt: die Geschichte vom schönen Max und den drei Jungfrauen, die eigentliche Komödie der Verführung."[19] He finds this drama "[. . .] zum Bersten vollgestopft [. . .] mit Handlung und Problematik"[20] without according proper consideration to vital details of the play. Seduction for its own sake is not the focus of the play; instead, it is the selfish, materialistic force behind it which is capable of penetrating society on all levels.

Körner is also the most insistent critic in discrediting Schnitzler as a dramatist when he states: "[. . .] dass dieser Dichter, und zwar vor allem als Dramatiker, nach gewissermassen naturwissenschaftlicher Methode verfährt, indem es ihm weniger um die Gestaltung einmaliger Menschenindividuen zu tun ist als um die Findung psychologischer Gesetze, die aus der Begrübelung typischer 'Fälle' sich ihm ergeben."[21]

Offermanns in this respect demonstrates a deeper insight into Schnitzler's work in general, and into the plot and characterization in particular. His detailed and thoughtful analysis is the only one in recent years which addresses itself to the entire play. "Die Fülle der dramatis personae," he writes, "deutet auf die Absicht hin, ein umfassendes Gesellschaftspanorama zu entfalten. Und in der Tat entstammen die Figuren den verschiedensten gesellschaftlichen Schichten, vom Hochadel bis zum Kleinbürgertum."[22] The important aspect which carries this drama beyond the scope of all of Schnitzler's previous plays is the author's desire,

> die gesellschaftskritische, politische Komödie mit der Komödie des Eros zu einem neuen Typus einer universalen Gegenwartskomödie zusammenzuschliessen, die die Wechselwirkung von pervertiertem Eros und verhängnisvoller historischer Entwicklung aufdeckt in der Verknüpfung des Themas der erotischen Verführung mit dem Krieg-Motiv, das, keineswegs blosse Staffage, von Beginn bis Schluss in eine strenge Korrelation zum impressionistischen Weltverhalten der einzelnen Figuren gesetzt wird.[23]

Unfortunately, the significance of this play in its entirety, aside from Offermanns' valuable discussion, has not been recognized as yet in most of the newer Schnitzler research. Françoise Derré at one point calls this drama "étrange et passablement confuse"[24] and Christa Melchinger, influenced by Robert Musil's critical evaluation of the first performance of the play at the Wiener Burgtheater on October 11, 1924, remarks that *Komödie der Verführung* could hardly be counted among the more successful pieces in Schnitzler's dramatic works.[25]

Max Kammeyer, who looks at *Komödie der Verführung* from the standpoint of dramatic theory in the field of theater science, observes this: "Das Werk zeichnet sich durch einen ambivalenten Altersstil aus, der einer äusserst subtilen Regie bedarf. In seiner Zeit steht der Dichter mit diesem Anspruch allein."[26] He finds that the various "Spannungsmomente" produced in Act I and mostly in Act II are not carried through because the third Act takes place two months later and "alle angespielten Motive sind schon Vergangenheit [. . .] und der für das Hauptpaar dramatische Schluss trägt nur scheinbar die Konsequenz eines Spannungsbogens in sich. Tod und Liebe gehen in diesem Werk erst am Schluss eine dramatisch vom Stück schon gelöste Verbindung ein."[27] The central problem, as Kammeyer sees it, is stated in one sentence: "Drei Männer [...] werben um eine Frau."[28] All other characters are involved in what he calls "Reigensituationen aus den Nebenhandlungen."[29] However, Kammeyer's observation that death, as the solution of the problem of love between Aurelie and Falkenir at the end of the play, can be anticipated by the course of events throughout the drama, is debatable. The "Reigensituationen," which he mentions as involving the remaining characters, raises a further point of contention.

Sol Liptzin, in his chapter "The Curse of Understanding," concentrates his analysis exclusively on the Falkenir-Aurelie scenes, for "these alone justified the publication, in 1924, of *Komödie der Verführung*."[30] Aside from this oversimplified evaluation of the entire drama, he does provide valuable scholarly information with regard to the genesis of the play whose central theme seems to bear a striking resemblance to the tale of Erasmus and Dionysia in the prose work *Die Hirtenflöte* (1911).[31] Another valuable aspect of his work deals with Schnitzler's concern for freedom and understanding, concepts which meander as "Leitmotive" through his entire production. Particularly in his later works, Schnitzler maintains that an excessive amount of freedom will lead to a disintegration of one's personality, and that understanding, if carried too far, acts as a paralyzing force. "In the end these characters recognize that direful results might have been averted," Liptzin paraphrases Schnitzler's philosophy, "if freedom had been curbed by responsibilities, and if understanding had been overridden by passion."[32]

Willa Schmidt, in keeping with the title of her dissertation, concentrates on the three major female characters — Aurelie, Judith, and Seraphine —, pointing out the insight Schnitzler demonstrates as he portrays each of these three women in their strengths and weaknesses in relationship to the major male characters in the play.[33] Evan B. Davis, in his discussion of the moral problems, sees this play in light of "three concurrent plots; holding them together is the one man, Max von Reisenberg, who is the first lover of all three women. He is not the seducer, but the seduced."[34] His analysis does not seem to offer new insights and, in fact, completely ignores Schnitzler's moral and ethical concern with regard to the war, the manipulative practices in banking circles of society as a symbol for deterioration of the nation from within, the apathy of people in general toward current political and social issues. However, Section V of his dissertation entitled "Unpublished material" contains an important letter which Schnitzler wrote to Josef Körner on July 11, 1927, defending himself against undue criticism.[35] In this letter Schnitzler challenges Körner to compare notes on definitions prior to reaching haphazard conclusions and reveals his awareness and insight concerning literary and philosophic trends as they relate to the issues of his time.

Analysis of the drama

The term "Komödie": Indeed, Schnitzler's "Komödien" cannot easily be defined in the traditional sense of the term comedy which, ordinarily, in literary criticism denotes a work that ends without serious unpleasantness for the major characters. His play does not fit into this denotation because the social, political, and psychological issues raised are too complex and serious in proportion. Besides, Schnitzler did not concern himself with the theoretical application of the various genres. Instead, he sees life itself, the different life styles, as comedy. Each human being, therefore, is involved in this comedy, as he acts and interacts with others. In order to understand Schnitzler's works properly, Kilian has devised a method of interpretation which he bases on the analysis of both form and content, and on the recognition that in Schnitzler's view comedy is a structural as well as a socio-anthropological category. The latter term designates a pattern of human behavior that is determined by a person's psychological make-up or social norm, and is related to the problem of inadequacy of language as a means of communication. [36]

The key factor which hampers the free flow of communication, as will be shown, is the problem of solitude in the sense that the individuals hide behind a mask or façade. They do not dare to peel off their outer shells. They do not release themselves to the highest and the best within, and they are therefore incapable of showing each other their true inner Self. They create barriers to trust and openness, fairness and honesty in achieving a clear expression of their feelings on various levels. The presence of fear wipes out the opportunity to express true love; doubt, distrust, and fear of ridicule after an open communication close the door to truth.

We see this in the relationship between Falkenir and Aurelie. When she announces that Falkenir is her choice as a husband, he is overcome by doubt and fear: "Bist du denn auch sicher, Aurelie, dass du dich nicht täuschest?" (869), and he considers Arduin or Ambros better suited to be her husband for various reasons. Aurelie's genuine answer points to the fact that she only wants to be herself in a marriage relation, trusting that Falkenir desires her as she is: "Dir, Falkenir, das weiss ich, werde ich kein Triumph und kein Gleichnis sein, dir bin ich Aurelie" (870), but he does not recognize the truth in her words. The next argument, regarding Falkenir's fear of losing her because of her youth and her unawakened desire to explore the adventures of the world, is also encountered maturely, when she states: "Sie lockt mich nicht, diese Welt, diese 'lebendige' Welt. Was ich von ihr gehört, geschaut, verstanden, gibt mir keine Gelüste, sie aus der Nähe kennenzulernen. Ich habe meine Mutter gesehen, wie sie wiederkehrte aus jener Welt, die du meinst, und müde und zerrüttet an der Schwelle unseres Hauses niedersank" (871). Yet, Falkenir is insensitive to Aurelie's true inner nature as expressed in her words. However, when he meets her again in Act III, he has learned several lessons with regard to human relationships. He carefully pays attention to each of her concerns and has come to value responsibility and truth, as well as love, in a relationship: "Ich bringe sie aus der Einsamkeit von hundert Tagen und Nächten mit, und sie ist besser als alle Weisheit, — sie heisst Liebe" (951). In Schnitzler's aphorisms, published posthumously, he reflects upon this human dilemma:

> Schmerzlicher, als dass wir niemals die Wahrheit zu hören bekommen, ist, dass wir sie auch beim besten Willen niemals aussprechen können. Denn was wir auch sagen, der andere hört ja die Wahrheit nicht, die wir ihm vermitteln wollten. Was von unseren Lippen kam und was in des anderen Seele dringt, ist niemals das gleiche. Es ist schon im nächsten Augenblick nicht dasselbe mehr: es kommt auf so viel an, was mit deiner Wahrheit und mit deiner Wahrheitsabsicht nichts mehr zu tun hatte: es kommt darauf an, was der andere hören wollte, wie er zu dir steht und so weiter. [37]

Besides looking at "comedy" in terms of human behavioral patterns, there may be still another reason why Schnitzler used the term "Komödie" in his title. [38] The author may have had the time of Greek comedy in mind, especially the period known as "jüngere Komödie" under its main representative, Menandros (ca. 343-294 B.C.). In his comedy the chorus counted twenty-four persons and the number of players on stage at one time was also larger than in tragedy. [39] What is further mentioned about Menandros parallels the characteristics of Schnitzler as well:

> Menendros' Stücke benutzen die traditionellen typischen Figuren der Komödie und vermitteln uns

ein buntes Bild des Lebens; 'das Beste ihrer Wirkung kommt aus der versöhnlichen Milde dieses hellsichtigen Beobachters und seinem echten Glauben an die Möglichkeit des Guten im Menschen;' über allem steht 'unverrückbar das Bild edler Menschlichkeit.'[40]

This, too, is Schnitzler's message in *Komödie der Verführung*. As he probes deeply into human nature, he finds no man to be perfect, but he sees the potential of nobility within each human being. All men are on different levels of evolvement and from time to time they go astray, they allow themselves to be lured away from their path. In his play the author examines these outer appearances ("Verführungen") which seem to have stronger attraction than the individual's guidance from within.

The term "Verführung": "Verführung" in the title of the play likewise provides for a choice of connotations, because "Verführung" means also "Verlocken." "Verleiten" with its further shades of meaning involves such terms as "Reiz," "Zauber," "Anziehung." The following analysis shows that these terms significantly relate to the various characters who move through the different episodes of the drama.[41] As each word increases in degree of negative connotation, so will many characters be involved in a gradual decline of personal values which, in turn, becomes instrumental in weakening the fiber of the whole society Schnitzler portrays.

Triangularity: *Komödie der Verführung*, therefore, is a carefully chosen title in that it suggests an aspect of triangularity right from the beginning, and is as important as the title of the previous play *Die Schwestern* was for its triangular constellation of the women characters. Urbach in his monograph on Schnitzler summarizes this phenomenon as follows: "In allen seinen Werken versuchte Schnitzler, den Menschen in allen seinen Möglichkeiten zu gestalten. Das Formprinzip seiner Jugend hat er in seinen späten Dramen auf die Durchführung einer Dreierkombination reduziert und konzipiert, die immer wiederkehrt, ohne das Geschehen einzuzwängen oder die Satzinhalte zu verstümmeln."[42] Not only characters, but also episodes and symbolic detail are arranged in triangularity. In addition, the play has three acts, with the second act highlighted by its division into three distinct scenes. Each scene has a triadic structure as well.[43]

The basis for the symbolic detail in triangular arrangement is provided by the constellation *Eros-Krieg-Märchen/Imagination*.[44] The aspect of Eros, in particular, produces a number of triangular combinations. Most of these combinations show the consequences of perverted love and form a polar opposite to genuine love, which is mankind's great harmonizing and healing principle. Genuine love is the spiritual force that can bind together the whole human family in that it seeks what is good everywhere and in everybody. In this form it creates order and continuity in a person's life. The drama, however, shows what happens, when this order changes and allows love to be perverted. This misconception of love has destructive results of far-reaching consequences. Beyond the individual sphere, it affects the fiber of society, fine arts, politics, and the fate of an entire nation. Schnitzler demonstrates this decay in his play *Komödie der Verführung*. He shows how individuals through the process of the various forms of allurement are out of control of their lives and affairs, how the loss of individual authority reduces them to becoming reactors to their own personal life. Because they have moved away from the center of their being and have attempted to seek solutions to their problems in outer ways, they are vulnerable to negative influences from various levels within their environment. Schnitzler builds upon this universal truth and shows how "Verführung" can be one such negative influence. In its range from enticement to seduction and temptation, it only temporarily alleviates feelings of hurt, rejection, false pride, anger, loneliness, in favor of a state of well-being. The after-effect is often seen in even deeper despair and the loss of personal integrity, or a permanent realization for the better may have been gained, or the person may remain insensitive and become even more self-centered. Schnitzler in his panoramic treatment of the process of "Verführung" has created his characters to fill the entire spectrum.

Comparison between Max and Casanova: At first glance *Komödie der Verführung* promises to continue where the previous play *Die Schwestern oder Casanova in Spa* left off. Max von Reisenberg assumes Casanova's role as adventurer and becomes successively the lover of Aurelie, Judith, and Seraphine. In relation to the adventurer they seem to be the counterparts of Flaminia, Anina, and Teresa. But the appearance proves deceptive, because the women characters in *Komödie der Verführung* have reached a different level of emancipation. They have a greater desire for self-fulfillment and are in search of true identity. However, the motives behind these desires should be examined, because Schnitzler allows us to recognize inherent weaknesses. It would be unfair, though, to relegate them to the role of female counterparts to the adventurer figure at this point.

Max himself differs from Casanova in several ways. In contrast to the flamboyant figure of Casanova, who excites women not only by his personality but also by such colorful incidents of his past as the story about his escape from the Italian prison, Max is a "local boy," the son of an ennobled jeweler, with a keen interest in increasing his father's wealth. This money draws especially high interest in the bank Westerhaus owns (866). Max does not risk his fortune in gambling as Casanova did, to be wealthy one day but poor the next. It is ironic, however, that Max ends up poorer than Casanova, for he did not heed Judith's advice to withdraw before Westerhaus could go bankrupt (866, 908, 969). Max is also less active in his love affairs than Casanova. Urbach observes in this regard: "Max ist Wegbereiter, nicht um der Verführung willen ist er da, sondern wegen der Verführten, die durch ihn ihr Schicksal erfüllen [...]."[45]

Each of the three women controls her relationship with Max not only in terms of duration, but also in the degree of emotional involvement. Max plays a somewhat passive erotic role. It is the woman who asks him to come, who kisses him and dismisses him again.[46] There is an element of truth in Körner's rather flippant appraisal of Max's situation: "Er wird genommen, er nimmt nicht; er darf diese Mädchen geniessen, aber er besitzt sie nicht [...] die Frauen nehmen ihn hin zu flüchtigem Genuss —, wie sonst der Mann ein Dirnchen nehmen mag."[47]

On the other hand, Casanova does not see himself as seducer either; at least his reply to Andrea does not admit to it:

Verführt' ich jemals? Nein, ich war zur Stelle,
Wenn just mit holder Zauberei Natur
Ihr Werk begonnen. Auch verriet ich keine,
Denn ewig dankbar jeder blieb mein Herz (684).

This element of discretion is more pronounced in Casanova than in Max, partly because Max does not have to fear the revengeful jealousy of cuckolded husbands, and partly because Max is not by nature a secretive man. Everyone knows, "er hat [...] viel Glück bei den Frauen," and his last experience, according to Seraphine, was with Aurelie (862). Judith heard the story in more colorful details: "Man weiss ja, Sie heiraten Aurelie" (908). Yet, the truth is that Max is more inclined to feel at home with Judith and Seraphine than with Aurelie, for he admits to Judith: "[...] zuweilen war mir — unheimlich in ihrer Nähe" (909). This uneasiness originated at the garden party when Max returned Aurelie's jewelry. He had found it by the pond, and in the ensuing conversation was abruptly reminded of tragic incidents (873).[48] Other incidents surrounding Aurelie may have contributed to his uneasiness as well. He was the first one to dance with her after her engagement to Falkenir, and he was also "zur Stelle" (in Casanova's terms) at the end of the ball when Falkenir had broken off the engagement and sent Aurelie into a state of shock. The charm of Max's personality differs also from that of Casanova. Max's sensuality is natural, almost child-like, and so are his affections.

Max-Judith: When she asks: "Sind Sie wirklich so ein Kind? Oder ist das auch Affektation?" (908), Judith assumes these to be alternatives. Even though Max wears the costume of a domino, everyone knows who he is and finds him in time of need, whatever that need may be. His relationships are friendships more than anything else. His often unselfish disposition creates an atmosphere of honesty. He is trusted as a friend to the point of brother and sister-type relationship but rejected as a husband. His first experience with Judith brings this to light. She does not want to bind herself in marriage to him, but she discusses honestly her feelings with him for "wir zwei sind vom gleichen Blut" (865). As such she likes to refer to him as companion; they are "Kamerad" and "Kameradin" (866, 867, 908).

In Act II this idea is carried one step further. Judith reveals that she does not feel uneasy around Max at all. He is happy to hear that: "Warum sollten wir einander unheimlich sein? Wir sind ja vom selben Stamm" (909), which gives him further encouragement to speak his mind: "Wir gehören ja zusammen in einer herrlichen und verworfenen Weise. Ach Judith, wollen Sie nicht die Meine werden?" (909). Two adventurers, for Judith wanted to become the "grand cocotte" of Europe," (907) ought to settle down together! In the last Act, they finally drop the formal "Sie" in exchange for "du," but Max is rejected in favor of Arduin whose trip "ins Ungewisse" (942) promises more adventures.

Max-Seraphine: With Seraphine, the informal relationship is immediately achieved in spite of her initial objections (860). To catch Max's attention, she threw at first one rose, then two more in his way, and he quickly wants to reciprocate by finding white lilac for her. Max treats Seraphine with the same honesty he later receives from Judith. As Seraphine reminds him that she does not wear a mask, he answers: "Ich glaube doch. Nur aber weisst du's nicht. Dein Aug', dein Mund, dein Lächeln — alles Maske. Was gilt's, mein Kind, bald kenn' ich dein Gesicht" (860). He intends to become acquainted with her true nature, at which point he is interestingly enough on formal terms with her, even though he calls his relationship with her "schwesterlich" (881). This concept of sibling-like harmony and reconciliation was treasured by Casanova, too (735); Max also shares with him the attitude of gaining pleasure just for the moment. At the end of Act II, Max is completely bound up in his erotic affair with Seraphine. Yet, at the beginning of Act III, he had an assignation with Judith. For several days and nights they enjoyed each other's companionship, which Judith abruptly ends on account of her other plans with Arduin. The final separation which Judith demands is a "unerträglicher, ein tödlicher Gedanke" (930) to him, but it is soon forgotten after he meets Seraphine the same morning.

It is the day of her concert debut in the resort town of Gilleleije, an event which, Max admits to Ambros, he had "vollkommen vergessen" (936). Only the present moment is important to Max, and this attitude accounts for the constant change in his mood and disposition.[49] Max does not forget the past, however, for he recreates the mood of their previous experience of passion and tries to persuade Seraphine into marriage, since he is the father of her child. These actions resemble Max's conduct in Act II, during which he had a passionate encounter with Seraphine only a few moments after parting with Judith, to whom he had proposed marriage. In this respect Max differs from Casanova whose life did not allow for commitments and responsibilities such as marriage, although he may have handled his life differently had he been given another chance (691).

It is Max's nature that makes him unconvincing in his desire for deeper relationships, because he is not even in tune with his innermost being. The age-old question, "Who am I?" is posed again, this time with an ironic twist. Instead of asking himself to find the answer, he is asking Seraphine to tell him "was für eine Art Mensch ich eigentlich bin" (878), and she is not too shy to comply with his request. She sees him as being "eitel, treulos und leichtsinnig" (878). None of these characteristics is helpful in a marriage. One of his answers is significant: "Nun ja, ich halte was auf mich. Aber von mir nicht sehr viel" (878). He is more concerned with his outer appearance and what other people may think of him than knowing his own self-worth and having a healthy self-image, i.e., he has little self-respect. As Seraphine puts it, he is "viel zu elegant" (881) to be truly himself, and she reasons that this falseness shows in his superficial talent for playing the piano: "Sie haben einen weichen Anschlag, manchmal ein bisschen zu süss, nicht sehr viel Rhythmus [. . .]" (880). She does not take him seriously as a musician, much less as a husband.

Max, who finds Aurelie "unheimlich," Judith "rätselhaft" (926), and only seems to be at ease when he is around Seraphine, is finally corrected and advised to look at himself: "Das wird wohl mehr an Ihnen liegen, Max, dass Ihnen die Frauen so rätselhaft erscheinen" (926). With regard to his talent, Seraphine advises him: "[. . .] seien Sie froh, dass Sie es nicht nötig haben, ich meine, dass Sie von Ihrem bisschen Talent nicht leben müssen wie — andere Leute" (927). On the other hand, Seraphine's father, the old Kammersänger Fenz, is not objective and realistic at all. He considers Max "eine eminent musikalische Natur" (918). In the meantime Max is good enough to provide the accompaniment for Seraphine, who uses every moment to polish her own performance.

Seraphine's music becomes a symbol of her personality. Her violin was enticing in the first act, because she wanted to attract Max's attention (861). He responds to the music so that he can invite himself at a later time: "Da werden Sie nichts Übles daran finden, wenn ich Sie frage, ob ich nicht gelegentlich einmal mit Ihnen musizieren dürfte" (880). It is music again which provides for a close relationship in Scene 3 of Act II. In Act III, Max speaks about her personality as well, when he compliments her music: "[. . .] dein Ton [ist] weicher, voller, wärmer geworden" (969). The tone of her musical instrument corresponds to her vocal instrument, the tone of her voice which reflects her personality. Max finds more warmth expressed in her personality. One reason may be the circumstances of her pregnancy, which in the lives of most women is a joyful time. She is fulfilled through Max; her relationship with him has given her greater maturity and identity. Although he is the father of her child, one last truth she must tell him: "Zum Heiraten bist du ja noch lange nicht erwachsen genug" (971).

In the end Max is alone again as he prepares to report to his regiment. He was instrumental in helping each of the three women find her own path, but his attraction was not strong enough to gain a wife. His interest in women, as well as his outlook on life, lacked depth, honesty, and integrity. His desire to avoid the commitments and responsibilities which are part of a balanced existence such as a marriage, was so dominant that it prevented him from experiencing true fulfillment in life.

Lack of identity and flight from reality: Schnitzler exposes this lack of identity and flight from reality in other characters such as Gysar, Fenz, Braunigl, and Prinz Arduin as well, as they gather at a "nächtliches Frühlingsfest" (847) in the latter's park. Although this spring party was not designated to be a masquerade ball, the majority of the participants hide their identity behind a mask and costume, most men wearing a "halboffenen Domino" (847) over their summer suit and the ladies donning light summer dresses. Only Julia appears in a domino. The common denominator of the guests is an attempted flight from reality. Although these guests are well aware of their different social backgrounds, their means of escape from reality is the same: erotic or political perversion, as the details of the analysis will show. Schnitzler uses Acts I and II to develop his critique upon this pre-war society, which includes members of the nobility and the educated bourgeoisie as well.[50]

Fürstin Franziska von Degenbach represents the former, and Kammersänger Eligius Fenz the latter group. Franziska is in charge of the ceremonies; her committee has organized this fund-raising event for charitable reasons (848). Not without pride does she reveal why Arduin's park was opened to the public (848). Westerhaus in his capacity as bank director was another major contributor to the charitable event of the evening. "Ich muss Ihnen noch im Namen des Komitees für die generöse Spende danken" (848) is her opening remark, as Westerhaus enters the stage, and her words entice him to throw a few more gold coins on the table. This gives him added attention and makes up for the lack of it in other areas of his life. The need of recognition is also present in Fürstin Franziska in her desire to gain attention. She likes talking about herself, which does not always contribute to "keeping up the good image." A case in point is her newspaper reading which is limited, according to her own comments, to the following sequence of sections: theater and art news, events from the court room, local reports, and the advertising portion. "Nur mit der Politik," she admits, "will ich nichts zu tun haben" (849), one reason perhaps why she does not pay attention to Heyskal's advice to spend her summer in a safer place than near the Russian-Polish border (902). Her ignorance reaches the climax of Schnitzler's satiric characterization when she says: "[. . .] ich fürcht' mich nicht. Die Russen, die ich kennengelernt hab', das waren lauter hervorragend nette Menschen" (903). She is unconcerned because her information about war comes from rather dubious sources. Exzellenz Greising (the name may indicate his state of mind) told her that war would be "ein wahrer Jungbrunnen für die Menschheit" (902). Braunigl's careless remark, "Ein Krieg würde zweifellos reinigend wirken, nicht nur in politischer Hinsicht, auch ethisch und moralisch sozusagen" (902) is equally useless toward giving her a better understanding.

Eros-Art-Poetry: Franziska's intellectual interest is limited to theater and arts, and she gives the reader an insight into the "depth" of her knowledge on three different occasions. Ambros Doehl, the poet, needs no special introduction in her estimation for "der Name [. . .] fängt ja an, weltberühmt zu werden" (851). He writes verse, we know, for Judith is obliged to him "für die Terzinen" (851). Later Franziska exclaims: "Aber wer kennt nicht Eligius Fenz, unseren berühmten Kammersänger, Mitglied der kaiserlich-königlichen Hofoper" (853). However, Fenz's career has long since ended, and he is only an honorary member now. Nevertheless, he is easily impressed by such kindness, genuine or not, and in turn extends an invitation to her for his daughter's wedding. Nor is Gysar, the painter, unknown to Franziska, because she has been his model for "die schlummernde Venus mit der roten Rose an der Brust" (850). Heyskal discovered the identity between picture and model and suggests now to Skodny a visit to the modern gallery. This explains why Gysar, upon reaching the stage, kisses Franziska's hand "etwas zu vertraulich" (849), and she, in turn, disposes of him by dancing with him (853).

Thus, Eros-Art-Poetry is the triangular combination which surrounds Franziska, just as Eros-Art-War is the constellation in Max's life. Schnitzler points out in this way how the upper classes and the writers and artists of the time avoided politics, with the disastrous result of two World Wars. Both Max and Franziska are satisfied with shallow experiences in matters of love, art, and life in general instead of searching for a more complete and meaningful purpose in life. Each character corroborates this superficiality which typifies their society as a whole.

Eros-Art-Age: The Character of Fenz combines the motif of age with Eros and art. In his conversation with Falkenir he condemns the process of aging as a legend which needs to be destroyed. "Wissen Sie, Herr Baron, was das Alter ist? Nichts als eine Intrige, die die Jugend gegen uns einfädelt [...] mit sechzig fängt das Leben im gewissen Sinne erst an" (875). Even his favorite role as Don Juan, he tells Falkenir, was twenty years ago only warbled, not sung because "nur ein Sechzigjähriger kann den Don Juan singen" (875); and to give proof of his voice he sings "die Champagner Arie" from Mozart's *Don Giovanni* for Falkenir until his daughter Seraphine reminds him of the cool night air which will affect his voice. The drama ends with the same aria; this time, he is indeed not singing but warbling, according to the stage direction: "Beginnt leise wieder die Champagner Arie zu trällern" (974).

Schnitzler shows here clearly the state of confusion within Fenz. He depreciates his earlier career, where he probably was a celebrated baritone, in order to avoid the present reality: he no longer is a member of the opera ensemble; his voice no longer projects strongly; he no longer is at the zenith of his life. One of his hopes at this time, of course, is to be again on stage. The opportunity to travel with Seraphine will give him a chance to pursue his own interests in this direction (915).

Both his daughters seem to play the game of youth with their father. Seraphine stands on his side: "Wie schön du singst, Vater" (875) [...]. Was fällt dir ein Vater. Bist du nicht jung, bist du nicht schön?" (859). Elisabeth, however, tries to help her father face reality: "Es wäre dir ganz gesund, Vater. Da kämst du vielleicht drauf, dass du am Ende doch kein Jüngling mehr bist" (858). This is her counter-argument to his concern of becoming a grandfather too soon, if she marries Leutnant Leindorf now. But Fenz remains in his world of illusion regarding his age and profession, because he wants to be in the limelight again.

He interprets every event in light of this hope. In Act I, the two female dominoes call him "Graf Almaviva" and "Don Juan" reminding him of former baritone roles in Mozart's *Hochzeit des Figaro* and *Don Giovanni*. But he assumes that they will relate an important message because "es soll sich allerlei vorbereiten in der Oper. Direktionswechsel und dergleichen" (859), and he follows them into nothing more than an adventure. Yet, it all ends before it really began (874), thus indicating that his career as an adventurer in love has come to an end as well. When in Act II his colleagues from the opera do not come to the wedding, he interprets their absence in his favor in light of significant changes at the theater. In reality, like attracts like, and only the previous generation, the senior Don Juan Meyerhofer and Devona, known for her role as Donna Anna, have shown up for the wedding. He treats them like patron saints from ancient times: "Ach ja, lasst es Euch nur schmecken, meine guten Alten [...]" (919), and refuses to realize, how much he truly is one of them. His own opera career has ended long ago, but as a voice teacher he presently helps others enter the field. Judith is one of his "most talented pupils" (853), he earlier told Franciska proudly. But Seraphine quotes her father differently: "Der Vater ist gar nicht so entzückt von ihr. Er findet ihre Stimme keineswegs ersten Ranges" (926). The manner in which Fenz admonishes Albine and Ida to pay more attention to their vocal practice every day seems to hint at the level of their present talent (917). How important voice work is for the expansion of volume is indicated by the example of "la divina Devona," as Fenz calls her sentimentally. "Aber von sieben bis halb acht morgens, auch als sie schon weltberühmt war, übte sie ihre Vokalisen. Also nehmt euch ein Beispiel, ihr kleinen Canaillen!" (917). On the other hand, Fenz may not be a first-rate teacher if one judges by the type of pupil he attracts. Nevertheless, the fact that Fenz is interested in developing talents within the younger generation is perhaps a mark in favor of this otherwise ambivalent character.

This ambivalence is demonstrated in his estimation of Judith as an artist. Yet, as was already pointed out, to his daughter Seraphine he talks quite differently. Another example is the "wahrhaft fürstliche Grossmut" (877, 919) which Fenz sees at times in Franziska. But he is not consistent in his thinking, particularly when we recall his talk with Ambros: "Dem Künstler ist Fürstengunst gefährlich" (856).

Eros-Art-Dilettantism: Ambros, the dilettante-poet, represents another aspect of the triangularity which can be called Eros-Art-Dilettantism, provided that the latter term is applied to a larger frame of reference. Ambros shares this constellation with Max, a dilettante in his own way, for in combination with the artists Judith and Seraphine, Max is not only a dilettante in his musical talent, but his passivity and insincerity make him also a dilettante in matters of the heart, particularly in his relationship with Aurelie. After he spent the night with her, he waited three days for her call instead of contacting her for reasons of interest and concern. His insensitivity may have aroused feelings of guilt within Aurelie and may have driven her into the hands of Gysar more easily in an attempt to free herself from emotional pain. She had the desire to see Max again, for when he finally appears she says: "Oh, ich bin froh, dass du da bist [...] warum warst du gestern nicht da — und vorgestern? Drei Tage lang sah ich dich nicht! Wo bliebst du? [...] Ich glaube wohl, dass ich rief; — du hast's nur nicht gehört" (896).

Judith and Seraphine, of course, never show any feelings of longing so openly. With regard to their talent, they never had the ambition to reach for the stars. Seraphine always knew, "dass ich nie das werden kann, was ich selbst darunter verstehe" (880), but her interest in the violin at least saved her from involving herself in the monotonous occupation of "Telephonfräulein" (880). Judith, on the other hand, who in her unrequited love for Westerhaus was deeply hurt, may have become a "Nähmamsell" (907) in outer ways as well. So she uses her voice to aim at becoming "die berühmteste Kokotte von Europa" (907). Interestingly enough, Ambros turns out to be the most unassuming character among them all. Except for Franziska, who calls him "weltberühmt" (851), and Judith, who openly presents him with a rose in gratitude for the "Terzinen" he wrote (851), the audience would not know much about Ambros' literary career. "Leben und Kunst," therefore, represent harmonious aspects in Ambros's personal experience; they are not polarities struggling for expression. Offermanns sees a change in Ambros taking place in the course of the play "zum patriotischen Journalisten, der seinem Publikum dessen Pflichten im Kriege einschärfen wird."[51]

This tendency to journalism was established at his initial appearance when, questioned by Judith about his relationship to Arduin, he admits: "Ich bin nur so eine Art Geheimrevolutionär bei ihm" (851), showing that he plays a certain role in Arduin's political involvements. It also indicates that Ambros deliberately functions behind the scenes, which is the reason for his low-key answer to Judith, as the word "nur" would indicate. In modern political terms, Ambros may be called a speechwriter, in the light of Arduin's poor talent for communication on his own. Thus Ambros, like Max, is qualified to fit into the previous constellation of Eros-Art-War as well. Act III reveals more about him in this direction, as he meets Arduin. As journalist, he seems to be better informed than Arduin about the latest developments on the political front, which prompted him to arrange for a private motor boat to reach Copenhagen in time for the last train across the border. On the other hand, Arduin has just completed various diplomatic missions and may know more of military intelligence than Ambros. One could speculate on Ambros' journalistic involvement in these missions at Arduin's request, which would have enabled Arduin to deliver valuable intelligence. Perhaps this discussion is simply an exercise in testing each other's confidence and trustworthiness anew, now that war has broken out in spite of Arduin's mediations on highest diplomatic levels.

When placed upon the triangular diagram which accompanies Schnitzler's theoretical work "Der Geist im Wort und der Geist in der Tat" (AuB, 135f), we find Arduin the politician in juxtaposition with Ambros the dilettante-poet (Literat) on the lower part of the triangle, both ranking in the category of negative "Geistesverfassungen." Although Schnitzler states: "Es gibt keine Übergänge von einem Typ zum anderen im gleichen Dreieck" (AuB, 138), he admits that occasionally one finds a journalistically inclined politician which in the case of the two characters of Komödie der Verführung needs to be reversed into a "politically engaged journalist." Thus, it would seem justified to rank Ambros in his "Geistesverfassung" slightly higher than Arduin, especially if the aspect of Eros is taken into consideration.

Offermanns views Ambros as a character, "dem gleichfalls jede erotische Bindung misslingt."[52] Actually, the play leaves its audience in suspense about Ambros' erotic contacts, with the exception of his desire to marry Aurelie. Because Aurelie's choice was Falkenir, it is possible to speak of an unsuccessful relationship. But the contacts Ambros has with all other women characters in the play are merely acquaintances. There is no indication that Ambros desired any closer relationship. This can be seen most distinctly in the way Ambros addresses the women, never during the entire drama varying from the formal manner of address when he speaks with them. Even with Aurelie he never uses informal address, which would, of course, be the natural manner in an erotic relationship.

We have seen the change take place in the case of Max and his relationships with Judith and Seraphine. He addressed them always by their first name; although formally at first. The relationship between Max and Aurelie is even more formal. He calls her "Gräfin," and she addresses him Herr von Reisenberg (889-90). In Act II, of course, they are on first-name basis and say "du" to each other. Ambros' conduct, therefore, compared with that of Max would prove that the poet was not an adventurer like Max or Arduin.[53] He only once fell in love. As an artist, he stands apart from all other artists in the play. He certainly cannot be compared to Fenz, either by age or ambition or erotic behavior. To mention the painter Gysar even remotely would truly constitute an insult to Ambros. Thus, it appears that Offermanns' argument is lacking in substantial proof.

There are other inaccuracies in Offermanns' interpretation of Ambros as well. Ambros cannot be relegated to the status of "eine zweite Schicht mittlerer Figuren."[54] His presence is particularly important in Act III when he is concerned in a selfless way with Aurelie's protection. To call him an "impressionistic adventurer"[55] seems to be wrong on both counts. The only remark which is not explained at any other time in the play is the one made by Fenz, from which the audience can glean that Ambros was once a frequent visitor there (856). Elisabeth confesses to Leindorf that she was in love with Ambros and that he wrote poems to her (861); but then he also shared "Terzinen" with Judith (851), and their relationships were platonic. Even the roses he gives and receives in Act I are in harmony with the tone of the evening. He does express his feelings mildly when Seraphine throws her roses to catch Max's attention: "Ich habe alles gesehen. So verfahren Sie mit meinen Rosen [...]" (861), but these words do not give any clue to the audience to assume a deeper relationship. Even his boat ride with Aurelie in Act III is nothing more than acquiescence to a passing mood of hers (946). Since Ambros at that time is her guardian until Falkenir arrives, he certainly would not have misused his privilege and responsibilities. Besides, Aurelie appears to exaggerate the story in order to impress Arduin.

With regard to the "impressionistic" behavior, I have not been able to find substantiating evidence. On the contrary, Ambros is one of the few characters who is well balanced on every level of his being. When he recognizes that Aurelie's choice has not fallen upon him, he rises beyond his personal longings and stands ready to help Aurelie later during the time of her greatest need, toward the end of the play. In Act II when Max is concerned about Aurelie and urges Ambros to exert his influence, since his relationship with her is based on pure friendship, he speaks with complete self-authority: "Es ist zu früh [...] sie muss ihren Weg gehen [...] ihr Schicksal spiegelt sich in meiner Seele wie das Bild eines Sterns in einem dunklen Weiher. Er geht seine vorgeschriebene Bahn; kein Sterblicher kann sie stören" (922). Yet, when the time is right, Ambros stands ready to extend his hand unselfishly. Because he spends his vacation every year at Gilleleiji (919), he takes Aurelie under his protection in the expectation that this peaceful atmosphere may heal her soul and calm any disturbing emotions. He is content to let their relationship rest on friendship and writes Falkenir to take over his responsibilities. He also cautions Arduin: "Es wäre unverantwortlich, auch nur mit einem Wort an den mühselig errungenen Frieden dieser verstörten Seele zu rühren" (945). Ambros knows from deep within that nothing will be gained by reproaching Aurelie for her past conduct. Genuine affection alone can provide an atmosphere of healing, which can be maintained only by non-judgment and true forgiveness. Therefore, Ambros does not allow Arduin an opportunity for criticism. Unfortunately, in his encounter with Aurelie, Arduin does not heed the advice of his absent friend.

The maturity and honesty in Ambros show not only in his relationship with Aurelie, but also in his positive convictions about Seraphine, when he points out: "Und wenn es mit der Zeit zehn Liebhaber werden sollten, die bleibt ewig rein" (863). He also defends Max against Braunigl's accusations: "Ich finde, dass junge Leute, wie mein Freund Max einer ist, einfach durch die Tatsache ihres Daseins die Atmosphäre der Welt freundlicher und anmutiger gestalten. Warum noch Leistungen von ihnen verlangen? Verlangen Sie Leistungen von einem Schmetterling? Vom Frühlingswind?" (905). As flattering as Ambros can be in his evaluation of a person, he is capable of unwavering honesty when he thinks it necessary, as in his conversation with Judith (907). It is important to question Judith's thoughts, that is, whether she really means what she has been saying.[56] Did Judith really want to become a "grande cocotte." Ambros may have startled her but perhaps caused her to think about her words more deeply. What was the reason for her statement? It was spoken under the pressure of deep emotional hurt. That hurt needed healing. But in her case, that need did not really surface and receive attention. It was repressed and finally replaced by a love affair with Max, and at the end by the anticipated adventure with Arduin.

Ambros seems to find the right words for every situation. When he studies Julia's picture in Westerhaus' home, he becomes aware of his host's anxious suspicion that a nude picture of his wife exists somewhere. Ambros, who certainly is aware of Gysar's practice in this respect, finds a word of protection for him: "Um Künstler bilden sich immer Legenden, Herr Präsident" (901), thus diverting Westerhaus' trend of thought and preventing futile wrath.

The analysis of Ambros has shown him evolving into greater maturity through his unselfish, honest nature — ever ready to help and to give of himself. He demonstrates sensitivity toward the feelings of others, a trait which helps him to find always the right comment in every situation.

Unfortunately, this cannot be said about Gysar, the painter. He represents the lowest aspects of perversion within the constellation Eros-Art-Dilettantism. Offermanns' evaluation of this character is pertinent: "[...] Verkehrung der Kunst in ein absichtsvolles Mittel zu nicht-künstlerischen, partikularen Zwecken, nicht auf Befreiung zielend, sondern wiederum auf 'Verführung' im engeren und weiteren Sinne. Gysar, der Scharlatan, sieht in seiner Malerei vornehmlich die Gelegenheit zur Verführung seines jeweiligen Modells. Die Kunst ist nurmehr Vorwand."[57]

When Gysar arrives on stage, he wears a domino over his summer suit, a mode of dress which is in keeping with his intentions for the evening's festivity. Most of the male characters use this costume to hide their identity. But in Gysar's case it symbolizes his incapacity to face himself and to evaluate sincerely the motives he chooses to fulfill his life's purpose through the expression of art. As he appears, he uses his artistic ability as a means to perverted ends. Act I reveals some of his past activities and shows him actively in search of new "victims." His outer appearance aids him in this endeavor, in that he is charming and good-looking, "über vierzig Jahre alt, glattes, schwarzes Haar, dunkler Spitzbart" (849). He greets Franziska too intimately, but then her picture as "schlummernde Venus" (850) is publicly displayed in the modern art gallery, a testimony of the kind of relationship they have had. It is Heyskal who has discovered her identity with the nude in the picture, and he tells Skodny of the discovery along with further revealing details: "Wissen Sie denn nicht, dass er von jeder Frau, die ihm sitzt, zwei Bilder malt? Das eine offiziell im Kostüm und dann ein anderes —" (850). We also know from Judith that he painted her sister Julia three years earlier. This picture hangs in the banker's home, but Westerhaus suspects a nude picture to exist somewhere else which he has not yet discovered, as he confides to Ambros (901). Gysar sells these pictures, which he paints without commission (852).

His new erotic target is Judith, although his question is posed rather inconspicuously: "Wann darf ich Ihr Portrait beginnen" (849). Westerhaus suggests, perhaps in an attempt to save her from becoming a "victim" too soon, that Gysar wait until she is a famous singer, not giving Judith a chance to answer for herself. This prompts Gysar to be much more direct with Aurelie. Once he had the triumph of dancing with her, a dance she accepted reluctantly in the end only to please Falkenir. Because Aurelie is not inclined to answer his incessant question, he boldly tells her: "So will ich nicht mehr fragen. So sprech' ich's einfach aus. Sie sollen es nur wissen, Aurelie, ich *werde* Ihr Bild malen" (885). He declares all his other pictures void: "An dem Ihren erst, Aurelie, vermöchte ich der zu werden, der ich bin" (886). Aurelie finally declares him a "coxcomb" and sends him away, but he swears not to begin another picture until he has completed hers.

Gysar is not able to paint a straight portrait of Aurelie. He has been trying for two weeks, and three attempts have failed so far (891). Aurelie, in spite of the disappointment with Falkenir, is in remarkable control of her emotions. She keeps the distance between herself and Gysar and finally suggests that he postpone painting her picture, especially since hundreds of women are waiting to be painted, and Arduin is also in line for a picture in order to add artistic expression to his yacht. But Gysar insists that no other work is left for him in this world but to paint her picture, and finally he reveals his idea of the painting he wants to do: "Himmelslicht über Ihre Haare, über Ihre Stirn, Ihren Hals, Ihren Nacken, Ihre Hüften, Aurelie. Sie müssen kommen. Mein Haus steht allein. Um den Garten hohe Mauern. Wir sind wie auf einer Insel im Weltmeer" (893). But Aurelie remains sceptical about his talent and openly reveals her concern: "Wenn es am Ende auf nichts hinausliefe, als auf eine Art von betrügerischer Herauslockung?" (893), and Gysar admits: "Nun, so hätten Sie sich eben verschenkt, Aurelie [...] hätten einen Menschen, der Sie anbetet, glücklich gemacht [...]. Ist das so wenig?" (893).

Act III develops in the absence of Gysar the destructive consequences of the painter's association with Aurelie; the final blow occurs when Arduin mentions triumphantly his possession of the nude picture. As Offermanns points out, Gysar's "Produkte dienen entweder einer vordergründig-eitlen gesellschaftlichen Repräsentation, oder aber sie verleiten, wie die Darstellung der nackten Aurelie, zu einem fetischhaften Bilderkult, wenn Arduin vor diesem Akt einen aus Zerrformen der Erotik und der Anbetung der Idee gemischten Götzendienst verrichtet."[58]

However, Gysar's villainies go beyond the framework mentioned in Offermanns' statement above. Actually, Gysar causes indirectly the destruction of lives as a consequence of his perverted actions. Hence, he represents the man who contributes greatly to the decay of moral and ethical values that is already afflicting the society of prewar Austria. When he said to Aurelie, "an dem Ihren erst, Aurelie, vermöchte ich der zu werden, der ich bin" (886), the ironic double twist was not apparent as yet. But if we think of him as a villain, then he reached the culmination of his perverted art by destroying two people in the process. If he portrays hundreds of women in society, and always paints a second uncommissioned nude picture of them which he then sells to influential circles in society, one can imagine the aggravation he causes the many cuckolded husbands, of whom Westerhaus is an example.

For three years Westerhaus has observed a change within his wife Julia toward open marriage. He is also aware of the orgiastic celebrations behind the garden walls of Gysar's house, as he hints: "In seinem Garten feiert man andere [Feste]" (850). The change in his wife has destroyed Westerhaus' marriage by making him openly jealous and possessive. This may explain in part his uncontrolled behavior toward Julia, when he decides to leave the party with her. Unrestrained, as previously in his encounter with Gysar (850), he tries to find out the reason for her silence: "Sind dir die Lippen von Küssen wund?" (864). When Braunigl and Ambros are shocked about such unkind behavior and try to object, Westerhaus defends himself: "Was wollen die Herren? Sie ist mein Weib, ein Weib, eine Sache, gekauft wie irgendeine andere. Ein reinlicher Handel, meine Herren. Wollte Gott, es gäbe keine schlimmeren" (865). This statement carries several levels of meaning, but one of them certainly relates to Gysar and his abuse of art for sexual seduction. For Westerhaus knows about these orgies and tries to expose Gysar publicly. Gysar calls his parties candid, more sincere in contrast with the masks and dominoes, but Westerhaus disagrees with him violently (850). It gives him a chance to vent all the hatred accumulated against the painter who has destroyed his marriage, turning his wife against him to the point of criminal involvement and the actual death of her husband later in the drama. The cause of all this misery is the villain Gysar.

Eros-Art-War: Gysar may even be responsible for Westerhaus' accelerated interest in high-risk monetary speculations to the point of gambling recklessly on the livelihood of war. This is the sort of conduct that places Westerhaus in a triangular combination of Eros-Art-War. Art, to be sure, is not his metier, and he only became involved in it in a negative way through the experiences with Julia after her portrait was painted by Gysar. However, within the triangular constellation it is the aspect of art which exerts direct influence upon the other two angles. His family life suffered, and this may be one reason why no children were born to the marriage. He therefore has turned all his attention toward the banking business and its adverse enticement to pursue high-risk speculations. Being neglected by his wife, he searches for recognition elsewhere, because money buys everything (849). This may have been the motivation for his "generöse Spende" (848) to charity. When he threw a few more gold coins on the table as he received a glass of champagne, he may have done so in anticipation of added attention. "Das ist ja beinahe schon zu viel" (849), comments Franziska, and Braunigl echoes "ein solcher Grad von Noblesse ist beinahe schon unmoralisch" (849). For people like Rittmeister Skodny, who do not have much money, it is a fiction, but not so for Braunigl who knows money buys all sorts of things, and not for Westerhaus, who can buy everything with money, even a wife (865). Such a disgracing assessment negates the individuality of any human being, but more severely that of a marriage partner; it reduces Julia indeed to an "object." Hardly any reconciliation seems possible under these circumstances; in fact, Julia's only desire is to be freed from the man who bought her in marriage. Cruelty is answered by cruelty: Julia is plotting against her husband.

Money has gained seductive powers over Westerhaus in the political arena as well. Apparently, he is thoroughly informed about the most sensitive international political developments and takes advantage of this in his speculations and manipulations on world money markets. Arduin's question directed to Westerhaus, "Werden wir Krieg haben?" (852), starts the process of entwining the erotic and political themes of the drama. Westerhaus knows about war, for he is in touch with colleagues in France, England, America, and Japan; according to Arduin, bankers are responsible for the timing of wars (852). [59] Arduin fears Westerhaus' warning not to wait until "Hochsommer" if he desires an undisturbed pleasure trip aboard his yacht. Later, in Scene 2 of Act II, Westerhaus' prediction is even more precise, when he tells Judith "dass es keine drei Tage mehr dauern wird, — und die Welt steht in Flammen" (900).

The telephone in Westerhaus' office rings almost constantly, as he receives reports of the newest political developments. One such development, known under the cover word "Kameltreiber," refers to the Berlin-Baghdad-Railway project between Germany and Turkey (898-900). England had a key interest in this issue because of her shipping activities on the Euphrates river. On June 15, 1914, the exact day on which Act II takes place in this drama, an Anglo-German agreement was initiated, which "settled the Baghdad-Railway problem, the Germans promising not to construct the line south of Basra and recognizing England's preponderant interest in the shipping on the Euphrates. The agreement reflected a real desire on both sides to remove many outstanding colonial difficulties."[60] It caused Westerhaus' financial ruin, for his speculations were based on the outbreak of war. Offermanns' interpretation of Westerhaus overlooks this fact of history. He observes a shift of roles within Westerhaus from an earlier erotic adventurer to a "Kameltreiber."[61] However, Westerhaus and his bank took part in the financial backing of this railway project. Because of the Anglo-German agreement, no war has come about as yet; consequently, no profit for Westerhaus and his banker friends abroad materialized.

In his argument with Judith Westerhaus reveals: "Auf die Geschäfte könnte ich am Ende verzichten, aber auf die Gefahr —? [. . .] Das Risiko, das ist der Sinn meines Lebens" (900), thus giving himself fully over to the dangerous consequences of temptation. He is totally aware, "dass man hohe Chancen auch hoch bezahlen muss" (900). His abrupt decision to go to the bank office seems to indicate that he will direct his attention now to these projects involving even greater risks. What were the issues? They can only briefly be outlined here because the discussion of a detailed historic background would go beyond the intent of this interpretation. In addition to Austria's involvement with the various Balkan disturbances during this time, there were preparations in the making to assassinate the Archduke Francis Ferdinand who was obstinate against certain Austrian interests.[62] This assassination came about on June 28, 1914, at Sarajevo, sending Europe into conflagration.[63] The death of the Archduke is anticipated in the drama by Westerhaus' suicide, thus the banker is the victim caught in his own net (911).

Yet, the causes of this net's tightening around Westerhaus can be traced to Gysar. Westerhaus would not have taken such high risks in combining his financial speculations with a gamble on war, had he felt responsible toward wife and children. "Ich habe keinen Sohn" (900) is his answer to Judith, who questions his reckless involvement. He does not make world history, but he has the talent to project into the future. "Es ist mein gutes Recht, von dieser Gabe zu profitieren" (900). By using his financial abilities for war speculations, Westerhaus employs his talents as perversely as Gysar.

Suicide, of course, was not part of the original conspiracy which Braunigl and Julia had planned against Westerhaus. Braunigl only wanted him arrested for his illegal financial speculations so as to be free to carry out his own erotic plans for Julia. Next to Gysar, Braunigl represents the worst element in this declining society in that he betrays his public office for erotic adventure, in addition to causing the death of another person. Max relates later to Ambros: "Und Braunigl ist suspendiert, wie Sie wohl gelesen haben. Es stellte sich heraus, dass zur Verhaftung von Westerhaus kein rechtlicher Grund vorhanden gewesen war" (936). Nothing more is said in the drama, but the audience certainly is urged to ponder this point of superficial justice. Is suspension from office a just punishment for causing the death of another human being?

In line with the principle of triangularity Schnitzler presents two more examples of Braunigl's decayed moral and ethical fiber. War to him "würde zweifellos reinigend wirken, nicht nur in politischer Hinsicht, auch ethisch und moralisch sozusagen" (902). Schnitzler calls such enemies of peace "Phrasendrescher," and acquaints his audience with them by developing such a character in the play (AuB, 210). Franziska knows "Exzellenz Greising," the second character of the Braunigl category. According to the Fürstin, Greising considers war "ein wahrer Jungbrunnen für die Menschheit" (902). The third example of the Braunigl type of corruption occurs in the legal procedures of the courts. Graf Merkenstein is sentenced to one year in prison for the duel that killed Max's father; yet, eight days later, he is pardoned and free again.

Schnitzler adds to Braunigl's questionable competence as a civil servant the arrogance of his personal life. During the evening of the spring party, social snobbery moves him to compare himself with other members of society. He remembers vaguely that Ambros is "Schriftsteller — nicht wahr?" (850), when the poet arrives in company with Arduin. Skodny from the ranks of the military comments: "Seine Hoheit lassen sich gern herab" (850), a remark which draws a quick correction from Gysar, the painter: "Vielleicht, Herr Rittmeister, ist es in diesem Falle Ambros Doehl, der sich herablässt?" (850). Later on, when Westerhaus is publicly outraged over his wife Julia, Braunigl dares to pass judgment: "Welche Zustände! Ein Sumpf!" (865). Yet, it was he who had approached Julia earlier with the enticing and tempting question: "Wann werden Sie mir gehören? [...] Fordern Sie, was Sie wollen. Mein Leben, meine Ehre ..." (864), thereby contributing most actively to the anger within Westerhaus and to the moral and ethical corruption within society in general. Furthermore, he betrays his own personal friend cold-bloodedly.

In Scene 2 of Act II a third example of Braunigl's negative character is given as he criticizes Max von Reisenberg for having no profession other than "Verführer." Max is not a useful member of society, in Braunigl's view. Ambros, however, drawing upon his creative talent in speech, has the perfect retort in defense of Max. He strikes out against Braunigl's arrogance: "Sie glauben doch nicht, Herr Staatsanwalt, dass solch ein Mensch, wie zum Beispiel Max [...] einer ist, an äusserem oder innerem Wert auch nur das geringste gewänne, wenn er auf dem Graben Uhren und Ringe verkaufte [...]. Oder wenn er Rekruten einexerzierte? Oder wenn er Verbrecher, eventuell auch Unschuldige ins Gefängnis schickte? Oder in irgendeinem Büro Akten schriebe?" (905). The remark regarding the prison is certainly aimed at Braunigl and the decaying judicial system he stands for in his capacity as public prosecutor, who does not want to face the facts about these illegal court-room practices. This contrast between illusion and reality is apparent throughout the play. Most of the characters analyzed try to escape reality by living in some kind of imaginary realm, regardless of the triangular constellation they represent.

Eros-Art-Fairytale/Imagination: The realm in which Prinz Arduin lives has an unrealistic quality which will be considered next. To bring him into closer focus, the constellation Eros-Art-Fairytale/Imagination is suggested.

A fairytale, according to current English diction, is an unbelievable story because of the absence of true-to-life characters or the presence of fantastic (untrue, to the brink of fantasy) characters or events. One finds, of course, no such elements in *Komödie der Verführung,* a drama of adultery, villainy, war manipulations and suicides, unless one understands Schnitzler's antithetical use of the term "Märchen." André Jolles, who includes the fairytale in his discussion of "Einfache Formen," concerns himself with the "Geistesbeschäftigung des Märchens."[64] In terms of its form it is, according to him, an expectation "wie es eigentlich in der Welt zugehen müsste."[65] This question, "How must things happen in the world?" commands an ethical judgment which is different from that based upon action in terms of Kant's question "What must I do?" Jolles calls it "Gefühlsurteil" when he writes: "Im Gegensatz zur philosophischen Ethik, zur Ethik des Handelns, nenne ich diese Ethik die Ethik des Geschehens oder die naive Moral, wobei ich das Wort naiv in demselben Sinne gebrauche wie Schiller, wenn er von naiver Dichtung redet. Unser naivethisches Urteil ist ein Gefühlsurteil [...]."[66]

Jolles, therefore, expands the "Geistesbeschäftigung" of the "Märchen" effectively in two directions, "[...] einerseits greift und begreift sie verneinend die Welt als eine Wirklichkeit, die der Ethik des Geschehens nicht entspricht, andererseits gibt sie bejahend eine andere Welt, in der alle Anforderungen der naiven Moral erfüllt werden [...] kurz es muss ein Anti-Märchen geben."[67] This then is the definition which Schnitzler seems to elucidate, when he employs the term so frequently in the drama.[68] The antithetical use of "Märchen" can be further illustrated by the historic accuracy of the play which, according to Jolles, diminishes the strength of the "Märchen-Charakter." "Historische Örtlichkeit, historische Zeit nähern sich der unmoralischen Wirklichkeit, brechen die Macht des selbstverständlich und notwendig Wunderbaren."[69]

Jolles includes in this observation also personages, "[...] auch sie müssen jene unbestimmte Sicherheit besitzen, an der eine unmoralische Wirklichkeit zerschellt. Wenn der Prinz im Märchen den Namen eines historischen Prinzen trüge, so würden wir sofort von der Ethik des Geschehens in die Ethik des Handelns übergeführt werden."[70] "Handeln," however, relates to the question "What must I do?" which Prinz Arduin does not ask himself seriously. It is the critical point at which he departs into the imaginary realm.

There are various indications throughout the play that the Prince is out of touch with reality on most levels of existence: his personal life and love affairs, his military and diplomatic career, the realm of responsibility and commitment as a member of society. In Act I he wears under his black Atlas domino an Austrian "Husarengeneraluniform," but he admits in Act III himself, he is not just "Generalmajor der österreichisch-ungarischen Armee" (943), he also carries "den Titel des Majors in einem französischen Kavallerieregiment" (943). In addition, Castle Rodegna near Florence is a family possession — his mother resides there; he still enjoys being called Prinz von Perosa, although that "Grossherzogtum" no longer exists (943) and it is not without celebrating his vanity that he tells Ambros: "[...] italienisches, englisches, wahrscheinlich auch etwas slawisches Blut fliesst in meinen Adern [...]" (943), for his loyalties are uncommitted to any of these countries.

It is true, diplomatic missions have led him recently to many governments in an attempt to halt the mobilization for war, but perhaps his lack of responsibility has been a cause of the failure of his services to Austria. He simply did not recognize the importance of his task. He was aware of only one possible reason for this appointment: "Richtiger gesagt, man hat sich meiner verwandtschaftlichen Beziehungen mit den meisten regierenden und abgesetzten Fürstenhäusern Europas erinnert [...]" (941).

Obviously, Arduin did not use these beneficial circumstances to his advantage in his diplomatic missions. But then, communication is not one of his strong points. His conversation with Ambros in Act I about Aurelie and Falkenir is comparable to a monolog because, for the most part, Ambros' remarks involve only one or two sentences (853-55). His rendez-vous with Judith was barely long enough to invite her as a guest aboard his dream yacht. Act II reveals more details of this fifteen-minute romantic encounter at the garden party. Furthermore, he does not even know "wer die Dame ist. Ich habe sie nur einmal gesprochen, da war sie maskiert" (942). When Arduin visits Aurelie unannounced in Scene 1 of Act II in her home to renew his marriage proposal, a different kind of communication problem occurs between them. Arduin is interested to hear more about Aurelie's sudden agreement to see Gysar on his terms, whereas Aurelie wants to know about Arduin's recent travels.

Aurelie:	Woher kommst du eigentlich?
Arduin:	Davon später. — Es ist nicht im Ernst deine Absicht, das Haus Gysars zu betreten?
Aurelie:	Das Haus und den Garten; — wenn der Himmel heiter bleibt. — Du warst in Griechenland und Italien?
Arduin (rasch):	Und in Frankreich und England. — Weisst du auch, wohin du dich begibst, wenn du zu Gysar gehst?
Aurelie:	In das Atelier eines grossen Künstlers. — Du bist in geheimer Mission gereist, wie man erzählte?
Arduin:	Ein Atelier? — Nächstens kommt die Polizei und hebt das Nest aus. Weiber laufen dort herum, wie Gott sie geschaffen.
Aurelie:	Eine komische Idee, dir diplomatische Missionen anzuvertrauen." (895)

Their separate ranges of interest are pursued simultaneously in this dialog; neither is genuinely concerned for the other. Aurelie in her attempt to smooth over the Gysar-Arduin encounter takes the latter's recent political career of diplomatic assignments as target for her questions; Arduin, whose pride is hurt by Aurelie's preference for Gysar, deliberately reverts the conversation to the artist. Although Arduin is unwittingly telling the truth, his own motive is selfish, another adventure in love, particularly since his memory of that night of his first proposal to Aurelie had already vanished "ins Unwirkliche, Unwahrscheinliche, niemals Gewesene" (855). Yet, he assures Aurelie, "Alles, was ich getan, war ja nur um deinetwillen — das Gute und das Üble, alles für dich" (895-96).

Arduin is playing "Komödie" which allows him to escape any responsibility for his actions. When he tells Aurelie, "du scherzest und spielst Komödie" (896), he is only projecting upon Aurelie that which is going on within himself. Act I had already revealed his love affair with Julia (856), and Act III tells us about his appointment with Judith for his pleasure trip. Still, he tries to impress Aurelie with his yacht: "Für dich, ich wusst' es immer, ist es gebaut und fahrbereit. Es trägt deinen Namen, und, wenn du willst, ist es dein - wie alles, was ich besitze. Komm mit mir!" (947). His last triumph over Aurelie, of course, is her nude picture on shipboard which he bought from Gysar, the very same man he had earlier despised for tempting Aurelie to follow Gysar into his infamous gardens. Arduin at that time would even have fought a duel with Gysar, had Aurelie not stated her position thus: "[...] bin niemandem Rechenschaft schuldig als mir selbst [...]. Hiemit ist die Angelegenheit ritterlich beigelegt" (894).

There exists a polarity between Arduin and Gysar in several ways. As adventurers, both are perverted in their sexual expression; both use lies as a means to their adventurous ends; both use similar terminology in their cajolements: "Haben Sie irgendeinem Menschen

Rechenschaft abzulegen" (894) was Gysar's question to Aurelie. "Bist du irgendeinem Menschen [...] Treue schuldig?" (947) asks Arduin. Both are misdirected in their appreciation of art, whether it be Gysar's orgiastic cult or Arduin's idolatry, a pseudo-religious picture cult: "Jeden Morgen, jeden Abend will ich vor deinem Bild meine Andacht verrichten, so gläubig und sehnsuchtsvoll, wie ich vor keinem Altar noch gekniet habe" (949). Both operate from a low level of consciousness, threatening the very existence of human life. Whereas Gysar is indirectly to blame for at least three deaths, Arduin's aggressiveness indicates that he is ridiculously often trigger-happy.[71]

Eros-War-Fairytale/Imagination: It is this aggressiveness which relates him to another triangular constellation, that of Eros-War-Fairytale/Imagination, all three motifs occurring consistently throughout the play. However, more emphasis is placed upon Arduin's imaginary realm. The first impression of him is that of a "Märchenprinz" with a "Märchenyacht," picking up his guest at a distant "Märchenstrand" where "Meeresgott" and "Wassernixe" still exist, to begin "eine Fahrt ins Ungewisse." He adds Aurelie to his "Märchenreich," for when she came to Franziska's evening party, "da war es nicht anders, als finge ein Märchen an" (855). But this "Märchen" had already started in early childhood, when they both played with their ball by the pond. It reminds us of Grimm's fairytale *Der Froschkönig*, where this enchanted green creature fetches the ball out of the well for the little princess. She does not want to play with him because he is too ugly, but later falls in love with him when he changes into the handsome prince. Many references in the play relate to this imaginary, indeed fairytale world.[72]

But it is also Arduin who carries the motif of war into the play, when he asks Westerhaus: "Werden wir Krieg haben?" (852). Westerhaus, like Braunigl, has his own reasons for being interested in war. Even people such as Fenz are involved in the war question, for his daughter Elisabeth is about to marry Leutnant Leindorf. Fenz is fearful that she may be left behind with three uncared-for children, but Leindorf asserts positively: "Die Kriegsgerüchte sind unbegründet" (858) which shows the irony that those closest to the source know the least. Elisabeth is already well indoctrinated by her husband-to-be, for she remarks: "Börsenmanöver, das weiss jeder Mensch" (858). Franziska echoes naively what she has heard from Greising (902), and even Julia needs to be cheered up to take her mind off the planned conspiracy: "Einen Walzer oder einen Trauermarsch" (906). The waltz, of course, relates to Act I in its gaiety, and the funeral march anticipates the happenings of Act III. Skodny adding the waltz title "Weltuntergang" (906), which he has heard recently. In Act III, each one of the characters is caught in the net of war, whether it be the hotel director who sees his profits for the summer season dwindle (933); Fenz and his daughter Seraphine, who do not seem to have a full house for the evening's concert (938); or Arduin, who with his "Märchenreise" aboard the "Märchenyacht" tries to escape commitment to any country: "Dieser Krieg bricht nicht nur gegen meine Voraussicht, sondern gegen alle menschliche Vernunft aus. Ich tue da nicht mit, weder auf der einen noch auf der anderen Seite" (954).

Such false pacifism is disloyal to the country of Austria, where he is a citizen, for Arduin's load must be carried by others in addition to the services they already give. In the end Max is the only one who is prepared to report to his military unit, except for Falkenir, who would have been ready to serve after he had brought home Aurelie according to his plans.

Eros-Illusion-Release: But none of the plans that Falkenir has ever made in life turns out favorably. What distinguishes him from Arduin is his desire to face the issues of life and not to run away from them into uncertainty. Falkenir is the only male character in the play who undergoes an inner transformation and in the end has gained better human qualities as a result of his reflection and contemplation. Aurelie when compared to other female characters, Judith in particular, has likewise opened her life to many changes, but they were painful for the most part, due to her lack of discernment and control over her life. Yet, in her endeavor to cope with life, she ranks higher than Judith, who after her experiences with Westerhaus withdraws from life and moves through her isolated adventurous experiences in a cold, detached manner, void of any feelings from her heart, to escape finally "ins Ungewisse" with Arduin. Melchinger writes of her: "Judith [...] wählt den Weg in die Welt der Liebeleien. Von so vielen Schnitzler-Gestalten unterscheidet sie sich durch die illusionslose Bewusstheit ihres Handelns. Sie unterliegt nicht der Gefahr, den Schein der Wirklichkeit zu verwechseln, da sie angesichts des einzig Sicheren und Gewissen, angesichts des Todes, die Flüchtigkeit und Unbeständigkeit menschlicher Bindungen erfahren hat." [73]

When Falkenir appears on stage in Act I, it is shortly before midnight and the major activities of that evening have already reached their peak, thus paralleling Aurelie's late appearance at the very last minute of the appointed time. Aside from Westerhaus, Falkenir is the only character who does not wear a domino at this spring evening ball; indeed, his interest is far from seeking amorous adventure. He is one of the three suitors who has come to hear Aurelie's choice of husband. The audience already knows much about him through the conversations between Ambros and Arduin, Aurelie's other suitors. At the end of Act I the picture of him is complete. A diplomat by profession, he now lives secluded from the world as a scholar and recluse in Italy, the perfect country for his archaeological endeavors. He and his family are considered "Sonderlinge" in the eyes of the world, because "sein Vater hat buddhistische Studien getrieben" (854). Falkenir himself has adopted this contemplative-meditative state of consciousness which gives him extended sense perception, "die ewigen Ströme rauschen zu hören – die dunklen, ewigen Ströme, die unaufhörlich fliessen von Mann zu Weib und von Weib zu Mann, zwischen Geschlecht und Geschlecht" (872), as he tells Aurelie, who has chosen Falkenir to be her husband. Falkenir is older than Aurelie by approximately fifteen years; he was a friend of the family and her guardian in time of need, when her parents died. Falkenir is afraid that Aurelie confuses love with what really is a feeling of confidence and friendship toward him; he also fears the possibilities hidden in her youthful inexperience and so refuses to accept her sincere avowal of love and devotion.

Aurelie: In deiner Stimme ist mir das Echo, in deinem Auge mir der Abglanz der Welt. Ich will nichts anderes, will nicht mehr von ihr, als was mir aus deiner Seele widerklingt und -strahlt.

Falkenir: Diese Bescheidenheit, Aurelie – steht dir, gerade dir nicht an. Wenn irgendeine, so hast du ein Anrecht auf die wirkliche, auf die lebendige, die unermessliche Welt, die dir in einem Menschen, so teuer er dir sei, niemals beschlossen sein kann. (871)

Yet Aurelie has no desire to experience this vivacious world, for she still carries within her the emotional trauma caused by her mother's style of life: "Suchende und Gejagte, Unersättliche oder Berauschte schienen sie mir alle, die Glücklichen wie die Elenden. Die Welt, aus der sie kamen, regte in mir eher Schauer auf als Sehnsucht" (871). A relationship with Falkenir, she is confident, will allow her to be herself (870). With Arduin she might have been "eine Beute oder ein Triumph mehr" and with Ambros "unter tausend Spielen und Wandlungen des Daseins – auch ein Gleichnis" (870). These three examples demonstrate Aurelie's awareness of what she does not want to be or experience in her world. She expresses less certainty about her true Self and the purpose of her life in companionship with Falkenir and is contented with a reflection of the world as it is represented in his eyes, an echo of the world as heard in his voice (871).

Falkenir, on the other hand, does not seem to value his Self too much, although to give oneself truly is the highest form of sharing in any relationship. "Ich, ein Mann ohne Zukunft und Überschwang, dem die Schläfen zu ergrauen beginnen, der nichts zu geben hat als sich selbst" (871). In the tone of a mature, wise, benevolent friend he explains to Aurelie that her true being presently remains smothered under the image created by the prejudices of her birth and upbringing. Aurelie, he continues, does not yet know her true Self, but if she is free of the limitations of marriage, she will be able to follow her deepest drives, to discover that Self. Therefore, he no longer believes they are suited for one another.

Offermanns considers this advice "die einzige Hilfestellung, die Falkenir Aurelie bietet" before he points out where Falkenir fails miserably, that is, "als er die für den Kulturprozess notwendige Dialektik von Trieb und Formung ignoriert [...] und nicht gewahrt, dass gerade die Erkenntnis des 'dunklen' Lebensstromes die erste Stufe eines Individuationsprozesses ermöglicht." [74]

It appears, however, that Falkenir did not extend any "Hilfestellung" to Aurelie at all because of his ignorance in matters of psychology and human understanding. If he truly was a friend and committed to a meaningful marriage with Aurelie, he would have helped her to recognize that hidden splendor within herself. Instead, Falkenir's changed attitude toward her as a marriage partner was motivated by fear, which he seems to justify with the memory of his first wife. She became insane and committed suicide as a result of her repressed desire for freedom, as Falkenir views the incident.

These experiences in his first marriage left him with guilt feelings and distorted his concept of freedom as it relates to marriage. He now seems to think that marriage poses a limitation to freedom; yet, the outside world including the marriage partner does not provide the freedom sought — it is solely an "inside job." But Falkenir has not looked at himself in complete honesty; hence his anxiety and distrust of Aurelie's expression of love for him. At this point, Schnitzler seems to use Falkenir to express his own convictions which are found in *Buch der Sprüche und Bedenken*: "Nicht früher darfst du dich von einer Frau geliebt glauben, ehe du nicht sicher bist, ihre ganze erotische Sehnsucht auf dich allein vereinigt und alle anderen Möglichkeiten ihres Wesens, auch die geahntesten zur Wirklichkeit erlöst zu haben." [75] Falkenir is not sure of Aurelie's exclusive love because of his own limitations in that area; therefore, he seeks a solution by sending her away to experience that unlimited freedom of expression.

When Falkenir tells Aurelie repeatedly that she does not know herself as yet (870, 887), he really recognizes the truth of his own condition. One can see in others what one has within himself. From a psychological point of view Falkenir is given to negative thoughts which function as mental inhibitors. Fear, distrust, anxiety, guilt, disbelief, selfishness are blocking his true life expression and distort his concept of freedom. Falkenir has not found a way to accept love and trust and, therefore, he does not know how to reciprocate love and trust. [76]

His first wife loved him, yet he seems to have doubted it. Perhaps he was suspicious and did not trust her until the issue reached serious proportions, the crisis being the death of his wife which "sollte mir dafür zeugen, dass sie nur mein und dass sie für alle Ewigkeit nur mein war" (872). Now the same situation arises with Aurelie. She is young and beautiful, with the world at her feet, so he doubts her fidelity, because he thinks he knows her better than she does herself, just as with his first wife. "Da ich sie liebte, wusste ich die Gedanken, die sie selbst zu denken, wusste ich die Taten, die zu tun sie selbst niemals gewagt hätte" (872). By withdrawing his hand from Aurelie's, Falkenir is not aware that he draws to himself the same experience which he so desperately tries to escape. He thinks to return freedom to Aurelie (888), without realizing that he never took any freedom away from her. Freedom begins within a person, with the feelings about oneself and others.

Aurelie never expressed feelings of limitation. On the contrary, she hoped to grow and develop in her relation with Falkenir. She looked to him as a companion, who because of his station in life would be able to help her achieve more self-confidence and balance. She probably resembles Falkenir's first wife in this respect so closely that it may have frightened him off. Falkenir is working exclusively with his intellect in matters where his heart should decide. The author summarizes this aspect as follows:

> Hat man zu einem Gegenstand, zu einer Frage, zu einem Menschen nur eine intellektuelle, verstandesmässige Beziehung, so hat man keine. Denn gerade das Intellektuelle ist relativ; es ist durch neue Erfahrungen etc. Veränderungen unterworfen. Nur auf die gefühlsmässigen Beziehungen kommt es an; sie sind die reichern und die wahrern. Ihre Motive liegen im Unbewussten, vielmehr in Vergessenem, Zusammengefasstem. [77]

Act III presents Falkenir as a transformed character. Three months of solitude have given him a chance to reflect upon the meaning of human relationships and to gain perspective on the events which occurred earlier in the year. He realizes the mistake he made in sending Aurelie unprotected into the world, when he should have taken responsibility in marriage. He offers her "Sicherheit, Zuflucht und meinen Namen" (951) and he does not feel as one "der über dir steht. Wenn es hier etwas wie eine Schuld gibt, so liegt sie bei mir allein" (950). But responsibility is not his only motivation in wishing to marry her now; he has grown within himself to a state of unselfish love and a real sense of forgiveness. The past lies behind and shall not be permitted to interfere; whatever the future may bring, it is not a point of concern now. Only the present matters and for that reason it is his desire "dass dir für alle Fälle eine Heimstatt gewahrt sei — woher du auch kommen, — für welche Ferne du sie wieder verlassen magst, — eine Heimstatt, deren Frieden niemand stören darf, —: mein Haus" (952).

Falkenir's attitude with regard to the past, present, and future stands in complete contrast to Schnitzler's own convictions. In *Buch der Sprüche und Bedenken* he writes: "Das Vergangene abgetan sein lassen, die Zukunft der Vorsehung anheimstellen — beides heisst, den eigentlichen Sinn der Gegenwart nicht verstehen, die überhaupt nur so weit als Realität gelten kann, als sie durch Treue des Gedächtnisses das Vergangene zu bewahren, durch Bewusstsein der Verantwortung die Zukunft in sich einzubeziehen sucht." [78] Schnitzler stipulates this demand that man in his conscience must feel responsible toward his fellow men in increasing measure. Especially in their interrelationships human beings must become aware of their mutual responsibility and must not withdraw, whatever the cost. Neither fright of outer difficulties and involvement, nor fear of inner pain and disappointments, justify a negligence of this basic obligation.

Falkenir is also aware that a marriage needs mutual attention, because "Liebe — heisst Bangen, Kämpfen, Werben — Lieben ist: in jeder Stunde neu sich erringen müssen, was man liebt; bereit sein, zu verzichten, wenn es das Schicksal will — und Heimat bedeuten, immer wieder Heimat, aus welcher Fremde auch die Geliebte wiederkehre — und in welche Ferne sie sich sehne" (964-65). In this respect, Falkenir has gained the same wisdom that Casanova shared with Andrea at the end of the play *Die Schwestern oder Casanova in Spa*. Aurelie is not readily convinced of the truth in Falkenir's words, for she does not see clearly the change which has taken place within him. She does not comprehend how he would be strong enough to withstand past realities in his life, when he had been frightened by future possibilities in their relationship. But Falkenir feels: "Möglichkeiten sind unheimlichere Gespenster als Wirklichkeiten, die vergangen sind" (953).[79] This concept that possibilities are worse than realities has its polarity also in the terms "Sehnsucht" and "Erfüllung," an idea which Andrea outlines in *Die Schwestern oder Casanova in Spa:*

> Als wäre Sehnsucht nicht
> Um Tausendfaches schlimmer als Erfüllung,
> Weil sie fortwühlend in der Seele Gründen
> Den reinen Lauf ihr bis zur Quelle trübt —! (670)

This issue first raised here no longer has an ideal solution in *Komödie der Verführung,* as if Schnitzler were tightening the ethical boundaries with each later drama. Aurelie picks up the words "Sehnsucht" and "Erfüllung" after Falkenir has successfully passed all the tests she imposed upon him, just as he had subjected her to trials in Act I.[80] Yet, Falkenir's transformation, she feels, was based on his longing; and what would happen, she asks, when after their consummation one morning the ghosts of the past would stand around their bedside and be stronger than Falkenir's and Aurelie's combined power to overcome them? (965). The past, Aurelie senses correctly, can be forgiven, but the challenge is the aspect of forgetting the past. Schnitzler seems to draw for his characters conclusions similar to Hofmannsthal's for his protagonist Andrea in *Gestern:* "Was einmal war, das lebt auch ewig fort."[81] Only Schnitzler speaks in terms of the soul: "Was unsere Seele am schlimmsten abnutzt, das ist: verzeihen ohne zu vergessen."[82]

The souls of both Falkenir and Aurelie are tormented. They want to forgive and forget, but Aurelie wants to know what will happen if this past breaks through again. Their answer is that they would end their lives, and it is this oath given to one another which seals their marriage vows and starts supposedly a new morning in their lives. Aurelie now considers herself his bride (965).

Before they sit down with Ambros for breakfast, she asks for patience a little while longer: "[...] ich komme wieder — in Weiss — wie es einer Braut geziemt" (966). The ensuing conversation between Ambros and Falkenir about Aurelie is of vital importance because "dieses gefährliche Spiel mit Möglichkeiten" has already begun for Falkenir. He wonders whether Aurelie's emotional disturbance may not be her true nature, and whether that which seems to be "ein allmähliches Erwachen [...] eine beginnende neue Klarheit," whether this new condition may not be a façade, perhaps unconsciously erected (967). Since both of them, Falkenir and Aurelie, have the ability to hear "die ewigen Ströme rauschen" (872, 965), Aurelie in her new state of "clear seeing" ("Klarheit" in this case translates as perspicacity) is able to tune in to Falkenir and thus to recognize the "Gespenster" which are already crowding in on them. Therefore, according to their mutual oath, it is time for her to leave and join "die ewigen Ströme" as her final resting place. Falkenir, fulfilling his part of the oath, joins her and "ganz glückselig lächelten sie" (973), as if their earthly tribulations were over now.

Aurelie's action, which ultimately draws Falkenir into the circle of death, is therefore a consequence of the oath they swore to each other. It saved them apparently from a life of torture on the earth, because Aurelie could not have spent one moment longer in her past, the experiences with Gysar having been the most devastating to her mind; and Falkenir, after the experience with his first wife, and perhaps being constantly reminded that Aurelie's despair is the result of his failure to act maturely in honoring his marriage proposal the first time, would have had to carry a tremendous mental burden. Their deaths — as described by Gilda — came to them as a joyful relief, a cherished opportunity to begin anew.

From a healthy critical distance, however, one would have to ask whether this oath and its consequences were really a blessing in disguise for these two characters. If one sees in it nothing more than a suicide pact, then the entire marriage was void of any true commitment to a loving, caring companionship. Schnitzler as a physician certainly was aware of the high suicide rate in Austria, and would indeed not condone it as a wise solution for certain emotional problems. In his Aphorisms he writes: "Im heiteren Drama pflegen die Autoren meist nur die Mängel ihres Charakters [...] zu verraten."[83]

The life styles of nearly all characters show weaknesses of one kind or another. As each one lives with the flaws instead of trying to eliminate them, these characters create certain situations in which they yield to temptation of many kinds — comedy in Schnitzler's work stands for life styles. However, the life styles of Falkenir and Aurelie are indeed of an extremely complex nature and difficult to reconcile with any aspect of comedy.

Referring to Falkenir's new understanding of the meaning of love (964-65), Andreas Török considers this a completely new aspect in Schnitzler's artistic development: "Also bedeutet die Liebe hier eine Verantwortung, etwas Ethisches; ein bei Schnitzler bisher völlig fehlender Bestandteil der Liebe wird jetzt zur Hauptsache."[84] Török may have overlooked that this new idea can be traced to *Die Schwestern oder Casanova in Spa*. It was Casanova who asserted for the first time that love cannot possess and cannot be possessed, that it does not bind and cannot be bound; that love can only enjoy and be enjoyed. This new idea forms the basis for Casanova's argument with Andrea over fidelity and the meaning of "Wiederkehr" instead of "Heimkehr."

The main argument in Török's article is concerned with an explanation regarding the double suicide in light of Aurelie's blissful smile, the happiness in her face as she sank, embraced by Falkenir, into the water. Most interpretations to date, according to Török, have not found a satisfactory answer.[85] Referring to Aurelie's happiness, Török concludes: "Sie kann nur auf eine — zugegeben: bei Schnitzler völlig unerwartete — Weise restlos gedeutet werden: hier tritt der Romantiker Schnitzler zutage, und der Tod ist ein Liebestod, ganz im Wagnerschen Sinne [...] welcher Opernfreund fühlt sich durch die obige Beschreibung nicht sofort an den Schluss vom 'Fliegenden Holländer' erinnert?"[86] He admits the changed roles which Falkenir and Aurelie assume when compared to Senta and the Holländer, and finds more proof of his theory by looking at the strikingly similar stage directions in both productions.[87]

It is true, the water symbolisms in connection with the idea of redemption through death are comparable, but the most important aspect in any comparison between Wagner and Schnitzler is the significance of the oath, which is not considered by Török. Falkenir honored his oath to Aurelie, just as Senta did when she joined the Holländer with these last words: "Hier steh' ich treu dir bis zum Tod!"[88]

"Der Tod wird gewählt," according to Bernhard Blume, "in einem Augenblick der Hochstimmung, in einem Gefühl des Überflusses."[89] Urbach in his commentary on Schnitzler sees death in this way: "[...] einzige Möglichkeit der Versöhnung."[90] "Selbstmord," as Urbach observes particularly in the late dramatic works, "bedeutet nicht nur Reaktion auf eine ausweglose Situation, er kann von den Gestalten Schnitzlers auch als bewusste Entscheidung und freiwillige Aktion begriffen werden, als Verfügung über die eigene Person, die unabhängig von äusseren Repressalien getroffen wird. Selbstmord kann als Selbstbestimmung und nicht nur als Selbstverlust gedeutet werden."[91] Mme Derré, on the other hand, describes this suicide as "résolution désespérée,"[92] thus giving expression to the thought that mutual death in Schnitzler's work is nothing more than an act of resignation or despair. She sees proof in the fact that even altruistic love, as in the case of Falkenir, "ne parvient jamais à unir deux êtres par d'autres liens que ceux de leurs corps."[93]

Körner considers Falkenir together with Amadeus (*Zwischenspiel,* 1906) and Erasmus (*Hirtenflöte,* 1911) as "lieblose Narren."[94] This appears, at least in the case of Falkenir, an oversimplification, because he reaches a realization of what he has done in pushing Aurelie out unprotected into an alluring world. As we already pointed out, his original release of Aurelie was caused as much by intellectual pride in his seeming insight into her nature as by his belief that he could offer her but little joy and happiness because of his age. These motives are less selfish than Amadeus' desire for self-indulgence or than Erasmus' intellectual curiosity as to Dionysia's true nature. Falkenir has demonstrated a true transformation because he has been able to understand and forgive Aurelie as well as himself. But just as the men's motivations become progressively freer of subtle variations of selfishness, so the effects on the women become more devastating: Cäcilie shudders in her security, but retains her integrity; Dionysia is filled with disgust at her experiences; but Aurelie is shaken to the core of her being and appears to lose her sense of reality.[95] The question may be raised with regard to the responsibility taken for another person. The men gave their women freedom, not license, but the women did not use their freedom well. Of course, the other part of the question concerns the viewpoint of these women. Did they really consider their new state of affairs as "freedom?" They may have felt utterly rejected and unable to cope with this feeling in a psychologically sound way.

Schnitzler, as so often in his work, refrains from condemning any one of his characters; he shows merely the ignorance due to unawareness in the various states of consciousness; he describes for his audiences the slow process of spiritual evolvement, the trials and errors associated with this growth. The poet has compassion for all of human nature, yet those characters who step forward in life and are prepared to make the necessary changes in harmony with their inner nature seem to be valued somewhat higher. In his *Buch der Sprüche und Bedenken,* Schnitzler writes about it this way: "Schlimmer betrogen, wer aus Angst vor Enttäuschung immer wieder sein Glück versäumte, als wer jede Möglichkeit eines Glückes ergriff, selbst auf die Gefahr hin, es könnte wieder nicht das wahre gewesen sein."[96]

At the close of Act I, Falkenir was such a "Betrogener," for he missed the happiness of marriage due to his various fears, but in Act III he is on his way to overcoming these inner obstacles in that he adds responsibility to his life, even though his insight comes too late to begin a marriage with Aurelie.

Aurelie had likewise to cope with fear. The events of her mother's life, her father's involvement in the duel, the parents' unhappy quarrelsome married life and their subsequent death are the reasons for her withdrawal from society. A sense of guilt, shame, and fear kept her secluded in her country home at Merkenstein for more than two years. Her nature is somewhat obscure, prompting her aunt Franziska to call her "unberechenbar." She thinks everything is possible with Aurelie, and she would not be surprised if Aurelie disappeared into a convent (852). Her suitors have less insight than her aunt and speak of her as a sprite. Indeed, there is a romantic air about her — who else would have the fancy of appointing the hour of midnight during a garden festival to let three lovers know which has won her heart and hand in marriage?

Of course, outer details contribute to the imaginary atmosphere also. There is the castle park which has been opened to the evening's guests. They for the most part hide their identity behind a mask or costume. Two of Aurelie's suitors have arrived in their domino costume as well, and it is significant that she chose Falkenir, who came without such trapping. He is best suited to help Aurelie leave her adolescent role and enter a more mature life. Then, there is the pond frequently present in fairytales. Aurelie loses her mother's jewelry there and, interestingly enough, Max von Reisenberg returns it to her, for his father had created this last piece before his death, probably to pay back favors (872). Aurelie at this point still feels very self-reliant and independent of anybody's advice. Not even her fiancé is able to influence her with his superstitions about the jewelry, although in other ways Aurelie is most submissive toward him in questions regarding their future (886).

After Falkenir's withdrawal, however, Aurelie is so humiliated and stunned that she loses her sense of balance. This is symbolized by her sudden decision to throw away the jewelry into the pond as Max approaches her. Twice more she changes her mind suddenly in an attempt to escape from her own Self, only to face each time more serious consequences. After withstanding Gysar's temptation courageously in Scene 1 of Act II, she suddenly agrees to come to his house and garden which draw her more dangerously into the net of erotic adventure. Previously, she had spent the night with Max just as his father had done with her mother, only Aurelie did not lose her heart and mind in this affair (897). In Act III, a third sudden change occurs when Aurelie, after dressing in white, is seen with her boat on the waters of the ocean instead of returning to Falkenir and Ambros for breakfast, as she had promised. When the two men go after her, she jumps to her death (972). Thus, the imaginary atmosphere of Act I which continues more intensely in Act III, is actually leading into a more crucial reality of life: the date of August 1, 1914, signifies the outbreak of the war and coincides with the time in Act III.

Schnitzler's message seems to demonstrate two points: It is impossible to ignore social, economic, and political developments by simply hiding behind a world of illusions. The author develops the war issue as an example. Most characters in the play tried to ignore the political events until they were forced to make arrangements to reach the last train leaving Copenhagen for Germany. Furthermore, in the realm of human interaction it requires strong effort to erase guilt feelings of the past between two people on the premise of forgive and forget, because memories of the past can enter the present unexpectedly and loom over their lives dangerously, thereby destroying peace of mind and harmony.[97]

The water symbol played a distinct role in Aurelie's endeavor to release that past. As a child she played by the pond with Arduin. Later in Act I she throws her mother's jewelry into the pond to cleanse herself symbolically of negative memories related to her mother. In Act III Arduin is ready to release into the water her picture painted in the nude (949), so as to let go of her past experiences with Gysar. Aurelie herself has a natural attraction to the water at the beach resort: every morning she takes a boat ride, Gilda reports (968). With Ambros, Aurelie is on the boat at night, and in the morning she sun-bathes by the water. The water seems to have become a natural element for her, similar to the experience reported about Gilda's mother, who, like Aurelie, disappears into the water for her final resting place.[98]

Offermanns presents a different view in this respect when he writes: "Aurelies und Falkenirs Vereinigung im Meerestod wird von Schnitzler deutlich als ein pseudomystischer, also illusionärer Vorgang dargestellt, der lebenszerstörend ist und mit dem Ausbruch des Krieges zusammenfällt."[99] It ends, of course, the "Zauberstimmung" at the summer resort Gillileije, but it does not seem to end in destruction for Falkenir and Aurelie. Gilda's account of these last moments emphasize six times the smile which accompanies both of them (972-73). Their death reconciles their earthly differences in what is to them a freely chosen act of self-determination rather than self-loss.[100]

Her life appeared to Aurelie nothing more than a dream-state. At one point in Act III, she recognizes suddenly how "real" Arduin was and all the others as well: "Es tut einem in der Seele weh, wie wirklich ihr alle seid. Drum hab' ich mir vorgenommen, Euch von nun an nur mehr zu träumen. Das ist bequemer und lustiger" (947). Even her bacchantic experience in Gysar's garden arouses the question within her: "War es Traum oder Wachen? Ich weiss es nicht" (962). Yet, only after this particular night is she able to identify with the picture Gysar painted of her. She recognizes for the first time the hidden side of herself, her genuine sensuality. It frightens her mainly because she does not seem to know how to control this aspect of her being. Her upbringing suggests that it must be rejected, for it is sinful "und vermutlich wirken noch die Widerstände gegen ein freies erotisches Leben nach, die sich in ihrer Jugend bereits gebildet hatten, da sie die tragische Folge des Ehebruchs ihrer Mutter mit ansehen musste und dadurch sehend geworden auch das Unglück, das die geschlechtliche Liebe bei anderen hervorrief [...]." [101]

Her withdrawal into herself allows her to bridge both ends of the spectrum, to lead a dual life, so to speak. Intuitively she conveys to Max the direction her life may take to its very end: "Mich schaudert. — Und doch ist es schön, allein zu sein. Wieder allein [...] zwischen einem Glück und dem anderen. Zwischen einer Lust und der anderen. Zwischen einem Tod und dem andern [...]" (898). This duality reaches greater proportion in her experience with Gysar's picture, especially as she relates her feelings to Falkenir after the orgies in Gysar's garden: "[...] — und wusste nun: dieses Bild log nicht; Wahrheit, von der ich nichts geahnt [...]. Dies Bild ist Aurelie — ich selbst aber, wie du mich hier siehst, bin nur ein Bild. [...] was ich tue, das ist der blasse Schatten meiner selbst" (962). When she rejects Arduin for the third time, she repeats again, this time in stronger terms, that she does not belong to anybody and therefore no man should claim any rights: "Aber kein Mann auf dieser Erde, und hätt' ich mich in jeder Nacht an einen andern verschenkt oder verkauft — wird niemals auch nur diese Fingerspitzen berühren, wenn es mir nicht beliebt [...]" (948). And further: "Dies aber sag' ich euch, in meiner Nacktheit und in meinen Sünden gehör' ich mir allein. Keiner nahm mir was und keiner kann mir was geben. Was soll mir Scham, da mich keiner doch kennt?" (950).

In her defense against Arduin she appears detached, cool, almost boastful, but it really is a measure of protection. She knows that in his adventurous life style, he mistakes sexual desires for genuine feelings of love; thus, when she rejects any intimate relationship it is not a matter of being afraid to love, to give herself — rather to avoid becoming another entry on his record of love triumphs. So she adopts a playful attitude, for his feelings are no more genuine than her own. He plays "Komödie," which gives him the ability to recognize the same in Aurelie. "Du spielst. Ja, Aurelie, du scherzest und spielst Komödie" (896). Aurelie's choice of words in conversation with Falkenir is quite different, even when she challenges him by telling him her experience with Ambros which could have turned into another love affair, had Ambros not remained the gentlemanly friend he had always been (964).

In light of this discussion, it becomes obvious that there can be no agreement with Körner's assessment of Aurelie: "Aurelie ist eben keine wahrhaft freie Frau, sie nimmt sich bloss Freiheiten heraus, sie handelt nicht in einer selbstverständlichen Ungebundenheit, sondern aus Trotz und Widerspruch, sie ist nichts als ein aufrührerischer Sklave." [102] The women who really struggle to become free for various reasons are Julia, Judith, and Seraphine. Aurelie's desire was to enter the protection of married life that would shelter her from the dangers of the outside world. She did not want to play a role in various love affairs, but to experience a one-to-one relationship. In addition to her devotion to Falkenir, there was almost a trace of submission apparent (886), which in the hands of the wrong man such as Gysar became an impediment to recognizing her own true identity. She identifies more readily with the nude picture he painted of her.

However, LoCicero blames Falkenir for Aurelie's dilemma, when he calls it a "plight caused by a man whose 'knowledge' was greater than faith at a crucial moment." [103]

"Maske und Lüge bin ich," she tells Falkenir, "was ich spreche, was ich schaue, was ich tue, das ist der blasse Schatten meiner selbst" (962). Although Schnitzler has harsh comments about people such as Falkenir,[104] he also points out the dangers encountered as in the case of Aurelie, when she moves away from the center of her being, no longer follows her inner guidance, and instead places her self-authority and self-control in other hands. When she no longer was true to herself, she could not find truth anywhere else, and thus the whole experience of living took on the character of insincerity in her estimation.

Schnitzler observes in his *Buch der Sprüche und Bedenken*: "Manche flüchten sich in den Wahnsinn wie andere in den Tod; — und beides kann sowohl Mut, als Feigheit sein." [105] Falkenir took flight into death, and his act may be considered courage in the sense that he honored the oath he gave to Aurelie. Aurelie escaped into madness and death in the absence of courage to go on living, resulting perhaps from lack of energy to straighten out her life, paired with a lack of confidence in herself to undertake such a task. Thus, death in this self-imposed way is a means of overcoming; but it served at the same time as a bridge for Falkenir and Aurelie to find each other in full acceptance of the uniqueness and individuality of each other, and the right to be one's own self. The experience of sharing, communion moves them beyond the event of death to a true understanding of Eros. They finally reached happiness at the end of the play, which lifted both of them from their individual worlds of illusion and separateness into a dimension of release and renewed integrity. Therefore, the triangular combination for Falkenir and Aurelie suggests the aspects of Eros-Illusion-Release.

The water symbolism associated with the pond which earlier related to significant steps in Aurelie's development, reaches at the end of the play even more importance in relation to Falkenir's and Aurelie's decision to release themselves from life into the vast waters of the ocean. This mysterious, unfathomable, effervescing element has attracted and repelled various characters in the play, some of whom were only mentioned, as for instance Gilda's mother. The ocean is also the element from which everything originates and to which everything returns. It becomes thus a powerful symbol of human striving and challenges. Henkel/Schöne point out in this connection: "Das Leben fliesst so schnell, wie das Wasser des Flusses, dem Meere zueilend, flieht, ohne zurückzukehren. Wenn wir geboren werden, werden wir fortgerissen, und es ist uns nicht gegeben, unseren Lauf zurückzuwenden oder eine zurückgelegte Lebensstrecke zu wiederholen." [106] It takes courage and strength to remain successfully in the stream of life by trusting one's ability to turn challenges into opportunities for increased knowledge. Aurelie in her present state of mind does not feel the strength to master real life because, in line with Schnitzler's antithetical use of "Märchen," she would have to ask herself the question: "What must I do? " But she has only enough courage to face herself in death, to be released from the forceful currents of life.

The triangularity of *Eros-Krieg-Märchen/Imagination* served as a basis for the analysis of characters in *Komödie der Verführung*. Almost every character added another aspect to the angles of Eros and Imagination. In some characters "Imagination" was synonymous with fairytale. Those characters connected to the issue of war also related to the rest of the triangle.

The triangular meaning of "Verführung": A second major triangular constellation is derived from the various meanings of "Verführung." Its general meaning of "allurement" branches out into the meanings of enticement, seduction, and temptation. The discussion regarding Gysar-Aurelie may show that the painter moves through all three stages in his persuasion to paint her picture. In Act I, when he is dancing with her, he is "enticing" in his conversation, for we recall that Aurelie only accepted this dance upon Falkenir's urging (877); later, he is more forceful when he bluntly tells her that he shall paint her picture (885). In Scene 1 of Act II he first seduces her morally by overcoming her own scruples[107] as he questions her: "Haben Sie irgendeinem Menschen Rechenschaft abzulegen? " (894), referring to his suggestion to come into his house and garden. Finally, he tempts her into the orgy which Aurelie tells Falkenir about in Act III (962). At that point, Gysar had overcome in her any "objection or conscience or better judgment" [108] and was strictly following the promise of pleasure. Another example can be seen in Max. He was enticed by Seraphine who throws at first one rose, then two more in his way to draw his attention (860). Judith also entices him by throwing herself into his arms, thus agreeing that they "wollen lieber tanzen" (867). At the end of Act I, Max is at hand when Aurelie is overcome by shock in view of Falkenir's strange resolve to break up the engagement. All three enticements end in seductions, Max being the seduced.[109] In the case of Judith and Seraphine, there is temptation on Max's part to create a more permanent relationship through marriage. With Judith he proposes to go to Dresden (865). When he is tempted by Seraphine, he wants to be her companion for the concert tour at first (927, 970), but later he changes his mind and delivers a marriage proposal: "Möchtest du mich nicht zum Mann nehmen, Seraphine, wenn ich zurückkommen sollte? " (970).

Not all of the various characters move from enticement to seduction and temptation with a partner. Julia serves as an example. She is enticed by the evening's festivities and, more seriously, the jealousy of her husband moves her on to further frivolous seductive action with Arduin in spite of the arrogance with which he treats her (856). With her approach toward Arduin, of course, she tempts her husband into anger and public outrage. Westerhaus, on the other hand, is enticed by the power of money which gains seductive force over him in the political arena. Finally, he gives in to temptation to pay the highest price for even greater risks (900).

Polarity: In addition to the principle of triangularity in this drama, the aspect of polarity is also important and recurs consistently in Schnitzler's late dramatic works. Such values as "Liebe" and "Treue" have to be considered in an antithetical way because Schnitzler's characters emphasize repeatedly that there is no ultimate proof of love and fidelity. It is impossible to find out the truth from the other partner, since his inner nature remains a partly opened book at best. What appears to be a sincere devotion to the marriage may suddenly be questioned by one of the partners; once distrust and doubt form roots, the situation can hardly be rectified to mutual satisfaction. Falkenir's first wife as well as Aurelie serve as examples in this respect. Their sincere efforts to prove love and faithfulness to Falkenir were made in vain.[110] In the early part of the play Falkenir did not have the courage to trust. This may be seen as immaturity. Yet courage is one of the absolute virtues which Schnitzler stipulates in his scale of ethical values; the others being "Wahrheitsdrang," "Treue," "Sachlichkeit," and "Verantwortungsgefühl." [111]

Each one of these values is introduced in Schnitzler's play but hardly any character with the exception of Ambros is able to live up to them. Therefore, these values appear in juxtaposition: "Treue-Liebe," "Wahrheit-Lüge." Human beings are so complicated in their emotional life that they may betray their relation through infidelity. "Weil diese Personen wissen," points out Müller-Freienfels, "wie unbeständig die Menschen sind, dass in jeder Frau die heimliche Anlage zur Dirne und in jedem Mann die geheime Sehnsucht, ein Verführer zu sein, stecken, können sie auch nicht an eine echte Verwirklichung der Ehe glauben, die eine dauerhafte Liebe und Treue voraussetzt."[112] Instead of expressing truth, the mask and domino in the first act serve to perpetuate the lie. Even Falkenir was not sincere in his advice to Aurelie in the early part of the play; instead, he claimed to know more about her than she herself. In his endeavor to withdraw from his marriage proposal he lost his objectivity and shied away from real responsibility.[113]

The inversion of truth is also seen in Scene 2 of Act II. Julia, who is involved in the plot to arrest Westerhaus, is asking Judith to tell her the truth about the situation. When Judith asked her: "Du hast gewusst, dass man ihn verhaften wird?", Julia replies with a lie: "Was fällt dir ein? Geahnt. Vorhergesehen" (912). Earlier, Julia had suggested that all three of them go to the opera to see "Der Maskenball," an ironic countertwist between the lie at home and the truth unmasked during the masquerade ball on the opera stage.

In Act III Max resorts to the lie in his answer to Ambros: "Judith ist in London, denk' ich" (936), although he has just left her hotel room. Neither is he truthful in his encounter with Seraphine (938). Aurelie is also inverting the truth when she sees herself as nothing more than a mask and a lie, and only Gysar's picture is "Wahrheit, von der ich nichts geahnt" (962). However, her love for Falkenir seems to be based on truth — Ambros is vouching for that (964).

The fluid state of their minds, which Falkenir and Aurelie express as "die ewigen Ströme" (872, 964, 965), creates the effect of "slipping away" not only from the truth, but also from the reality of their environment. The state of "Träumen" and "Wachen" is especially apparent within Aurelie throughout the play but reaches the culmination, when she recalls her experiences in Gysar's garden (962). Every aspect told represents a polarity, transforming the story into a mystical vision. She speaks of "Frauen" and "Jünglinge," "Licht" and "Finsternis," "Umarmen" and "Töten," "Geigen" and "Flöten," "Schweben" and "Gleiten," "Aufjauchzen" and "Ersterben," "Minuten" and "Stunden," "Traum" and "Wachen." In the end she feels at one with the picture and at one with the harmony of the all-encompassing universe (962). Falkenir in his polarity concept of "Möglichkeiten" and "Wirklichkeiten" sees dreams as uninvited guests which clean up the table, leaving the hosts behind with dry and thirsty lips (953). Judith envisions her future as a dream. After her experience in the mortuary she seems to have gained a deep realization of life in all its wonders and dismays, so that "alles was noch kommt, wird nur wie ein Traum sein von einem Dasein, das eigentlich schon hinter mir liegt" (930).

Other polarities such as "Jugend" and "Alter," "Leben" and "Kunst," have already been discussed in light of such characters as Fenz, Ambros, and Gysar. It is not convincing, however, that the motif of aging occupies the center position of the drama, as Körner has stated.[114] The women characters are young, and among the main male characters only Falkenir mentions once his "Schläfen [die] zu ergrauen beginnen" (871), although he is hardly forty years of age. This is only one of the reasons he presents to Aurelie in defense of his changed mind regarding the marriage. Later in the drama, it is Falkenir, who establishes a new aspect of polarity with his concept of "Heimat" and "Ferne." It is his desire to offer Aurelie "für alle Fälle eine Heimstatt [...] woher du auch kommen, — für welche Ferne du sie wieder verlassen magst [...]" (952). He repeats his offer again in all sincerity (965), for he has learned his lesson in responsibility and commitment during several months of solitude. This realization of providing a home tends to replace Falkenir's earlier concern with age.

Schnitzler has already presented this concept of "Heimat" and "Ferne" in his play *Die Schwestern oder Casanova in Spa;* in *Komödie der Verführung* he resumes it and develops it further in order to show the senselessness of any flight into illusion and imagination, because the reality of life cannot be betrayed. However, as one changes his attitudes toward life, he will discover that life itself takes on a different color. In this respect Schnitzler confirms: "Eine Illusion verlieren heisst, um eine Wahrheit reicher werden" (*BdSp.*, 224). Yet, he cautions: "Doch wer den Verlust beklagt, ist auch des Gewinnes nicht wert gewesen" (*BdSp.*, 224). Falkenir is haunted by possibilities about Aurelie's state of mind immediately after she leaves to change her dress. That nullifies in the end all the gains Falkenir made in more than a hundred lonely days. Falling back on possibilities is here synonymous with Schnitzler's "den Verlust beklagen."

Comparison with other late dramatic works: Festivities take place in both dramas. They are arranged in *Die Schwestern* at the end of the play to provide the main characters with an opportunity to lay aside the various personal differences. However, the atmosphere of festivity in *Komödie der Verführung* barely disguises the corruption present within the various levels of society such as the moral and ethical issues concerning the pending war, the manipulative practices in banking circles, the tainted procedures in the judicial system as a symbol for the deterioration of the nation from within, the apathy of people in general toward political and social issues. Therefore, no reunion of major characters is possible at the end. Yet, the festivity held in Prinz Arduin's park itself was arranged for purposes of charity. In that respect it differed from the one in *Die Schwestern*. Santis organized his banquet there for selfish reasons, mainly to aid his personal finances by proposing an extravagant gambling party afterwards.

The titles of the dramas had each significance for the interpretation of the play, only in *Komödie der Verführung* it proved to be much more complex. The term "Casanova" in one play is synonymous with "Verführung" in the other. But the characters involved in "Verführung" differ by comparison. Max von Reisenberg, the so-called seducer, is a greatly diminished adventurer, as was shown in the comparison with Casanova. Rather than being an agent, Max is the instrument by which each of the three women characters — Aurelie, Judith, Seraphine — acts to enter her particular future. Thus, the triangular combination seen in *Die Schwestern* occurs in more complexity in *Komödie der Verführung*, as demonstrated in the women, the adventurers, and other detail of the play. Of the three adventurers present in *Komödie der Verführung*, only Max was involved with all three of the women. In this respect, he has the same key position as his counterpart in *Die Schwestern*.

In summary, this analysis focused on each character in the play and discussed their interrelationships from which developed the various dramatic happenings. The constellation of *Eros-Krieg-Märchen/Imagination* and its various triangular combinations crystallize Schnitzler's key ideas and concerns. A true expression of love toward another person requires involvement and concern. Herbert Lederer considers this new love the " 'better' kind of love, to which many of Schnitzler's characters aspire, a love which is the fulfillment of life and for which death holds no terror, a love, however, which only the positive few can ever reach."[115] Schnitzler has shown these difficulties repeatedly in the play.

The motif of war relates directly to Schnitzler's personal view on the subject. He called himself a liberal and advocated the ideals of humanitarian liberalism, as is especially apparent in his essays *Über Krieg und Frieden*[116] and "Aufzeichnungen aus der Kriegszeit."[117] Both were published posthumously, a fact which may have contributed to the view critics hold about Schnitzler's apolitical attitudes.[118] These pages contain statements of profound wisdom which even to this day should not be taken lightly. Schnitzler observes: "Gewisse Epochen lassen ihre ganze Grauenhaftigkeit besonders darin erkennen, dass innerhalb ihrer zum grössten Unrecht werden kann, was sonst das erste Gebot aller Sittlichkeit scheint, nämlich die Wahrheit auszusprechen. — Epochen, in denen die Wahrheit nicht nur gefährlich werden kann für diejenigen, die sie aussprechen, sondern auch für diejenigen, die sie hören, sind im Innersten ungesund."[119] His concern for truth emerges as a key idea in all of his writings, whether he deals with human conflicts in various degrees, philosophical ideas and their frequently abstract systems, or the concept of the true artist vs. the dilettante. Eras in which the pursuit of truth becomes a dangerous undertaking are marked by violence. In his estimation, wars are only possible under three conditions, namely: "1. durch die Schurkerei der Mächtigen, 2. die Dummheit der Diplomatie, und 3. die Phantasielosigkeit der Völker."[120] The first two points are directly demonstrated by Westerhaus and Arduin; the third one was hinted at in different places.

"Jeder Krieg," says Schnitzler, "wird unter den nichtigsten Vorwänden begonnen, aus guten Gründen weitergeführt und mit den verlogensten Ausreden beschlossen."[121] It is true, however, that Schnitzler was not as much interested in what Hofmannsthal termed "das gesamteuropäische Wetter."[122] His creative work occupied immediate attention.

His primary interest there was to create human beings on the various levels of their expression of life. Even a war does not change human nature in its basic elements so rapidly. The characters he establishes after World War I are, therefore, still valid representatives of that period, and so are their themes.

In 1924, Schnitzler defends himself strongly in his letter to Jakob Wassermann:

> Ganz und gar nicht bin ich Ihrer Ansicht über die 'abgeschlossene, abgetane, zum Tode verurteilte Welt,' als welche Ihnen offenbar sowohl die in der 'Komödie der Verführung,' als die ringsum 'Fräulein Else' erscheint. Was ist abgetan, abgeschlossen, zum Tode verurteilt? Wer hat verurteilt? Wann soll das Urteil vollzogen werden? [...] Sind etwa die Typen, um nicht zu sagen, die Individuen, vom Erdboden verschwunden, die ich geschildert habe und wie ich hoffe noch einige Zeit hindurch zu schildern mir erlauben werde?[123]

A later letter to Körner in 1927 has the new morality of society and, more specifically, the themes of love and death as its topic. Again, it is a defense against wrong criticism.[124]

Schnitzler also addresses himself to the myth of a "sunken world" in his *Buch der Sprüche und Bedenken* by questioning the naive opinion on the part of critics regarding the essence of political, social, and ethical development within a short span of history; the phrase

> [...] von der 'versunkenen Welt' [...] (ist) so völlig sinnlos und verrät eine so naive Auffassung vom Wesen politischer, sozialer, ethischer Entwicklung, kurz ein solches Missverstehen aller Geschichte — (als wäre jemals im Laufe weniger Jahre eine Welt wirklich versunken — wäre es selbst so, — als hätte der Dichter das Recht nicht, die Gestalten einer versunkenen, auch einer eben erst versunkenen Welt heraufzubeschwören —), dass es nicht lange dauern wird bis zu dem Augenblick, da dieselben Leute das neue Schlagwort als lächerlich verhöhnen werden, die heute noch ihre kritische Überlegenheit zum grossen Teil von ihm zu bestreiten suchen.[125]

Offermanns attributes the meager success of Schnitzler's late comedies to the fact that the literary Expressionism was capturing the public interest at the time: "Der kritisch-reale Sinn von Schnitzlers Komödie widerstreitet der visionären Exaltation des expressionistischen Verkündigungsdrama ebenso wie der lebenstrunkenen Mythengläubigkeit einer nunmehr auslaufenden, vom Jugendstil wesentlich geprägten Dramatik."[126] However, the last act of *Komödie der Verführung* does contain some visionary aspects. It presents a different way of seeing the world, another level of reality. This is not to say that Schnitzler has become Expressionistic, but through characters such as Aurelie and Gilda he adds a mystical quality to the play. Aurelie not only sees people such as Arduin with an expanded awareness, but she also recalls her experience in Gysar's garden in a visionary way, thereby extending her world to include "das All." The triangular aspect of "Imagination" drew Arduin to our attention as well. Gilda, who is most familiar with the ocean waters because she has lived there all her life, also "adds a delicate nuance of mysticism to the scene."[127] LoCicero further encourages his readers to add another view to Schnitzler's already established reputation as a realist, when he cautions:

> It may well be that the failure to grant due consideration to the mystical content of Schnitzler's Weltanschauung contains one of the keys for false conclusions which stress ultimate scepticism out of all proportion to its significance in Schnitzler's view of the world and life. It is in the area of the

I-Thou relationship where the mystical — or that area of reality and truth which is not accessible to the cerebral capacity of man — has its most positive function in man, according to Schnitzler. [128]

The symbols of water and vision are definitely mystical elements in the drama *Der Gang zum Weiher* (1926), discussed in the following chapter. The study also focuses on the mystical aspects of I-Thou relationships in an effort to demonstrate Schnitzler's interest in matters related to intuition.

CHAPTER III

DER GANG ZUM WEIHER

Background of the play and statement of purpose

Although Schnitzler had reached a preliminary conclusion of this play by June 11, 1921[1] and had written in 1924 to his friend Georg Brandes "[...] und ein Versstück wird vielleicht auch bald fertig sein [...],"[2] this five-act verse play was not published until December of 1926 by S. Fischer Verlag, Berlin.[3] As a serious artist, Schnitzler rarely allowed publication of any work until he had convinced himself that it expressed truly his innermost convictions and that it had reached the most perfect form which he could create for it. As in other cases, this dramatic work was first conceived as a prose work entitled *Der weise Vater* in 1907. More sketches and notes were added between 1907 and 1914 and the new title *Der Weiher* given to it in 1915.[4] This new designation announces a shift in focus. In the final version of the drama water has even more significance than in the previous play *Komödie der Verführung*. This points to another aspect in Schnitzler's artistic career which heretofore has rarely attracted attention in the field of literary criticism. Eight months before his death (October 21, 1931), Schnitzler attended the premiere of the drama on February 14, 1931. During the first theater season the work had fourteen performances within two months.[5]

Upon first acquaintance with *Der Gang zum Weiher,* it is possible to become literally overwhelmed by the complexity of its thematic structure. For almost four decades Schnitzler had wrestled with essential problems of life, seeking to divest them of the conventional thought associations of his own time and place, in order to suggest their universal importance among mankind and to reveal all facets of their inner meaning. With some justice Josef Körner writes that even "der grösste Dichter" would find it difficult to force "so Mannigfaltiges zur Einheit."[6]

But was it unity which really captured Schnitzler's interest? Is it perhaps not more important to recognize that he concerned himself primarily with the diversity of human relationships as he observed them in the course of daily life, concluding that the ideal premises, such as unity and harmony, desirable for well-balanced personal interactions are rarely present. Schnitzler recognizes that these are worthwhile goals to strive for, but to attain them, one often experiences adverse states of mind first. Therefore, he emphasizes the dialectic pulse of the world, where polarities reign supreme. The analysis of this drama reveals that the antinomies of life are expressed in attraction and repulsion, intimacy and detachment, realism and surrealism, youth and age, art and life, life and death, peace and war, love and hate, selflessness and egotism, for gratification of physical desires and those of the psychic personality exist side by side, and often within the same personality.

It is the purpose of this analysis to show how Schnitzler's characters face the antinomies of life on physical, mental, and spiritual levels in an effort to achieve balance and restore inner peace. Beyond the desire for truth and well-being in their own lives they have an urge to better understand their relations to other people. The discussion indicates that Schnitzler's use of symbolism allows some insight into the mystical content of his

Weltanschauung. More than fifty years have passed since Körner wrote his assessment of Schnitzler's play. I share the predictions of recent criticism which states that "Many will come to regard this poetically beautiful play as one of his supreme achievements, a pinnacle in his lifelong struggle to express his uniquely personal view of life."[7]

Outline of the play

The action takes place in the mid-eighteenth century, paralleling in this respect the period of *Die Schwestern oder Casanova in Spa*. However, the setting in *Der Gang zum Weiher* is presumably Austria. The first act introduces the ex-chancellor, Freiherrn Albrecht von Mayenau, in peaceful retirement at age fifty, dictating his memoirs. He lives at a distance from the city, in his castle, previously just a vacation place (741). In his company are his unmarried sister Anselma, over forty but still beautiful (741), and his lovely daughter Leonilda, a precocious young woman of nineteen, who has recently finished her education in a convent. They expect the arrival of Sylvester Thorn, an aging poet and friend of Mayenau, who is returning to his homeland after ten years of self-imposed exile. Among the preparations for his visit are instructions from Leonilda to decorate the guest room in the tower of the castle with fresh lilac. Many branches have already wilted because Sylvester is several days late. Meanwhile, Mayenau and his sister speak about Leonilda, thus preparing for her late appearance on stage. Anselma expresses her concern for her niece as she tells the brother of Leonilda's nocturnal walks to the pond, a secluded place in the forest, where she has been bathing in secret. This activity in the solitude of moon-flooded summer nights is always climaxed by a ritualistic dance around an ancient stone. The chancellor does not share Anselma's worries; he only sees innocence in his child and insists that they both keep silent about their knowledge of Leonilda's secret, her nightly "Gang zum Weiher."

With the appearance of Leonilda begins the historical theme of the drama. She brings news from the village that war is imminent. The youthful Konrad von Ursenbeck, officer and son of the military commander, enters the stage shortly. He informs the chancellor that war with the neighboring state is unavoidable and conveys the hopes of his father, an old friend of the house of Mayenau, that the ex-chancellor will persuade the indecisive emperor without delay. The arrival of Sylvester Thorn interrupts their conversation and leads into Act II.

Schnitzler portrays both Sylvester and the chancellor so affectionately and in such detail that one could easily suspect a superimposed self-portrait. Sylvester has returned to Mayenau primarily to retrieve his past, captured in diary notes which he left in safekeeping with Anselma. Prior to burning each page in the fireplace, he wants to read his old writings again. Today he is confident of being able to compare himself with his own youth, thus preserving the sense of progress in his life. He is growing old, and he will soon be forced to admit that he no longer possesses the talent and vitality of his youth. He can try to forestall this conclusion by burning the papers and turning to the present and future, for he is in the process of preparing a home for the mistress he plans to marry and the child they are expecting. Sylvester meets Leonilda briefly, and she recalls all the fairytales he once told her in her childhood, hoping that he would add new stories. Meanwhile, the chancellor resumes the dictation of his memoirs, but the political discussions of the morning have excited his mind so that he stops the dictation.

Act III takes place late that evening; Sylvester has burned his papers and wants to leave the castle that same night. He is delayed by Andreas Ungnad, the secretary of the chancellor. In his role as a psychopath he entrusts Sylvester with a secret. Because Sylvester is conscious of his own egocentricity, he tends to see in his interlocutor a caricature of himself. While still baffled, he meets Leonilda, who with youthful admiration expresses concern about his future. This he interprets as a declaration of love. Flattered by Leonilda's words, he misunderstands them entirely and suddenly is prepared to desert the woman he supposedly loves. Instead, he asks the ex-chancellor for Leonilda's hand in marriage. Mayenau is appalled and speaks to his friend harshly. Finally, he tells Sylvester that he may return after he has put his own house in order. This decision will also provide time and distance for Leonilda to think things over. Should Sylvester still love her and find her the same, Mayenau will not withhold his blessing. Neither man is aware as yet that Leonilda is a free spirit and does not intend to bind herself in marriage. Anselma enters and intuitively knows what has happened. She withdraws with her brother into the darkness of the trees, from which they see Leonilda on her walk to the pond. Anselma foresees also Mayenau's reinstatement as chancellor and envisions for Leonilda the fulfillment of "ein fürstliches Geschick" (796-97).

The sudden appearance of Konrad returns the scene to the level of reality, as the threat of war looms more seriously now than ever. The document from the emperor restores to Mayenau all rights as chancellor. Mayenau, however, appears a disappointment to Konrad and the war party, for he will intercede only for the sake of peace. As he leaves immediately on this peace mission to the capital, Konrad stays in the castle impatiently. He wants to cool off and remembers the pond from his childhood days. Mayenau denies at first the existence of such waters, but his cryptic remarks made later on are actually intended to direct Konrad to the pond. When the chancellor returns from his trip to the emperor in Act IV, the inevitable, of course, has happened: Leonilda and Konrad have found each other and are "married before God" (832). A sharp argument follows between Mayenau and Konrad about the political situation and its consequences. The latter becomes suspicious of the chancellor's motives for keeping him at the castle; he sees in him nothing but an adversary and refuses to appear before the emperor.

Act V begins with the official return of Sylvester, who has had a brief encounter with the foolish secretary Ungnad in the previous act. He reports that his mistress and child have died in the travail of birth. "Von kaum geschloss'nen Särgen" (822), he comes still with the desire to marry Leonilda. Mayenau informs him of the changed circumstances, but only a long conversation with Leonilda convinces him of his wrong assumption. Mayenau is in error also about Leonilda's relationship to Konrad. "[. . .] mir beliebt es nicht [. . .] so bald mich zu vermählen" (832) she replies to her father. The last phase of the drama returns to the political scene. Mayenau has failed to preserve the peace. Konrad becomes more hostile as he disagrees in matters of strategy. He is finally free to leave, but Sylvester steps in his way by challenging him to a duel. The first shots of war are fired, thus averting Sylvester's provocation. While Konrad takes leave, not without properly addressing Leonilda and her father, Sylvester disappears unnoticed to start his walk to the pond. Schnitzler has no official exit for him. Ungnad, who followed Sylvester and observed his drowning in the pond, returns with this message to the house. His state of mind is very confused. Meanwhile, Mayenau prepares to move to the capital and Leonilda begs him to take her along because "dreifach gespenstisch schleicht Alter, Wahnsinn, Tod durch dieses Haus, / Nicht eine Nacht mehr will ich hier verweilen" (841). The work ends with the hope for early peace and a happy future for Leonilda.

Review of criticism

In Körner's view the drama does not hold together because the various themes are not developed in order of their priority.[8] He criticizes Schnitzler for the fact that his characters, happenings, and thoughts appear "mehr ersonnen als erlebt, mehr durchgrübelt als durchlitten [...]" and attributes the unsatisfactory impression it leaves with the reader to the circumstance, "dass der Dichter in einer seelisch-sittlichen Wandlung begriffen ist, die uns von ihm in jedem Sinne neue Werke noch erwarten lässt, die aber vorläufig nur zu einer zwiespältigen, unausgeglichenen Dichtung geführt hat."[9]

Sol Liptzin sees this work as an epilogue which Schnitzler wrote in loneliness and concern for age "in the last decade of a contemplative career" where "he gives utterance to his deep disillusionment with art as a substitute for active life, and to his sad recognition of the fact that fame is not in itself an end worth striving for."[10]

Françoise Derré, who in her detailed presentation of Schnitzler combines creatively historical, biographical, and thematic aspects, finds that the drama concentrates upon two aging characters: Thorn, the poet thwarted in his effort to recover wasted younger years through marriage with young Leonilda, and Freiherr von Mayenau, the statesman unsuccessful in his attempt to prevent the outbreak of war with the neighboring country. Her interpretation stresses the issue of war and peace, which she feels constitutes the center of the drama, "le heurt entre la bonne volonté des hommes et leur méchanceté, le conflit de la liberté avec le destin."[11] Although he is less carefully drawn, the emperor in this play is reminiscent of Rudolf II, as he is represented in Grillparzer's *Ein Bruderzwist in Habsburg,* for his weaknesses are marked by indecisiveness.[12] In Sylvester she seems to recognize an extension of Schnitzler's own experience, who like his protagonist, was suffering from discrimination, deliberate misunderstanding, and false criticism.

Martin Swales in his chapter, "Schnitzler's World: Restriction and Resonance," focuses on the "dialectic of attraction and repulsion" which "is central to Schnitzler's vision of human relationships."[13] This attraction can be felt toward another person, as Konrad experiences it with a young man in the opposing army. At the end of the play Konrad's main interest in war is to kill his "Doppelgänger."[14] Another form of "Doppelgänger," Swales shows, can be observed appearing in characters like Leonilda, Sylvester, and the Sekretär, who "have a sense of other people's existing as another part of their own being."[15] These states are further explored in an excellent article by Harold D. Dickerson.[16] He points out the "significance of the pond" as "the one symbol in the drama that gives coherence to its disparate and seemingly unrelated parts" because it is "both a place and a state of mind."[17]

Although all of the above interpretations contribute to an understanding of the drama, the analysis given by Dickerson is to date the most comprehensive effort in focusing on aspects of water and vision.

The present analysis explores the idea of unity in diversity from the standpoint of the polarity principle. In his late dramatic works Schnitzler creates frequently polar opposites in order to find answers in his search for truth and the deeper meaning in life. Often he establishes a synthesis which is equivalent to his concept concerning "die Ganzheit des Lebens." It also includes those states of consciousness beyond the rational mind. The tower symbolism in addition to that of water and vision is discussed in an effort to show how various characters in the play leave the firm ground of reality to seek answers from the higher mind.

Analysis of the drama

Symbolism: The symbolism begins with the carefully chosen title *Der Gang zum*

Weiher. "Der Gang" refers to the means, the path which various characters seek to get to their goal. The path is symbolic of life itself. It represents the burning path of life's desires. In connection with the second part of the title, "zum Weiher," the path to the water is important to all major characters in the play, because they recognize the pond as a point of reference which connects earlier experiences with the present moment and gives them a sense of direction for the future. For example, Konrad recalls his childhood days, when he was playing with Leonilda by the pond and one day lost her ball in the water. After a long day's journey on horseback, he now wants to return to the place and refresh himself (802-03).

For Leonilda, the pool seems to provide more than physical comfort, now that she has returned from the convent as a mature young lady, who is sensitive to the difference between life in a sheltered, restricted, cloistered atmosphere and life in a worldly environment with its social, economic, and political issues. During her nocturnal walks and activities at the pond she is seeking insight from the higher mind, that part of the mind which transcends the waking conscious and subconscious mind — the superconscious mind, the voice of intuition. With regard to the water symbolism Juan Eduardo Cirlot points out that "a secondary meaning [. . .] is found in the identification of water with intuitive wisdom."[18] Thus, the water represents mental potentiality, that is, unexpressed possibilities in the mind.

Commonly it is said that a man is "at sea" when he is in doubt about a mental process; in other words, he has not established his thoughts in line with the principle involved; he is not balanced. The sea is capable of production, but must come under the dominion of the formative power of the mind, the imagination. Leonilda is moved by the power of her imagination, whether she is dancing or immersing herself in the cool water. The waters, according to Cirlot, symbolize the universal convergence of potentialities which precedes form and creation.[19] Immersion intensifies the life force, and Leonilda certainly experiences in her nocturnal walks to the pond the awakening of her body as well, between mysticism and myth.

Sylvester, on the other hand, experiences the opposite: death and annihilation. In earlier years, the pond inspired his creative talent to tell Leonilda many fairytales, as they walked together along the water. When his endeavor of turning their friendship into a love relation fails, he loses the purpose in life and is ready to end it.

To Anselma who secretly observes Leonilda's nightly activity, the situation appears quite different. She is convinced that Leonilda engages in pagan worship which may lead her to other temptations as well. Indeed, she questions the wisdom of her brother and wonders, whether it was such a good idea "aus des Klosters Schirm und Frieden / Ein Kind — / [. . .] eh' sich ein Eidam fand, / In eine ringsum aufgetane Welt / Der Rätsel und Versuchungen zu stellen" (745). Hesitatingly, she tells him that she has been aware for a long time of Leonilda's nightly visits to the pond in the forest. She witnessed Leonilda's nocturnal swim and only "der Wellen Sang" (747) disclosed her proximity until she reached the other side, culminating in mystic dances around an ancient stone — "ein ungefüger Block" (748) — with arms outstretched, as if transfigured in the moonlight."[20]

Anselma's description, so vividly alive, seems to create a sensual atmosphere around the pond, Anselma herself being drawn momentarily into a magic spell as if she re-experienced her own years as a young woman and projected her feelings onto Leonilda. At this point Anselma's eyesight is transcending human limitation, when she recounts minute details from across the pond: "Es rinnen langsam / An ihrem Leib die blauen Tropfen nieder" (747). To her description on the physical level she adds mental and emotional aspects. In her mind's eye she observes the countenance of a god, embracing this beautiful naked child who gave herself "ahnungsheiss dem Blick des Gottes" (748). "Es war kein

Menschenantlitz," she confides to her brother, but it was attuned to Leonilda's spirit —
"es gab sich kund" (748) to the extent that Leonilda became aware of her own beauty in
the presence of the onlooking god: "Wie sie berauscht von diesem Wissen war, / Und zweifach trunken, weil ein Gott sie sah —" (749).

Anselma's vision is paralleled later in Act IV by an exceedingly charming and enchanting love scene between Leonilda and Konrad as they recall the moment, when they
— as if by magic — found each other at the edge of the pond and under its spell entered
together the domain of sexual love. The experience represents to Leonilda her initiation
into womanhood, answer to and fulfillment of her spiritual dance around the "ungefüger
Block" (748). This change within her is further evidenced by her firm attitude toward
Sylvester to remain on the level of friendship with him. To Konrad these nights of love
are the consummation of a strong attraction to Leonilda that began by the same pool in
their childhood days. He is so overwhelmed by his powerful feelings for Leonilda that he
prepares to leave the castle even before the Freiherr has returned. However, when Mayenau's arrival is announced and Leonilda unselfishly tries to help Konrad escape through a
side door, the young man reveals to her his real reason for leaving: "Noch eine dritte
Nacht an dich, / An diesen Mund, an dieses Herz gedrängt, — / Und all mein Wesen trankst
du so in dich, / Dass ich mit Leib und Seele dir verfiel. / Und davor war mir bang. D'rum
wollt' ich fliehn" (810).

The motif of flight as it relates to the pond is of antithetical significance to Sylvester
Thorn. In contrast to Konrad, Sylvester flees because of unrequited love for Leonilda.
Whereas Konrad, after the second night, draws away from the pond, the magic place of
his spellbound relationship with Leonilda, Sylvester is attracted to the pool in his final
moments of existence. ". . . als wenn / Der Waldpfad, den er ging, sich unsichtbar / Fortsetzte unterm Wasserspiegel," reports the Sekretär, "schritt er / Vom Ufer immer weiter
in die Flut — / Und immer tiefer, bis sie ihn verschlang" (838). Contrary to Leonilda's
experience in the water, which imparted vital energy to her, Sylvester's immersion brings
him death. Again, the path serves as a means to achieve a goal, which was not reached at
the edge of the pool. Watching Sylvester on that path, Ungnad felt the path continued
invisibly under the surface of the water. This may suggest a continuation of existence
beyond physical limitations. Reinhard Urbach points out: "Selbstmord kann als Selbstbestimmung und nicht nur als Selbstverlust gedeutet werden [. . .] er kann [. . .] auch als
bewusste Entscheidung und freiwillige Aktion begriffen werden, als Verfügung über die
eigene Person [. . .]."[21] The Freiherr feels that his friend decided his departure "mit
letzter Würde / Und eben noch zu rechter Zeit" (840). His thoughts this time are very
tactfully expressed in contrast to the blunt words he used in the dispute which they had
had previously.

Water in its different negative aspects represents weakness, lack of stability, negation
— all of which can be linked to Sylvester. In his lifetime he has not found the spirit of the
law which governs human existence in its actions and interactions. His selfish concept of
freedom and detachment let him always stand alone in the world, free of commitment or
obligation of any kind: "Und also schwebt' ich über fremder Erde, / Von Wurzelkräften
nirgends festgehalten, / Ein Gast und frei" (769). His adventurous life, exciting as it might
have been in younger years, has never taught him a sense of responsibility and concern for
anyone else; now the aging poet stands alone. He has never known the simplest but profoundest of human emotions, a loving feeling for another human being.

Too late Sylvester recognizes the futility of such an egocentric life and even the
changes he is prepared to make upon his return to the country are marked by weakness,
lack of stability, and dishonesty. On the one hand, he wants to prepare a home for his

mistress and the child they expect; on the other, he hopes for their demise so that he could be free for Leonilda: "In meiner Seele Gründen / Hab' ich's gewollt" (826). With these words he admits to Leonilda his feelings of guilt for having wished their death. He shows no remorse for having forgotten, or having been prepared to abandon them in favor of Leonilda. Every thought and word, of course, is recorded in his consciousness, and all the weak and characterless words and expressions gather in the subconscious mind as water collects in holes. Mayenau, who cannot hide his astonishment over Sylvester's return as suitor immediately after the funeral, receives this answer from him:

> Als Freier ging ich schon.
> Und gab ich an der Beiden Totenbett
> So heissem Schmerz mich hin, wie je ein Gatte,
> Ein Vater ihn gefühlt, — mich drein verlieren
> Wär' Schwäche; — zu verweilen, wo mich nichts
> Mehr hielt, wär' Heuchelei [...]. (822)

Sylvester's selfish attitude demonstrates a polar opposite to the author's own ideas which Liptzin captured in these words: "Schnitzler himself specifies in the codicil to his will, dated April 29, 1912, that, after his death, absolutely no one is to wear mourning for him. He forbids funeral orations and elaborate funeral rituals [...] he feels that no amount of oratory or weeping can warm the dead, and that the living should not succumb to gloom because of those who have passed on."[22] Schnitzler wanted to relieve everyone of a burden in the event of his death. Sylvester, on the other hand, burdened himself by wishing for the death of Alberta. In time of need there is nobody to sustain him. One such moment arrives in Act V, when the poet reveals the complete emptiness in his heart and pleads for acceptance of his marriage proposal. At that time Leonilda reaffirms her position of friendship and admiration for him as an eternal artist, because youth does not understand nor respond to the suffering of age and loneliness. As contorted as Sylvester's reply appears, it closes with the essential word which takes away any positive outlook on life: solitude (828).

It is again this despair that wells up in protest against Konrad's youth, when he challenges him with these lines: "Nur mir verstattet, [...] / Ein Abschiedswort Euch nachzurufen. Bube!" (834). It is a complement to Sylvester's earlier remark: "[...] 's wär eine arme Welt, / Wenn Jugend alles wär' —" (822). Even though he tries to end his life in a duel, the message about the outbreak of war at the border interrupts everything and he cannot even have the satisfaction of a "heroic" death. Ironically enough, the death by duel of one man is prevented by the bloodshed of many in war. But Konrad would not have agreed to such a fight, because it would have been "ein ungleich' Spiel" (834). He recognizes that Sylvester is "[...] wen'ger / Zu töten als zu sterben aufgelegt" (834). Therefore, the real issue is not moral but biological. It is a struggle not between the two personalities but between youth and age. As the Freiherr pointed out to Sylvester earlier: "Du bist ein ausgelesen' Buch, ein Name / Auf einem Grabstein" (823). The ensuing exchange between the Freiherr and Konrad allows Sylvester to leave unnoticed and start his final walk to the pond. He seeks the water to find not atonement but escape from this present state of affairs.

Water, however, stands not only for mental potentialities, weakness, negativeness, vital energy, regeneration, and birth; according to Arnold Whittick it is also a symbol of purification.[23] In this play so abounding with symbolism, there is the possibility that Sylvester's suicide can be interpreted as an act of purification. He is escaping from his egoism, thereby releasing himself from the narrow confines of his selfishness. In this sense his death is "inseparably linked with the theme of man's purification."[24] In Whittick's view death, as we commonly understand it, affects only physical man, while the rebirth is that of spiritual man, a dimension of which Schnitzler's characters indeed rarely are aware during their lifetime. "They pass their lives with no hope of ever penetrating the essential mystery," points out Dickerson. "But Schnitzler relieves the intransigency of this situation by endowing his characters with an instinctive and mystic awareness of life's secrets which enables them ultimately to come to terms with the unknown forces that both create and destroy them." [25]

It is hard to determine, however, where the Sekretär, the mad solipsist, stands in his "awareness of life's secrets." He looks upon other characters in the play as figments of his imagination. Schnitzler arranges to have scarcely any importance attached to Ungnad's notions, which, rather than a reasoned conviction, translate into a fixed idea bordering on insanity.[26] He is the only witness to the suicide: "Er sprang / Aus meinem Schädel in die Welt hinaus, / Wir waren zwei mit einmal auf der Erde" (838). The influence of the pond to which the Sekretär was exposed while watching Sylvester drown seems to have helped him clarify the "Doppelgänger"-problem he struggled with throughout the play. As he tells the Freiherr, Sylvester gave the sign for the rest of the world to come to life: "Nun leuchtet, braust es, heult, es lebt ringsum — / Und wider eine Welt steh' ich allein" (841). Thus, the Sekretär experiences a sense of separation which he might have picked up from Sylvester, who not only felt separated from the outer world, but also from the innermost part of his being.[27] Kammeyer sees in this character only a technical means to an end, namely, to carry out stage effectiveness: "Schnitzler stellt diese Figur als schweren Psychopathen dar, um an die Irrealität des gesamten Bühnengeschehens erinnern zu können. Der Zuschauer soll durch diesen allerdings nicht leicht zu durchschauenden Kunstgriff, wie schon in der Überleitung zum zweiten Akt, Abstand gewinnen."[28]

The term "Irrealität" is perhaps ill-chosen to describe "das gesamte Bühnengeschehen" because the drama also deals with politics and the looming war issue which certainly have a realistic basis. The important concept which dominates all four of Schnitzler's dramas discussed here is the principle of polarity.[29] Life's expression would not be complete without the two poles. William Rey summarizes this principle of composition as follows: "Letzten Endes also umfasst das Dasein für Schnitzler [...] alle Gegensätze, Kosmos und Chaos, Sinn und Unsinn, Gut und Böse, und verbindet sie zu einer Ganzheit, deren Wesen zwar geahnt, aber nicht mehr definiert werden kann," and concludes: "Angesichts dieser Ganzheit, deren Schrecken und Wunder ihn immer von Neuem faszinieren, wird Schnitzler zu dem, was Hofmannsthal einen Mystiker ohne Mystik nennt."[30]

On the one hand, Schnitzler's concern is the question of reality, but in order to understand reality, one must look at the opposite as well, which in *Der Gang zum Weiher* leads some characters to a search beyond the physical senses. Richard Specht calls Schnitzler a "Dichter der seltsamen Zusammenhänge."[31] Oskar Seidlin, who recognizes that the Schnitzler research has bypassed certain aspects of Schnitzler's work, summarizes these neglected sides of the author's artistic development by stating: "[...] es lässt sich kaum leugnen, dass hinter der eleganten Fassade, hinter der weltweisen und abgeklärten Skepsis, die gesamte Apparatur des Spuks und der Zauberei am Werke ist."[32]

Surrealism: Schnitzler has no ready answers to any of the problems posed, for he recognizes that it is not a condition he is dealing with but it ultimately narrows down to states of consciousness, states of mind. Quite often he has been misunderstood and harshly criticized for this.[33] "Was er immer wieder darstellt," observes Rey in defense of Schnitzler, "ist die Einsicht in die unerhellbare Hintergründigkeit des Daseins."[34] This impenetrable ambiguity is not only related to the symbolism of water and vision, it also finds application in the political realm discussed later. The focus again is on "Ganzheit." Herbert Cysarz in his excellent comparative study broadens the spectrum, when he admits: "Doch freilich ist Schnitzlers Erscheinungswelt immer auch ein Spiegelsystem, ein Medium unsichtbar-unsagbarer Mächte. Oft bilden sie gleichwie einen Schleier vor transzendierenden Weiten, bisweilen gewinnt sie ihr Relief wie unter metaphysischer Matrize."[35]

The influence of the inexplicable upon man, Cysarz's "Spiegelsystem," is seen by Gerhart Baumann as a two-fold activity which takes place "halb vor und halb hinter der Wirklichkeit [...]; die Gestalten erleiden dabei ein Doppelschicksal: ein unwichtiges, das sich an ihnen vollzieht, und ein wichtiges, das sie nicht erfahren. Die Mehrzahl verbringt ihr Dasein im Vorfeld des Noch-nicht-Eingetretenen oder im Schatten eines längst unwiderruflich Vollzogenen."[36] Sylvester belongs to this category. He lives either in the past or projects into the future, bypassing the only opportunity for constructive activity: the present. The first critic, however, who became aware of the conflicting element in Schnitzler's work is Körner, who wrote as early as 1921: "Wider Willen fast scheinen sich diese Okkultismen dem Dichter aufgedrängt zu haben, denn sein waches Bewusstsein liebt dergleichen durchaus nicht."[37] Perhaps Schnitzler's own ideas in this respect will help to clarify his position: "Das Wesen der sogenannten okkulten Erscheinungen liegt nicht darin, dass sie geheimnisvoller sind als tausend andere, die wir nur darum nicht als okkult bezeichnen, weil wir sie gewohnt sind, sondern dass sie sich den uns bekannten Naturgesetzen nicht einfügen, sondern ihnen gerade zu widersprechen scheinen."[38]

It seems that Schnitzler uses the natural laws known to science as parameters to place so-called "occult phenomena" in their proper perspective. There appears nothing mysterious about them to him; the mystery is only in man's mortal concept of them, because not all natural laws are known to man as yet. Thus Schnitzler, the natural scientist, the realist, allows space to grow, and this is reflected in *Der Gang zum Weiher*. Its complex symbolism includes that aspect of the work which Michael Imboden, in his examination of Schnitzler's prose works, calls "die surreale Komponente."[39]

Although the concept of "Surrealismus" originates in a movement in French literature, Imboden found a quote by Maurice Nadeau which redefines the term and allows its application to certain works of Schnitzler: "Die surrealistische Gesinnung, d.h. die surrealistische Verhaltensweise kommt [...] zu allen Zeiten vor, sofern man sie als die Bereitschaft auffasst, das Wirkliche tiefer zu ergründen, ohne es damit sogleich transzendieren zu wollen [...]."[40] Seen in this context, surrealism in the work of Schnitzler helps to complete "das Bild der Wirklichkeit und bringt es zu einer Ganzheitsdarstellung."[41] This total picture by necessity includes also phenomena which defy rational explanation, interpreted by Imboden this way: "Der Surrealismus stellt eine Welt dar, die dadurch mehrdeutig wird, dass sie nicht nur Oberflächen-Realität darbietet, sondern auch das Geheimnis jenseits des Verständlichen miteinbezieht. Die Gestalten der Dichtung leben in einer Alltagswirklichkeit, die durch das Hervortreten des Hintergründigen, der Dinge hinter den Dingen, brüchig geworden ist."[42]

Surrealism can be discovered not only in Schnitzler's prose works, but also in his dramatic production, and increasingly so in his late dramatic works. In *Der Gang zum Weiher* emphasis is placed upon "die surreale Komponente" as it occurs in the symbolism of water, vision, and the tower, discussed in the following pages.

Water and vision: The pond had immediate attraction for Leonilda, Konrad, and Sylvester. They were physically drawn into its seeming magic water for various reasons, whereas the Sekretär, Anselma, and the Freiherr kept a physical distance, but their mental activity displayed a vivid imagination about the pool. The Sekretär calls the pond "Zauberweiher" (838), because he witnesses an event peculiarly different from any of his previous experiences with water. The forest path in his state of mind magically seemed to continue for Sylvester directly underneath the water. In reality Sylvester is drowning, but Ungnad is not aware of it in this context. The spell of the water attracts him. The word "Zauberweiher" invites the immediate response from the Freiherr: "Wer sagt, dass hier ein Zauberweiher sei?" (838); yet, in his earlier conversation with Konrad he refused to give him direction to the pond because "Es heisst, der Weiher sei / Verzaubert, / Seit Märchenzeiten" (804). Adding to the "Märchen"-atmosphere, the Freiherr tells about evil spirits present there at night and nixies who are not necessarily from the spirit world, hinting at Leonilda's nocturnal dances (804-05).

The pond clearly has a deceiving influence upon the chancellor: Not only does he misguide Konrad by being vague regarding the existence of the pond, and by creating curiosity in Konrad with his reference to the nixies, but he is also duped by his own failing eyesight. His memory tells him the water "ist eher / Ein Sumpf zu nennen" (804), while Konrad can "swear" that he remembers from his childhood "Quellklares Wasser, wiesengrün umrandet, / Durchsichtig bis zum kieselblauen Grund" (804). At this point the Freiherr readily admits: "Vielleicht, dass Kinderaugen tiefer schau'n" (804), a comment prompted by his morning's activity in dictating another chapter of his memoirs. Dickerson, who correctly recognizes "that the eye plays a role only second to that of the pond,"[43] concludes that "in youth the chancellor had also enjoyed the mystic vision of 'Kinderaugen' and was able to grasp intuitively the common bond of humanity that joins all men."[44]

Indeed, in his case it was a special bond, for when they were twelve years old, the Freiherr felt a great sense of loyalty toward his playmate who was to wear the crown of the emperor later (751). This loyalty turned into a deep friendship with the emperor which seemed "ewig unzerreissbar" (783). As everything in human nature is subject to change, he learns that this "Band von Mensch zu Menschen [. . .] zerriss, wie jedes Menschenband" (783). There is a parallel yet different experience in Konrad's military life which draws again upon the water symbolism in the meaning of separateness. A small brook divides two opposing armies, and each side is carefully patrolled because they await orders to go to war against each other. Instead of feeling hostile toward one another, Konrad has found a friend of his age and rank across the water: "Und unbedenklich spinnt sich das Gespräch / Vertraut und heiter über das Gerinnsel, / Das uns zu Füssen weiter Grenze lügt" (763). They talked about everything and even embraced as friends and brothers before Konrad received orders to go to the chancellor and then to the emperor (764). But suddenly Konrad experiences a change. The friend becomes an enemy: his "Kinderaugen," which could see clearly to the depth of the pond before, suffer blurred vision; no longer are they a source of light, inspiration, and understanding: "Und nicht eher / Will ich ihm wieder Aug' in Auge stehn, / Als — meiner Schmach in Blut mich zu entsühnen — / Ich's mit gezücktem Degen darf und muss" (764).

Distrust and suspicion interfere with his intuitive nature. He questions the chancellor's honesty in his dealings with him, and when he finds Leonilda by the pond one night, he is uncertain two days later whether she may not have waited for somebody else, and wonders who may have seen her and been with her on other nights. He reasons that the place is "nicht eben unzugänglich" (808) and hardly doubts "dass auch vom Dorf ein Weg zum Weiher führt" (808). The chancellor, however, is convinced that nobody else ever saw his daughter because nobody knows the gate and the path "Und zu dem Weiher führt kein zweiter Weg" (749). Anselma, too, considers the path unknown to anybody and only sees a "weglos abgeschied'nen Weiher" (747), which lifts this location from the physical into the mental realm: it becomes a state of consciousness in the lives of certain characters. In fact, she equates this pond with "einem schillernd grünen Riesenauge" (747). It is the single eye which suggests one-pointedness and a spiritual equivalent to the possession of two eyes, which in human beings conveys physical normalcy.[45] Imboden calls this spiritual intuitive vision "Blick nach innen."[46]

According to Cirlot, it is the center of clairvoyance and vibrational perception. However, it also relates to the "symbolism of the number three: for if three can be said to correspond to the active, the passive, and the neutral, it can also apply to creation, conservation, and destruction."[47] All three processes are likewise related to the symbolism of water in the drama, constituting an ongoing cycle in nature from start to completion. The water has creative as well as conserving and destructive powers, forming a cycle in nature which also relates to the life cycle in man. Because of man's diverse emotional nature, life is complex. Schnitzler demonstrates this complexity in his drama *Der Gang zum Weiher*. Each character has reached a certain station in life which becomes the motivating factor for his human actions and interactions. Together they convey the author's concept of "Ganzheit," a total experience.

The life-giving forces of the pond have their complement in the human experience of love as it came to Leonilda and Konrad; while the destructive forces of the water correspond to death, as seen in Sylvester's case and to an extent in the clouded mind of the Sekretär. Anselma and her brother are the characters who are neither positively nor negatively affected by the pond. They observe everything from a distance: Anselma watched her niece from afar during the latter's nocturnal activity at the pond. Mayenau draws his sister into the darkness of the trees, as Leonilda begins her walk to the water another time. In their own personal experiences brother and sister come more closely in contact with the forces of fate than others, because they believe in such powers. An example is Anselma's status as an unmarried woman. Whatever happiness prevails in her life, she never experienced the joy of sharing it in an intimate one-to-one relationship. It is easiest for her to dismiss any future possibilities of companionship in the name of fate. There is a hint that Sylvester may return for her sake, but Anselma has released this affinity from her mind: "Ich und er ... / Wie lang ist das vorbei — wenn's jemals war!" (744). Time has indeed weakened Sylvester's memory because he addresses Leonilda with "Anselma?" (776), thus giving away, through gesture and the question mark in his voice, the difficulty he faces in associating the correct name with the right person. A second intervention by fate occurs toward the end of Act IV.

The Freiherr speaks of his guilt feelings toward Anselma for having prevented a possible marriage between the emperor and his sister, who, though equal on emotional and intellectual levels, "doch nimmermehr / Den kühnen Blick so hoch erheben durfte" (817). Anselma does not want unwarranted sympathy: "Hätt' ich mich für mich selber nicht bewahrt, — / Mehr als nur einem müsst' ich dann gehören. / Und dass ich's wusste, — das bewahrte mich" (818). Her brother's answer suggests a different viewpoint: "Und wär's vielleicht ein Dirnenlos gewesen, / Du hättest doch dein Frauenlos gelebt" (818). However, the question arises as to which of the two possible relations could have been meaningful to Anselma. Sylvester's negative attitude toward responsibility and commitment may have been more suggestive of a type of open marriage, especially in light of his suggestions to Leonilda (827). The question of "Dirnenlos" versus "Frauenlos" arises after Anselma and her brother have discussed the emperor and his unhappy marriage, which has just concluded. The Freiherr feels guilty toward the emperor also, for, in an effort to protect his own sister, he also guided his friend in another direction. The whole country might have experienced happier times had he not given distorted advice (818). Although these guilt feelings are self-inflicted, they constitute a heavy burden. In addition, the Freiherr was dismissed as chancellor, an event which for years unpleasantly interrupted his friendship with the emperor. Fate, therefore, has left its mark on both their lives.

Although the neutral attitude which Anselma and the Freiherr have toward the pond is more pronounced on the physical level, it should be pointed out that on the intellectual level Anselma is very active. Her intuition produces a prophetic vision three times in Act III. Intuitively she knows that Sylvester is serious about Leonilda (796). She also predicts that her brother will be reinstated as chancellor (796) and, at that time, should consider taking Leonilda along so that "a princely fate" (797) may be fulfilled, especially since the year of mourning for the death of the emperor's first wife has just ended (797). Anselma speaks "seherisch," according to Schnitzler's own stage instructions (797).

The end of Act V emphasizes Leonilda's intuitional gift again. In her mind's eye, the process of Sylvester's disintegration and return to the "All" speeds up "Und wesenlos zu nichts sein Bild verzittert [...] Denn keine Welle bringt, / Was jemals in des Weihers Tiefe sank, / Nicht Ding noch Mensch bringt je die Welle wieder" (841). The "Ding," of course, may relate to the event in Konrad's childhood, when he lost Leonilda's ball, which never surfaced.

Sylvester and the Sekretär, on the other hand, are blind to inner vision and the truths that are revealed. In fact, the opening lines of the drama emphasize the "meist offenen, wie ins Leere schauenden Augen" (740) of the Sekretär. The same emptiness is present in Sylvester's eyes, for he is not able to remember his experiences from younger years for the purpose of adjusting to his present station in life. Instead, he had to undertake a long journey in order to read his diary notes again. By physically releasing page after page of his past into the fire, he believes himself able now to direct his efforts and aspirations to the present and to the future. But in his limited, ego-bound expression of life, Sylvester is imperceptive, unable to effect a release of the past intellectually. He is blind to the necessity of facing himself with honesty. It is impossible for him to recognize the natural progression in life from youth to age; neither can he see the difference between art and life, past and present. This intellectual burden in the end contributes to his self-surrender to destructive forces.

Among the minor figures Dominik deserves to be mentioned in this context. Although his physical station in life is only that of a servant, on intuitive levels he is more advanced than other characters in the drama. He has taught himself to concentrate on each letter that arrives in the mail: "Man lernt allmählich / Auch hinter unerbrochne Siegel schau'n" (741), which the Sekretär does not comprehend in its significance.

Even the term "Aug' in Auge" (764, 812) is used antithetically. On the physical level, Konrad wants to meet his enemy-friend "Aug' in Auge" in order to kill him; the chancellor, however, meets with the ambassador of the opposing country, on occasion that enables them to dissolve prejudice, misconceptions, inharmonies, arrogance and to step before the emperor as peacemakers (812-13). The chancellor, therefore, can be viewed as the balancing force in the drama. Not only does he influence Sylvester during his sudden outburst of passion for Leonilda, he also "cools off" temporarily Konrad's fanatic ambitions to involve his country in useless war with the neighbor. Although the Freiherr is not able to remove the blindness from their eyes — this task is one that each must do for himself according to his level of awareness, Mayenau's hospitality provides an opportunity for reflection.

Tower symbolism: It is probably no coincidence that the guestroom is located "im Turmgemach" of the house (772, 803), which at first is prepared for Sylvester's visit and later serves to accommodate Konrad. The tower, as well as the house, carries ancient symbolic meaning. House means consciousness. The idea of ascent and spiritual elevation is implicit in the tower which connotes transformation and evaluation. Unfortunately, Sylvester does not experience any change; he intends to run away from it, as indicated by his desire to return home on the same night he arrived. According to Cirlot, the tower "is a determinant sign denoting height or the act of rising above the common level in life or society."[48]

At the beginning of Act II, Sylvester has just returned to the life and social customs of his native city, and he now prepares to settle down with his mistress Alberta into marriage and parenthood. But he is still filled with misconceptions and distorted views about himself and his earlier life. He mentions his house "in der Residenz" in which he lived "So lang, bis man den Fremdling d'raus verjagt" (767) because his mother's ancestors came "aus fremden Land hieher gewandert" (767). He equates "Fremdes" with such negative terms as "verhasst," "niedrig," "gemein" without realizing that his erroneous thinking may have been the cause of his own flight into "fremdes Land." In his desire to rise "above the common level of life," Sylvester had submitted to self-imposed exile rather than ask his friends for help. It is Mayenau who interrupts Sylvester's distorted presentation to Konrad in an attempt to balance the scales of truth: "Kein Mensch hat dich verjagt" (768), he tells him, and had somebody tried, not only the law of the land but also his friends would have been strong enough to protect Sylvester.

This exile, however, was more than just physical distance from his friends and everything dear to him. It was at the same time an escape from his own self: "Mir selbst entronnen, / Ein and'rer wandelt' ich durch kühle, klare, / Von keiner Ford'rung überhang'ne Welt" (769). Although he was "Wunschlos und keinem als [sich] selbst verpflichtet" (769), he recognizes slowly that nothing was gained during these ten years: as a "fool" he left, and he is returning in like manner (769), for to run away from challenges is to never meet them. As he communicates his feelings to the Freiherr and to Konrad, he appears to reach a certain perspective over his life which helps him to untangle its intricacies.

However, the most important task of coming to terms with life's progression from youth to age seems to fail him. He takes his diary notes to the tower guestroom, the place of spiritual elevation, but he is not able to free himself from self-deception, from his concept that the power of language is superior to the intuitive insights of the inner eye and the human heart. Mayenau tries in vain to call Sylvester's attention to the power of the word which continues to linger in memory long after it has vanished from the page, but Sylvester does not accept memories at all. In his view memory is "Ein Ungestaltes, Nie-zu-Fassendes" (775), but the written word is "ein Zaubergriff" which connects "Verfliessendes, Verflossenes [...] / Und schafft, wenn's aus erfüllter Seele kam, / In übermächt'ge Wirklichkeit es um" (775).

Sylvester does not fit into the group of characters who, in Schnitzler's words, experience life three-dimensionally: "Man erlebt alles Wesentliche in dreifacher Art: im Vorgefühl (auch wenn man es nicht geahnt hat), in der Erinnerung (auch wenn man vergass) und endlich in der Wirklichkeit: diese aber bekommt erst ihren Sinn in Hinsicht auf Vorgefühl und Erinnerung."[49] Because Sylvester rejects memory, he is never able to come to terms with reality in the present moment. Instead, he is afraid that in later years he might discover that his past, the youth of his life, is better than the aging process of the present. By burning his diary, he believes he can destroy the domination of the past because: "Heute bin ich meines Sieges noch gewiss, / Ob über's Jahr, ob ich es morgen wäre? / Drum sei es heut gelesen — und verbrannt" (775).

But the past is closing in before he has a chance to reach the tower guestroom to destroy it. Leonilda leads him back in memory to the time when she was a child listening to the fairytales he told her. She proves to him: "Ich weiss sie alle noch — / In Worten nicht, doch besser als in Worten. / Sie träumen stumm in meiner Seele fort" (777). She is the second person who tries to awaken Sylvester from his lifelong deception, to assist him in removing the blindness from his eyes which are the windows of his soul. Just as the pond reflects in its "Riesenauge" the truth of his soul, his inner being. Yet he is afraid of the truth. Finally, Leonilda urges him to look into her eyes and see the reflection of his true nature: "Und siehst du mir nur lang genug ins Aug', / Erblickst du selber durch den Maskentrug / Dein mir vertrautes, wahres Angesicht; —" (778). His poetic talent shall create a new beautiful fairytale, and it shall belong to both of them as a child is shared by father and mother (778). Little is she aware yet of the dual role which Sylvester would have to play as father: However, she is keenly aware that Sylvester would follow her "trotz aller Geister — / [. . .] üb'rall hin, wo's [ihr] beliebt" (781).

Later on the drama reveals that Sylvester's experiences in the tower have not brought him any closer to present realities, for his reaction is the one usual to him, that of flight in order to reach less complicated territory. "Die Menschen hausen meistens nur im mittleren Stockwerk ihrer Lebensvilla," observes Schnitzler with his psychological insight, "dort, wo sie sich behaglich mit guten Öfen und sonstigen Bequemlichkeiten eingerichtet haben. Selten steigen sie in die unteren Räume hinab, wo sie Gespenster vermuten, vor denen ihnen schaudern könnte; selten klimmen sie zum Turme auf, wo der Blick ins Tiefe und Weite sie schwindeln macht."[50] Sylvester's abrupt change of plans would indicate his uneasiness at the prospect of spending the night high up in the tower. He is mentally unprepared for any uplifting experiences. Schnitzler is aware of two kinds of people when he says: "Manche Leute freilich gibt's, die sich just im Keller aufzuhalten lieben, weil ihnen im Dämmern und Gruseln wohler ist als in Licht und Verantwortung, und andere wieder klettern gerne auf den Turm, um den Blick in unergründliche Fernen zu verlieren, die ihnen ewig unerreichbar bleiben."[51]

If the basement can be compared to the past, then Sylvester tends to remain there for fear of facing his present and future desires. He wastes the precious moment, the only time for him to fill with meaningful activity. But in his tower symbolism Schnitzler considers a third group of characters and comes closer to describing Sylvester's state of mind: "Die unseligsten Subjekte aber sind diejenigen, die zwischen Keller und Turm ruhelos treppauf und treppab rennen und die zum eigentlichen Wohnen bestimmten Räume verstauben und verwahrlosen lassen."[52]

This restlessness within Sylvester is a result of his nonchalant nature. During his carefree life he had crossed paths with Alberta numerous times, only to drift apart again after a while. This time he wants to create a permanent relationship through marriage because they are "des Schicksals vorbestimmtes Paar" (773). This is a deception when compared to the statement he makes to Leonilda later (829). Furthermore, he tells Mayenau they stay together "um immer wieder, nach erfüllter Zeit, / Aufs neu' zu scheiden" (773). Mayenau in his balancing nature issues a warning, indirectly pointing to the responsibility and commitment involved in marriage: "Und dennoch denkst du ernstlich an Vermählung?" (773), but his words fall on deaf ears. This insincerity on the part of Sylvester, together with the fact that he is suffering from self-deception, apparently is the cause of his sudden change in marriage plans. In Leonilda's presence he misunderstands every word she speaks, especially when she touches upon the concept of sin in life: "Mit seh'ndem Aug' den falschen Weg zu geh'n" (789). This Sylvester interprets to mean that the right path leads along Leonilda's side. "Hielt Treue mir dies wunderbare Kind? / Und stürzt aus ihrem glaubensjungen Herzen / Sich Glaub' und Jugend endlich auch in meins —?" (789), he says, conjuring up his youth again, which he said he had come to leave behind by burning the pages of his diary.

Konrad, on the other hand, has little trouble with the tower guestroom. He has his first sexual experience during this stay. As soon as the chancellor leaves him at the end of Act III, he frees himself from the idea of adolescence (805). Suddenly, he knows "Ich bin ein Mann" (805). However, in Act V he is faced with a challenge with regard to his newly gained consciousness of being an adult, when the Freiherr for reasons of political differences demands his sword. The sword, as Whittick explains, is the symbol of power, authority, protection, justice, and knighthood.[53] When taken away, these attributes would reduce Konrad again to the status of adolescent. But Leonilda intervenes in the name of justice to let him be a free man (834). It is this new state of consciousness which leads him without difficulties to the pond, where he finds Leonilda likewise ready for her first sexual experience. The hours Konrad spends in the guestroom up in the tower are filled with his memories of that joyful experience. However, with the awareness of manhood often comes that of jealousy, and Konrad proves to be no exception. Two days later he begins to wonder why Leonilda was not frightened when he suddenly appeared and disturbed her nocturnal devotion. Something else puzzles him: "Mir war, als hätt'st du mich, nein Leonilda, / Nicht eben mich — nein, irgendwen erwartet" (808). Leonilda's simple but serious answer does not satisfy him, for there may be other paths that lead to the pool, and if so, who has seen her emerge from the pond on other nights? When she playfully leaves this possibility open, Konrad at the height of his jealousy wants to die, but not without taking her life also (809).

Whenever the chancellor is not present to balance onesided views, it is Leonilda who takes his place. As she stepped into this role with Sylvester, she now does so with Konrad. With distinct self-authority she places the situation in perspective: "Hab' ich in dem Augenblick, / Da wir verzaubert ineinanderglitten, / Zum Herrn dich über mich gesetzt? Gab ich / Mit meinem Heut mein Gestern und mein Morgen, —" (809), thus maintaining again the freedom of her own choice.

Her words are a firm rejection of Konrad's assumption that he now has a voice in what she does. She requires that he first earn the right through responsible behavior: "Nein? Jetzt gilt es erst zu werben. / Dein war die Nixe. Willst du auch das Weib, — / Mit Jünglingsfrechheit wirst du's nicht gewinnen. / Und auch die Nixe, gib nur acht, steigt wieder, / Wie sie emporgetaucht, hinab zum Grund" (809). Although Leonilda dislikes being called "Nixe," she now uses the word twice herself as a means to distinguish Leonilda, the woman, from the water sprite, an incomplete state of being. Seen in connection with the term "Jüngling," it indicates a state of spiritual incompleteness on both their parts; sheer sensuality without responsibility lacks the foundation of truly deep love that is desired in marriage. With the words "hinab zum Grund," she establishes the need to know more about her potential as a woman in order to feel the same harmony as she does with the forces of nature signified by the pond, which are the same forces that underlie the secret of life and love. Leonilda, this "âme indépendante et fière," as Mme Derré characterizes her,[54] represents the woman of the future, who moves beyond the conventions of a romantic idealization of love and marriage.

Leonilda's awakening: Her experience with Konrad also provides better understanding of her own feelings toward Sylvester. Davis points out that "she wakes from adolescence and dreamy fantasy into the reality of womanhood. Before the encounter with Konrad at the pool, she is vague, uncertain, and remote in her mind [...]."[55] Such generalizations contribute little to the interpretation of this important character. It is necessary to recognize that Leonilda actually becomes aware of deeper levels within her nature. This awareness helps her to realize that her attraction to Sylvester was not based on love but admiration. In the beginning of the drama she insists to her father: "Er lebt in mir" (754), because she was inspired by Sylvester's fairytales and his spirited artistic temperament, which impressed her so strongly as a child that Leonilda, the woman, could not forget him. As a woman, she has reached a new level of maturity; she refuses Sylvester's marriage proposal in lieu of friendship, which seems to her "das edlere Geschenk" (825), begging him to reciprocate forgivingly: "Lass mich nicht entgelten, / Dass ich nicht früh'r erkannt, was mich zu dir — / Das Kind schon übermächtig zu dir zog, / Und jenseits meines Irrtums bleib mir nah" (825). But mere friendship does not comfort Sylvester, who is longing for a youthful wife to regain his own youth. He does not understand Leonilda's new state of awareness and in fact is led to believe that she is "unter allen Frau'n auf Erden / [ihm] bestimmt von Anbeginn der Welt" (829). With these words he alienates her even more.

Leonilda is similarly upset at her father, who attempts to arrange a marriage ceremony to give his daughter honorably to Konrad before the young man leaves to meet an uncertain fate at the front. She however rejects even the thought of a wedding: "Verzeih, mein Vater, mir beliebt es nicht, / Mit wem's auch sei, so bald mich zu vermählen" (832). Without hesitation she grants to Konrad the same freedom which she desires for herself: "Frei zieh' er hin. Ich bleibe frei zurück. / Wie und — ob wir einander wiederfinden, / Weiss nur der Gott, vor dem wir uns vermählt" (836). Konrad accepts her terms, although he declares himself "feierlich verlobt" (836). However, when Leonilda emphasizes for the second time that Konrad should be free from any past memory to experience joyfully whatever life has in store for him (836), Konrad senses a note of farewell rather than a blessing or an assuring message from her heart that would give him courage during the lonely hours of his war mission.

Unity: The two parts of the play. In his desire to contrast matters of the heart with political issues, Schnitzler has carefully proportioned the two parts of the drama. It is unfortunate that this intentionally created balance of the plot has been mostly overlooked by Schnitzler critics. Körner insists: "Im 'Weihergang' ist das politische Geschehen, trotzdem es mit der Liebeshandlung im Grunde nichts zu tun hat, zu sehr ausgedehnt, macht sich mit seiner eigenen Problematik breit, benimmt der Haupthandlung Lust und Raum."[56] He fails to recognize that the "Haupthandlung" really spreads over two-thirds of the drama. In addition to the war issue pushed by Konrad and his father, the remaining part of the play deals with peace efforts on the part of the chancellor, as well as with the problem of friendship between himself and the emperor. This complexity is Schnitzler's tool to sharpen the conflict which arises from human action and interaction.

Further criticism is raised in terms of the various arguments. Körner asks: "Handelt es sich um das Problem des zum Weib erwachenden Mädchens? Oder um das der freien Frau? Um den alternden Mann? Um das Heimatproblem? Um den Pazifismus? Oder verbirgt sich der eigentliche Sinn des Stücks in dem wahnsinnigen Sekretär Ungnad [...]."[57] Schnitzler defends himself in a letter to Körner, dated July 11,1927, in which he can barely hide his anger and annoyance: "Niemals ist ein Einfall in mir mit solch zwingender Einheitlichkeit aufgetaucht, vom ersten Augenblick an [...] waren die erotischen Vorgänge in die politische Atmosphäre gestellt, das Verhältnis des Dichters zum Krieger, des Kriegers zum Politiker, der Leonilda einerseits zum Dichter, andererseits zum Soldaten war mir von Anbeginn an das Wesentliche, unter einem anderen Himmel als dem, den ich über es gespannt habe, konnten die seelischen Vorgänge, auf die es mir ankam, sich überhaupt nicht entwickeln [...]."[58]

Consequently, the drama does not outline a single problem, but deals with the complexity of life which affects human conduct. Schnitzler's insight into human nature reveals that there are no ready answers. He reproves Körner for not recognizing "die Notwendigkeiten der Verknüpfungen und die Verknüpfung der Notwendigkeiten" which "'hätten Ihnen aufgehen müssen.'"[59] Furthermore, he clarifies Körner's question with regard to "Probleme": "Es handelt sich ja in der Kunst — verzeihen Sie die Selbstverständlichkeit — überhaupt a priori nicht um Probleme, sondern immer nur um Gestalten und um das Schicksal der Probleme, in den vom Dichter geschaffenen oder der Wirklichkeit nachgebildeten Gestalten."[60]

Liptzin's observation, on the other hand, is more applicable than Körner's, when he says: " [...] though Schnitzler fails to solve the important questions which he poses, he does remove a maze of prejudices with which these questions are normally surrounded, so that they stare at us in their sphinxlike majesty."[61] They remain questions, indeed, "[...] denn Lösungen gibt es nicht," according to Schnitzler.[62]

Polarities: Schnitzler's dialectic approach allows him to show various aspects within one character as well as the relationship to others in the play. Leonilda combines within her filial love such natural polar qualities as loyalty and rebellion. So too does Konrad project the same opposites in his war interest. Leonilda is devoted to her father but rebels when he tries to hasten her into marriage. She shows loyalty toward Sylvester, for she not only remembers him and his artistic talent, but feels that he lives within her and tells her father that the same poet will return, who left ten years ago (754). Yet, when Sylvester wants to bind her to his side, she withdraws in protest. Konrad, eager to prove himself as a warrior, is faithful to his father's interests which stand in sharp contrast to Mayenau's philosophy as a statesman. The reader and audience are already familiar with the chancellor's viewpoint from his conversation with Leonilda, who carries the war issue into the play as a distinct antithesis to the aspect of Eros, likewise initiated by Leonilda. Her visit to the village that morning did not result in play, as her father suspected, but in a political discussion because "ein schwarzer Reiter" came through the village with documents presumably containing a decision to go to war. Pensively the chancellor questions: "Entscheidung — für den Krieg? — [...] Befehl zum Angriff? " (753). He imagines it possible, especially since the proper moment — as so often in the past — had already been lost because of the emperor's indecisiveness. It has always been this way, always is, and always will be the same: "[...] inmitten des Zufrüh und des Zuspät / Ratlos einher, von jedem Hauch erschüttert" (753).

"Encore que moins nettement dessiné," Mme Derré has opportunity to show, "l'empereur de 'Der Gang zum Weiher' n'est pas sans rappeler un autre célèbre monarque de la littérature autrichienne, Rudolf II tel que le représente 'Ein Bruderzwist in Habsburg'."[63] In her excellent discussion she discovers relationships between Schnitzler and Grillparzer in that they both deal in their dramas with polarities such as loyalty and rebellion, hesitation and action. These associations between the two great Austrian dramatists have hardly been noticed in earlier criticism. Five years later Swales points out: "The shadow of Grillparzer falls unmistakable on Schnitzler's 'Der Gang zum Weiher.' Human action is seen as an inevitable caricature of the intention from which it sprang."[64]

Unfortunately, Swales does not support his idea beyond this general statement. It is important to recognize the close relationship between these two monarchs. The emperor in *Der Gang zum Weiher*, like Rudolf, is a wise man but incapable of acting. He does not like to make decisions and so creates within himself a conflict between "Pflicht und Neigung." He also tries to ignore the demands of a changing society, thereby resembling Rudolf closely.[65] In Schnitzler's play the emperor is drawn between war and peace, between introversion and the public life of a politician, between thought and action, leaning toward a contemplative rather than an active style of life. He, too, has to deal with the conflict between individual interests and the welfare of the entire empire. There exists an antithesis between earthly anarchy and cosmic order, between his role as a human being and that of an emperor. This latter conflict has been the reason for withdrawing his friendship from Mayenau. As emperor he developed a strong feeling of distrust, which the chancellor recalls not without sadness in a conversation with Konrad: "düst're Hast" was disguised "als Drang zur Tat, / Unschlüssigkeit als kluger Vorbedacht, / Schwachheit als Güte, müd' geword'ner Hass / [...] als Gerechtigkeit / [...] kaum bezwung'ner Ekel [...] als Menschenliebe" (759-60). In Rudolf's situation there exists also a conflict between Protestantism and Catholicism, but this religious aspect is not apparent in *Der Gang zum Weiher*.

Instead, more emphasis is placed on intuition, present in degrees within all major characters. Mayenau is the first one to emphasize "Ahnung" when he answers Anselma: "Muss Leonilda *wissen*? Ihrer *Ahnung* / Vertrau' ich mehr als and'rer Wissenschaft" (744). William Rey explains Schnitzler's dialectic approach in these words: "Als überzeugter Feind eines jeden Dogmatismus, ob nun religiöser oder wissenschaftlicher Natur, entwickelt er ein dialektisches Denken, das von der Einsicht in den gleichberechtigten Geltungsanspruch des Gegensätzlichen beruht und durch die Bejahung der im Dasein angelegten Widersprüche eine höhere Ebene der Erkenntnis zu gewinnen sucht."[66]

It follows that Schnitzler in his dialectic thinking recognizes a deeper meaning in that which is commonly considered negative. In his *Buch der Sprüche und Bedenken* he formulates this idea as follows: "Das Sinnvolle hat nur Bedeutung, ja Daseinsmöglichkeit durch die Annahme des Sinnlosen [...]. Gerade der Schmerz über das unvermeidliche Scheitern des Menschen kann zur Quelle innerer Bereicherung werden."[67]

Sylvester experiences this kind of pain in his sudden passion for Leonilda, but instead of gaining inner strength and enrichment, he is overcome by despair. His polar opposite, Konrad, the warrior, is not successful in his political mission and withdraws to a position of rebellion, but in the end he is able to reconcile the differences with Mayenau. For the third time within seven weeks, he carries the same message to the emperor and this time invites the ex-chancellor to accompany him in order to lend more force and urgency to the task at hand. But Mayenau, who was forced to leave his political appointment seven years ago (759), declines his help. Even after he is reinstated as chancellor in Act III, he does not share Konrad's philosophy of war, namely, that this hostile encounter is an inevitable destiny. Instead, Mayenau believes in the power of thought whose energies have influence upon the cosmos: "Ich fühle nicht geheimnisschwer vom Schicksal / Mich überhangen. Über mir die Wolke / Ist auch nur Nebeldunst aus Menschenland, / Und am Verhängnis über mir braut so / Mein Will' auch mit" (802). Unfortunately, his peace mission comes too late, war has already broken out. In loyalty to the emperor, Mayenau joins his regiment, thus restoring a better relationship with Konrad.

Significantly enough, the "dialectic," in Swales's terms, of intimacy and detachment, of attraction and repulsion, which is a central issue in Schnitzler's vision of human relationships,[68] also plays an important role in the chancellor's loyalty to his emperor. In his memoirs the Freiherr recalls a certain attraction to an intimacy with the young man who was to become emperor. His position as chancellor increased the closeness and friendship between them. Yet, when the emperor detached himself, Mayenau ceased to maintain an active interest in his country and its destiny. To him Schnitzler gives his own view of intellectual pacifism, that war is a waste of human values and the triumph of injustice (761). Much to Leonilda's surprise, her father draws a distinction between "Reich und Vaterland." When he fails to accomplish this task, then the political power struggle invites duality, as seen in the conflict between the emperor and the marshal. If the emperor decides against the marshal's recommendation to go to war, which was outlined in the letter Konrad delivered, then Konrad is convinced the army will decide in favor of the marshal (765). In this event the chancellor speaks of rebellion, but Konrad calls it "obedience to the proper master" (765). Similarly, he is of the opinion that the letter to the emperor provided choice and not a threat, as Mayenau sees it.

This polarity between the conservative judgment of the older statesman and the liberal ideas of Konrad creates differences between age and youth. At the end of Act II Mayenau proclaims: "Und nach Jugend riecht die Welt!" (783); whereas Act IV ends with Konrad's disgusted expression: "Vergiftet ist die Welt von Greisenatem!" (806), an inner rebellion of youth against age. It is a sensitive issue with Mayenau, who corrects Konrad in his reference to Sylvester as "der sonderbare alte Herr" by saying: "Nicht eben alt, doch sonderbar, mag sein" (804). He needs to take this position, for whatever is said about Sylvester would also ring true for himself as Sylvester's friend. Konrad does not change his mind at all and indeed insists, when alone on stage later: "Ich bin ein Mann — und er ist grau und alt" (805), referring to Mayenau. Leonilda, on the other hand, looks at Sylvester differently. Interestingly enough, she is correcting her father: "Der, den ich meine, Vater, altert nicht, / So wenig jemals Jugend von ihm strahlte" (754). Age in her frame of reference is not an issue of chronology; she sees him in his spirit nature, forever young. Yet, at the end of the play she no longer has this idealistic view. Because of the most recent incidents of suicide and Ungnad's psychopathic behavior, the castle has turned into a nightmare for her, and she begs her father to be taken along to the court: "Vater, nimm mich mit dir. Dreifach gespenstisch / Schleicht Alter, Wahnsinn, Tod durch dieses Haus, / Nicht eine Nacht mehr will ich hier verweilen" (841).

Sylvester, however, knows that the storms of youth have gone by; his only chance to bring them back to life is by reading the diary notes, but the spirit of his youth (778-79) will not be redeemed, not even by way of Leonilda as a marriage partner. Twice Sylvester addresses Mayenau as "Freund meiner Jugend" (791), until he stands corrected "entschwund'ner Jugend Freund" and furthermore is reminded: "Schlimmer als alt — wir beide — nicht mehr jung" (792). The Freiherr, conscious of the limitations that age may impose upon him, agrees in the presence of Sylvester to accommodate himself to this situation of being no longer young on a physical level. These limitations, however, by no means have influence upon his mental capacities. He would call any man a fool if not "ein Geck" (793), because he knows that at this age a man may be able to conquer the heart of a teenage girl but not to keep her happy in marriage. [69]

Sylvester refuses to accept his friend's viewpoint, defending himself with these words: "[. . .] 's wär eine arme Welt, / Wenn Jugend alles wär' —" (822). This philosophy parallels that of Fenz, the old "Kammersänger" in *Komödie der Verführung*. Interestingly enough, Schnitzler discloses the age of neither of these two characters. The only reference with regard to Sylvester is contained in a letter to Brandes where he says: "In meinem nächsten Stück soll der neunzigjährige [sic] als Sieger übrig bleiben."[70] Because the final version of the drama did not grant the victory to Sylvester, it is perhaps safe to assume that Sylvester was not ninety years of age either, possibly closer in age to Mayenau. Schnitzler, of course, addresses himself to the problem of age and aging numerous times in his late dramatic work. His own conviction is perhaps best expressed in the letter cited above to Brandes: "[. . .] das Alter ist nur eine Intrigue, die die Jugend gegen uns einfädelt."[71] But another cycle of seven years expired in Schnitzler's life between 1924 and 1931, which left Jakob Wassermann with a different impression. He visited Schnitzler six months before the latter's death and recalls the following: "Was ihn von Mal zu Mal tiefer bedrückte, war die Tatsache des Alters und Alterns, die er sich nicht mehr verbarg. Ich [Wassermann] las neulich ein entzückendes Wort von Alice Berend: Das Schlimme im Altern ist nicht, dass man älter wird, sondern dass man jung bleibt. Damit ist der seelische Zustand des alternden Schnitzlers umfassend gekennzeichnet [...]."[72]

Wassermann's statement reverses Mayenau's earlier convictions: "[...] schlimmer als alt [...] nicht mehr jung" (792). This really amounts to a matter of attitude toward the complexity of this problem. Wassermann seems to come to the same conclusion about Schnitzler, when he writes: "[...] Mit jedem Atemzug wehrte er sich trotzig und angstvoll gegen das unerbittliche Gesetz, bis zum Zorn, bis zur Paradoxie oft, wobei zugleich der Arzt in ihm, der Denker, das aufsässige Kind zur Ordnung rief."[73]

Not only is Schnitzler the thinker at work in an attempt to come to terms with this problem, but especially Schnitzler the poet. Freud offers the following consolation in a letter to him: "Zum Schluss aber — ich weiss nicht ob Sie dieses Trosts bedürfen — lassen Sie sich sagen, dass der Dichter später altert als gewöhnliche Menschenkinder, und dass nach dem Dichter noch der Denker herauskommt."[74] Earlier, however, it was the poet whom Freud jealously admired in Schnitzler, because this poetic talent seems to have given Schnitzler access to knowledge which opened up for Freud only after laborious efforts of scientific research.[75]

This knowledge is based upon Schnitzler's dialectic approach to presenting a problem. The anger and indignation which Wassermann spoke of are not Schnitzler's last words about the deficiencies in human existence, such as age. "Auch Leid ist Gnade," we read in *Der Gang zum Weiher* (789). And his aphorism in *Buch der Sprüche und Bedenken* underlines this statement even further: "Dass wir geschaffen sind, das Unfassbare zu fassen und das Unerträgliche zu ertragen — das ist es, was unser Leben so schmerzvoll und was es zugleich so unerschöpflich reich macht."[76] It is truly an acceptance of human existence in all of its contradictions which Schnitzler stresses. In *Der Gang zum Weiher*, Mayenau is the character whose wisdom strikes a perfect balance between Konrad's unstructured vitality of youth and Sylvester's inability to see his age in proper perspective. His philosophy reveals a firm belief in the power of the spirit, which allows life's energies to expand within the context of responsibility and commitment. Friedrich Wilhelm Kaufmann observes this polarity of youth and age in a similar way: "In 'Der Gang zum Weiher' aber wird eine Synthese der ziellosen Vitalität der Jugend und der rückwärtsschauenden, begrifflichen Unlebendigkeit des Alters in der Forderung und Schaffung eines Jugend und Alter gemeinsamen höheren Zieles gewonnen."[77]

It is certainly exaggerated to say that the problem of aging forms the center of the drama, as Körner does.[78] Rey recognizes the situation more accurately when he stresses Schnitzler's view of the adventurer: "Es ist aber bezeichnend, dass sich in dieser Periode die Kritik Schnitzlers am Abenteurertum noch verschärft [...]. Hier wird der Abenteurer, auch wenn er Künstler ist, entlarvt als der grosse Egoist, der nie ein Opfer gebracht hat, der nie wahrhaft geliebt hat."[79] Therefore, Mayenau and Sylvester are opposite yet complementary characters; opposite because the chancellor is a man of action and not an egoist, a combination rather rare in Schnitzler's work; complementary because he, too, is unable to comprehend women's souls. He misunderstands both Leonilda and his sister Anselma. Worried by the thought that he might have sheltered Anselma too well, he now is in a hurry to arrange for Leonilda's marriage to Konrad. But neither as father nor as brother could he fulfill their destinies. Schnitzler goes with his ideas beyond the customs of the day, because in his drama each woman is responsible for her own life and essentially accepts the freedom of her own choice. But Mayenau is motivated in all his actions by a sense of responsibility, whether it be the war issue or more sensitive emotional matters within his own household.

In this respect too he is the opposite of Sylvester who really wavers between frivolity and responsibility. Most of his frivolous life has been given to debonair selfish pleasures. He has never committed himself beyond the narrow limits of "I, me, and my," and even now he withdraws from his commitment to Alberta. Herbert Lederer, discussing the problem of ethics, finds other ethical concepts which Schnitzler arranges in contrasting pairs such as: "Altruismus und Egoismus, Erlebnis und Sensation, Sachlichkeit und Opportunismus, Stolz und Überheblichkeit."[80] Each one of these concepts can also be found in *Der Gang zum Weiher,* for they are motifs, all connected to the central conflict in human relationships.

Another form of polarity can be recognized in the "Doppelgänger" motif, discussed by Swales.[81] Schnitzler presents this motif in different variations. Konrad, for instance, was attracted to the young man in the opposing army because they shared many interests; but when war is declared, he is eager to find his "Doppelgänger" again and destroy him, thus cancelling human relations in favor of political differences. Leonilda, on the other hand, feels Sylvester's existence as another part of her own being. Early in the play, she tells her father "Er lebt in mir" (754); later she urges Sylvester to capture his true self in the reflection of her eyes in an effort to erase his false identity (778). Sylvester, who for the most part cannot look beyond the periphery of his personality, constantly compares earlier images of himself or escapes from them. He tells his friend: "Mir selbst entronnen, / Ein and'rer wandelt' ich [...]" (769). The purpose of reading his diary notes again is "Den, der ich bin, an dem zu messen, der / Ich einmal war" (775), a false competition within himself. His own fierce egocentricity, the only thing he is conscious of, culminates in the encounter with the Sekretär. In him Sylvester tends to see his own "Zerrbild" (787). Andreas Ungnad is Schnitzler's most extreme version of subjective ideals. The "confusion of dream and reality borders on the insane," one reads in Liptzin's account.[82] Ungnad has strange notions about himself and the world: "[...] wenn ich sterbe, stirbt / Die Welt mit mir. — Herr Sylvester Thorn / zerfliesst in nichts, wenn ich mich von ihm wende" (786). Just the opposite occurs, however, and Swales describes it in this way: "Significantly, the collapse into total insanity of the Sekretär is parallel to and in part caused by the collapse of Sylvester Thorn."[83]

At the expense of any social relationships, this solipsist cultivated such extreme indulgence of and concern with the self that at the death of his only contact he sank into total oblivion also. Schnitzler's aphorism in *Buch der Sprüche und Bedenken* sums it up best: "Manche flüchten sich in den Wahnsinn wie andere in den Tod: — und beides kann sowohl Mut als Feigheit gewesen sein."[84] Sylvester's death is linked with the water of the pond and can be interpreted as his desire for purification rather than as a lack of courage.[85]

Other polarities in the drama are Anselma and her niece Leonilda. They are opposites in age and in their relationship to Mayenau and to the established order he represents. Anselma's cautious nature conforms to the rules of society. Susanne Polsterer, discussing the symbology of names in her study of women, asks the question: "Sollte es ein blosser Zufall sein, dass die einzige Aristokratin, die virgo intacta bleibt, weil ihr Bruder liebevoll aber streng über ihre Mädchenehre wacht, den Namen Anselma trägt, das bedeutet: 'Gott als Helm,' von einem Gott beschirmt?"[86] She ignores Anselma's own assessment with regard to "brüderliche Strenge" (818). Of her own choice Anselma leads "a useful life," Willa Schmidt points out, "is fulfilled and happy in her own way, and is loving and perceptive where others are concerned."[87] It is her own choice to forgo any intimate relationship (818).

Leonilda, however, is searching to find different ways. She is "an excellent example of Schnitzler's increasingly positive feelings about emancipation of women."[88] Though Leonilda, "the nixie," has given herself to Konrad, the woman Leonilda does not want to enter a permanent relation with him, sanctioned by either Church or State. The intimacy experienced with Konrad does not leave her with feelings of remorse, either; she only answers to her own conscience, which Liptzin considers as "inner fulness" or "conforming to the laws of her personality."[89] Boner, who was the first among critics to see Schnitzler's attitude toward women in realistic perspective, explains the change within Leonilda this way: "[...] sie gewann Konrad [...] die Übertragung des Glaubens an einmalige Idealität in gläubige Bereitschaft jedem Lebendigsein gegenüber. Sie wirft die Fesseln der Konvention von sich, da sie die wertvollere Fessel ihrer eigenen Konzessionslosigkeit fühlt. Sie vermag die Tragik eines Einmaligen durch die Annahme des Vielmaligen aufzuheben."[90] Boner's sensitive observation with regard to Leonilda's sexual behavior represents a sharp contrast to Polsterer's semantic interpretation of Leonilda's name: "Ich würde ihn als Leon + Hilda deuten, die 'Löwenkämpferin.' Die Kaltblütigkeit, Rücksichtslosigkeit und Entschlossenheit mit der die erst 19-jährige Baronesse im 'Gang zum Weiher' um die von Schnitzler's Frauen so hoch gehaltene völlige sexuelle Freiheit kämpft, würde jedenfalls diese Namensdeutung rechtfertigen."[91]

Attributes such as "kaltblütig" and "rücksichtslos" can hardly be proven through textual evidence. Leonilda's role in the drama is that of an emancipated woman who desires the freedom to choose and to decide her own fate, just as Anselma exercised choice to experience her life in harmony with her inner nature. Their physical desires are, of course, on opposite ends of the scale, perhaps as a result of age difference. On mental levels, however, Anselma and Leonilda are complementary characters. They both have highly developed intuitional gifts, and lead strong inner lives which give them self-acceptance and stability. Leonilda's nocturnal dances by the pond may be considered as freedom to express one's inner feelings in line with Wolfdietrich Rasch's findings about the dance, which he considers: "[...] als Mittel der Befreiung und Ausdruck jener geistigen Freiheit, Freiheit der Frau [...] als Ausdruck der übermässigen und nicht aussprechbaren Spannung."[92] The movements of the individual body and soul find expression in the dance and "mit diesem individuellen Ausdruck ist der Tanz zugleich Verbundenheit mit den überpersönlichen, universalen Mächten, mit den — wie man damals sagte — cosmischen (sic) Kräften."[93] Anselma quite accurately sensed Leonilda's spiritual experience and felt it was "kein Menschenantlitz" but "Blick des Gottes" (748). Rasch calls it "die Verbundenheit alles Lebendigen, der grosse Zusammenhang"[94] which made itself known to Leonilda. Seen in this larger context, the dance symbolizes "Lebenstanz" which never ends, but Rasch points out "seine symbolische Darstellung durch den Tanz eines einzelnen Menschen endet, wie das Einzelleben, mit dem Tod."[95]

Comparison with other late dramatic works: Schnitzler used the motif of the dance in addition to other symbols in the previous drama *Komödie der Verführung* as well. Each situation, however, is unique, so that a comparative study is in order. Leonilda carries out the dance in the quiet of the night, as if spirit was dancing through her. The joy which she expresses during the dances, as observed by Anselma from afar, signifies a sense of harmony with herself and the world around. her. This harmony is also with her during the day, when she frequently strolls through the meadows to pick flowers and explore nature.

The dance that ends in death for Aurelie, who is only six years older than Leonilda, was imposed upon her by Falkenir, who gained pleasure in watching her dance first with Max and later with Gysar. It was not a spiritual dance, although it likewise took place near the waters of a pond in the park. It became a fateful dance for Aurelie, for it changed the direction of her life. Her dance movements emphasized her youth and so prompted Falkenir to withdraw his marriage proposal. His action pushed Aurelie into a state of bewilderment. Gysar took advantage of her confused state of mind, from which she never recovered, and eventually she and Falkenir ended their lives by drowning. Leonilda, who is balanced on physical, mental, and spiritual levels, understands the concept of self-authority increasingly as the play unfolds. Aurelie, on the other hand, is motivated by a feeling of insecurity, hiding her true self behind masks. When a critic fails to recognize these subtle psychological differences which Schnitzler so carefully develops in the two dramas, it is easy to draw superficial conclusions such as the one in Körner's evaluation of Aurelie: "[...] sie nimmt sich bloss Freiheiten heraus, sie handelt nicht in einer selbstverständlichen Ungebundenheit, sondern aus Trotz und Widerspruch [...]."[96]

Willa Schmidt has corrected Körner's viewpoint with regard to Leonilda: "He thereby both distorts the character and misses the author's message, i.e. that women share with men not only the need to express their sexuality but also the desire to determine for themselves what course their lives will take regardless of their experience in this realm, rather than being compelled to bow to a hypocritical social code."[97]

The water symbol also pertains to both women. Whereas Leonilda is reticent about the refreshing bathing activity at night which leads her into the dance afterwards, Aurelie speaks freely about her boating on the ocean. To Falkenir, she relates her ability to hear "die ewigen Stürme rauschen" (964-65), just as he first confided the same phenomenon to her (872).

With regard to the contrasts between Mayenau and Sylvester, Schnitzler uses similar configurations in each of his late dramatic works, but his characters seem to grow older with each play he writes. Andrea and Casanova in *Die Schwestern oder Casanova in Spa* are young; the dominant male characters in *Komödie der Verführung* are about forty; in *Der Gang zum Weiher* and *Im Spiel der Sommerlüfte* they are in their fifties. The dialogs between these characters often express Schnitzler's deepest feelings and wisest thoughts. Liptzin compares them with Schnitzler, who is also growing older and observes that "they change form and clime, but they rarely leave him. They point to a dualism in his nature." [98] On the other hand, one must guard against identifying the author too closely with the characters he has created and the opinions they put forward. As Schinnerer points out: "Every creative artist will resolve the complexity of his nature by creating a variety of characters all of whom may be to some extent his spiritual and intellectual offspring."[99]

With regard to the major male characters in both dramas, *Komödie der Verführung* and *Der Gang zum Weiher*, Schnitzler contrasted youth and age. Arduin would like to marry Aurelie but is refused in favor of Falkenir, the older of the two. Konrad, on the other hand, who had no marriage plans at all upon his arrival at the castle of Mayenau, was "married before God" to Leonilda one night by the pond. Both men share a similar childhood experience in that they recall pleasant hours with their playmates at the pond (855, 803). Falkenir in turn did not believe in his "Spätglück"[100] and allowed his doubts to destroy not only a potentially happy marriage but also both their lives through drowning. An antithetical situation exists in *Der Gang zum Weiher*. The aging poet Sylvester Thorn reaches confidently for a "Spätglück," but is not able to capture it and so ends his life by drowning likewise.

In both dramas, therefore, water and death by drowning play a significant role. For Aurelie and Falkenir it is a joyful moment as they swiftly sink beneath the surface of the sea, "as if they were kissing," and smiling "blissfully" (973). For Sylvester it is "ein Gang zum Weiher" in utter loneliness and disappointment just in time to save his dignity, as the Freiherr puts it (840). Sylvester's name is significant. Sylvester is the patron saint for the last day of the year — in the drama Sylvester lives the last day of his life. In both of these works water transcends its natural qualities in that "Nicht Ding noch Mensch bringt je die Welle wieder" (841), predicts Leonilda, whereas Gilda knows with certainty "noch in dieser Nacht wird die See beide an den Strand bringen" (973). However, the Direktor had commented earlier that only "die irdischen Ursprungs sind, die werden von den Wellen ans Ufer gespült" (934), and indeed, when Gilda's mother drowned, the sea did not return "ihre sterbliche Hülle" (934). Gilda like her mother spends much time in the water, earning the description "Nixe," an epithet she shares with Leonilda as well.

The significance of the pond has already been discussed in this chapter, but it is also a central motif in *Komödie der Verführung*. In both dramas, emphasis is placed on the fact that no other paths lead to the pond (749, 808, 853), which would indicate that only certain characters are attracted to the pool. Indeed, these waters effect changes of inner direction not only within the lives of Leonilda, Konrad, and Sylvester, but also within Falkenir and, most ominously, within Aurelie. She lost her mother's necklace near the pond, where Max found it and returned it. If she were superstitious, Falkenir suggests, she would not wear it again, or she would throw it into the pond (873). At this point in the play, Aurelie is still in control of herself and her life, and does not follow this joking advice, but at the end of Act I she "löst ihren Schmuck, wirft ihn in den Teich" (889), thereby symbolically giving away authority over her life, self-identity, personal freedom, and power of choice.

A certain magic surrounds the ponds in both dramas. Leonilda asks Konrad: "Weisst du nur, ob ich mich selbst dir gab" (809). A similar question arises within Max, but he feels that Aurelie gave him "unendlich viel — nur nicht (sich) selbst" (897). Judith reminds Max of her individuality in a way similar to Leonilda's with Konrad (865). In each situation the woman character seems to view her experience remotely, removed from reality into a world of dreams.

Related to the pond is the park, present in both dramas, and the significance of the tree symbol. "Alleen" are frequently mentioned in *Der Gang zum Weiher*.[101] Sylvester was most creative when strolling with Leonilda down the "Alleen" to tell her fairytales. Leonilda's creativity inspired her dances under the trees by the pond. Mayenau and his sister Anselma seek shelter under the trees so as to remain unseen by Leonilda as she starts her "Gang zum Weiher" (796). In *Komödie der Verführung* all important aspects of the plot take place in the park under the trees (Act I).

The obvious symbolism about the tree is that it is capable of developing from a small seedling into a large, upright, calm, stable, sturdy plant with its roots firmly anchored in the ground. In that respect the symbolism relates to man and his ideal relationship to life. When man has strong roots, firm values, he is able to withstand the storms of life by drawing upon inner resources. Mayenau and his sister Anselma are examples. As father, he has been able to impart this secure feeling to his child Leonilda. Aurelie, on the other hand, experienced insecurity on account of an unstable household because of unfaithful parents. She conducts her own life without firm values. The adventurous characters such as Sylvester, Arduin, Gysar, Santis, and Casanova fall short of the qualities attributed to the tree as well. "The tree is one of the most essential of traditional symbols," points out Cirlot. "In its most general sense, the symbolism of the tree denotes the life of the cosmos: its consistence, growth, proliferation, generative and regenerative processes. It stands for inexhaustible life, and is therefore equivalent to a symbol of immortality."[102]

Schnitzler rarely elaborated on the question of immortality beyond his term "Aufhebung des Individuums ins All" for reasons he conveyed to Körner in his letter of July 11, 1927.[103] But as a psychologist he is interested in what Rey formulates as "Undurchdringlichkeit der Zusammenhänge" and "Ganzheit des Lebens."[104] It is the author's "Staunen vor dem einfachen Sein" which Rey considers a significant trait of Schnitzler's "religiosity."¹⁰⁵ "Wenn er es als Agnostiker auch ablehnt, den Schöpfer näher zu definieren," Rey continues, "der Ehrfurcht vor der Schöpfung kann er sich doch nicht entziehen."¹⁰⁶

Along similar lines, the symbol of lilac branches is used in both plays in an intriguing way, which rules out any argument suggestive of coincidence. From the many spring flowers Schnitzler selects lilac, a flower which prevails in many love songs as a symbol of spring and love, just as its scent permeates a garden. In *Komödie der Verführung* it is Max who shares his branches with the women who invite him later for closer relationships.¹⁰⁷ Twice Aurelie mentions "den Duft des Flieders" (890, 964), which influences her senses and allows her to glide willingly into the arms of a lover. The lilac branches in *Der Gang zum Weiher* serve to decorate the guestroom for Sylvester. Although the maids handle this task, they are directed by Leonilda who also watches carefully to make sure they are fresh each day (741-44). Because Leonilda worships the ideal poet in Sylvester and later rejects any closer relationship with him beyond friendship, it would be farfetched to assume sexual overtones similar to those of *Komödie der Verführung*.¹⁰⁸ The wilted lilac branches in *Der Gang zum Weiher* have symbolic importance in this respect. Sylvester's spring of life has long passed and his efforts to win Leonilda's love are likewise in vain, as predicted at the beginning of the drama symbolically through the wilted lilac in his room.

Not only symbols but also trends of thought provide a foundation for comparison in Schnitzler's late dramatic works. Just as the symbols imply deeper levels of meaning, trends of thought are re-examined for the purpose of deeper understanding and awareness. Ideas which in *Komödie der Verführung* were presented in triangular arrangement are considered as polarities in *Der Gang zum Weiher*. Foremost in Schnitzler's mind rank the ideas of war and peace because he wrote both dramas under the influence either of war or of its devastating consequences for Germany and Austria. In *Der Gang zum Weiher* this idea comprises one-third of the drama. The chancellor has played a great part in the history of his country and is shown now in his peacekeeping efforts, combining his capacity both as a diplomat and as a wise friend to the younger generation, represented by Konrad, who can see only the excitement of war. *Komödie der Verführung* emphasizes the powers at work in an effort of profitmaking by plunging the country into war; the drama also pointed out the irresponsibility in diplomatic and banking circles as represented by Arduin and Westerhaus. The ideas in *Der Gang zum Weiher,* however, move beyond the war issue to register also the abuse of the word "Vaterland," which Schnitzler had so often noticed in German and Austrian power politics. Alfred Apsler points out that the author "differentiates between Vaterland and Heimat" and explains that " 'Heimat' is the noble conception of home, 'Vaterland' the catchword of the politicians."¹⁰⁹

Schnitzler expresses this viewpoint through Mayenau, the wise statesman. Davis, on the other hand, emphasizes a moral adversity within Mayenau: "Once he has left his retirement, however, and moves in the field of power and action [...] the land becomes his fatherland, when he can use it to express his demand for power [...] . Albrecht sees only a field for action whether in war or peace."¹¹⁰ All indications in the drama, nevertheless, point out that Schnitzler's idea of pacifism was not intended to be merely an intellectual exercise.

The idea of "Heimat" is also picked up again in the context of love relationships, as a temporary place of peace and immunity to which a loved one can return after physical and emotional detours. In *Die Schwestern oder Casanova in Spa* it was Casanova who introduced this idea and considers that place as "Rast am Weg" (733), since in his frame of reference a more permanent place would pose a threat to his concept of freedom. In *Komödie der Verführung,* Falkenir has the desire to provide a temporary "Heimstatt" for Aurelie, "deren Frieden niemand stören darf" (952). In *Der Gang zum Weiher* the term

"Heimat" recurs most frequently.[111] The emotionally most intense expression comes from Sylvester, who would be so happy to watch over Leonilda's sleep even if it was only for one night (827).

Schnitzler judges progressively more severely the behavior of his "Abenteurer," for the deeper problem is the question of commitment and responsibility. These adventurers try to preserve a state of isolation because they shy away from either inner or outer relations with other human beings, in an effort to maintain unlimited freedom. They limit their emotional involvement to short periods of time and never attempt continuity and lasting relationships. Marriage looks to them like all other ties to family and country, that is, an encroachment on their personal freedom. In no way are they prepared to commit themselves to another being because they do not want to shoulder responsibility or any sharing-caring attitude. This desire for noncommitment is apparent not only in relationships with other human beings, but in other areas as well. It certainly is not by chance that these adventurers mostly belong to independent professions, for they would reject any activity that tied them down to regular working hours and a permanent seat of residence.

Müller-Freienfels concludes: "Gerade zu den Beziehungen zu ihren Mitmenschen zeigt sich immer wieder, dass sie nicht nur die äusseren, sondern ebenso sehr auch die inneren Bindungen fürchten. Sie scheuen im Grunde jedes echte, tiefgehende Gefühl für einen anderen Menschen, da sie auf diese Weise innerlich an ihn gebunden werden würden."[112] He poses the question whether or not these people really stand with both feet in the stream of life, and suggests: "Im Gegenteil, ein solcher Mensch, der niemals etwas von seiner inneren oder äusseren Freiheit einbüssen möchte, distanziert sich im Grunde vom Leben, will sich in einem Abstand halten. Dieser Gedanke der Distanz vom Leben und von den Menschen ist bei den meisten von Schnitzler's Personen auch der tiefste Sinn ihres gesamten Strebens nach Bindungslosigkeit."[113] Bernhard Blume, who discusses the problem of distance also, feels that these characters stay away from the "Strudel des Daseins [...] der ihnen unausweichlich mit Vernichtung droht."[114] He attributes this behavior to the life style "des Lebensschwachen, der in der Flucht sein Heil sucht."[115] Casanova is able to avoid serious consequences,[116] but Falkenir and Sylvester pay with their lives. As will be seen in the last drama, entitled *Im Spiel der Sommerlüfte,* a summer rain clears the air and returns everybody to their senses before it is too late.

The idea of "Gespenster" and "Geister" from the past invading the present moment form a close connection. The common denominator would be "die Macht der Erinnerung." In the last act of *Komödie der Verführung* Aurelie fearfully raises this question, but Falkenir believes they are both strong enough to avoid recalling the past for the sake of a harmonious marriage. But he himself is not able to do it, even moments after Aurelie has left him to change into a bridal dress (966-67). In *Der Gang zum Weiher* Schnitzler deals with these problems more in detail. Mayenau does not believe in "Geister der Vergangenheit" (762), yet tells Konrad about "böse Geister" which reign at night near the pond (804). But he is firmly convinced that "Erinnerungen" continue to glow (774), a fact he demonstrates most vividly by dictating his memoirs. Sylvester, on the other hand, discredits "Erinnerungen" (774), but "die Geister der Jugend" are so vivid in him that he needs to destroy them by fire in the hope that they may never return. Even Leonilda, who triumphed over Sylvester's "Geister" (781), wants in the end to flee her surroundings because they are "dreifach gespenstisch" (841) and quite real to her.

The question might be asked: Why was Schnitzler the rational scientist interested in these ideas? Ideas can be reduced to thought forms meandering mostly uncontrolled through the mind. As such they would fall into the same category of intuition and vision for which Schnitzler himself has the following definition: "Gewiss handelt es sich auch hier um nichts anderes als um eine nicht mehr zu kontrollierende Geschwindigkeit des Gedankenablaufs. Scheinbare Gleichzeitigkeiten von Eindrücken, die durch grosse Geschwindigkeit vorgetäuscht wird." [117]

To have a vision means to form a mental picture, "ein Bild." This idea of "Bild" occurs first in *Die Schwestern oder Casanova in Spa*, but it seems to become more important with Schnitzler as time went on. In this play the idea of "Bild" is central to the dispute between Anina and Andrea over the night she spent with Casanova, who had intended to be with Flaminia. Anina maintains that Casanova still takes along eternally "die Erinnerung dieser Stunde" (694), but Andrea insists "doch nicht dein Bild" (694), thus providing a basis to forgive and forget, because the whole affair can remain a secret between the two of them. "Erinnerung," therefore, is not identical to "Bild," although both are mental processes, because even Anina's picture would have to be a mental vision. In *Komödie der Verführung* the idea of "Bild" relates to Aurelie. The picture which Gysar painted of her and which she rejected at first for not representing her true nature, becomes more real to her as the play unfolds. In her outer life she lives up to the sensuality which Gysar's picture portrayed, until she finally transforms her entire being into the picture, thereby losing her inner balance completely. She reduces herself to "Maske und Lüge" (962) and suffers the consequences of this total rejection. The "Bild" is symbolic of replacing her self-image with a mask to hide behind. In her "Erinnerung," the devastating garden party at Gysar's house has grown into a mental monster, dangerously impairing her sanity. In this drama "Erinnerung" and "Bild" have become one and the same in a negative way.

The concept of "Bild" in *Der Gang zum Weiher* is related to Leonilda's idealistic vision of Sylvester. She tells him that in her mind's eye "dein ewig Bild hab' ich in mir bewahrt" (788). Looking beyond the personality, she beholds Sylvester's poetic soul which is forever perfect and pure. When he later pleads with her to marry him, she speaks about "dein edles Bild" (827), which refers to the neveraging spirit self of Sylvester. On the physical level, she knows that more than thirty or forty years of age difference are not a realistic basis on which to build a lasting marriage. At the end of the drama she speaks about Sylvester and visualizes how "wesenlos zu nichts sein Bild verzittert" (841) — perhaps as indication of Leonilda's concept of death. At that point all earthly riddles are resolved.

Connected with Sylvester is the idea of "Märchen" in this drama. Leonilda remembers the fairytales he told her in her childhood days, but he denies "Nein — Märchen waren meine Sache nie" (777). In Act V Sylvester renounces the idea of immortality as a fairytale and equates "Märchen" with "Lüge." In *Komödie der Verführung* the concept of "Märchen" received much more extensive attention. Since it was used there within the context of triangularity, one might conclude that Schnitzler redefined the idea of "Märchen" and narrowed it down again to its original meaning of telling stories, as Sylvester did before his exile.

In contrast to *Komödie der Verführung*, where the triangularities connected certain ideas with various characters, *Der Gang zum Weiher* emphasizes the characters in their triangular position. Mayenau stands between the emperor and Konrad, who is motivated by his father, over the issue of war and peace. Leonilda forms a triangle with Konrad and Sylvester with regard to the expression of love and marriage. Sylvester stands between Anselma and Leonilda in his effort to create a deeper relationship: the one with Anselma failed years ago; the one with Leonilda never gets started. Mayenau has a triangular relationship with Anselma and Leonilda in an effort to correct his mistake of overprotection.

The contrasts, however, seem to have been more important to Schnitzler, since he mentions them especially in his letter to Körner: "[...] das Verhältnis des Dichters zum Krieger, des Kriegers zum Politiker, der Leonilda einerseits zum Dichter, andererseits zum Soldaten, war mir von Anbeginn an das Wesentliche."[118] Many polarities are sharply delineated in the lines of various characters (759, 762). Especially significant is the contrast relating to the political part of the drama, i.e., the friendship between Konrad and the enemy soldier, and Mayenau and the emperor (763, 783), as well as the concept of "Aufruhr und Gehorsam" (765), "Treue und Verrat" (827), "Geisel und Gast" (830). Through Mayenau, Schnitzler emphasizes again his concept that opposition can be links of the same chain as "Wild und Jäger," "Herz und Pfeil," "Mörder und Opfer" (801), just as on ethical grounds "Schuld" is related to "Sühne," and "Verdienst" to "Tat" (801).

In summary, the results of the preceding analysis of the drama, *Der Gang zum Weiher*, add another view to Schnitzler's already established reputation as a writer concerned with complex issues. Imboden's conclusion regarding the prose works can also be extended to Schnitzler's late dramatic works: "Das scheinbar Immer-Gleiche der von ihm beschriebenen Welt hat weit auseinanderliegende Pole. Nicht wenigen seiner Gestalten gleitet plötzlich der feste Boden der Realität unter den Füssen fort; viele werden in die pfadlosen Bezirke des Geheimnisvollen hineingestossen. Von wem? Weshalb? Fragen, die in Hinsicht einer heilen Welt berechtigt wären, doch, auf doppeldeutige und unkontrollierbare Weiten bezogen, vergeblich gestellt werden."[119]

Considerable skill is required to treat in literary prose the complexity of this world, which extends, in Imboden's words, to far-reaching poles, often reaching beyond the area of scientifically acknowledged information, "that area of reality and truth which is not accessible to the cerebral capacities of man," as LoCicero formulated it.[120] The task seems even more complicated when the information needs to be compressed into drama form. But Schnitzler achieved it convincingly, proving that he is a better dramatist than critics have been willing to acknowledge. Imboden sees two factors as being responsible for Schnitzler's newly increasing interest in surrealism: "Nach dem Kriege verliert Schnitzler den Kontakt mit der Umwelt; sie versteht ihn und er sie nicht mehr. Ferner entfremdet ihn auch der fortschreitende Verlust des Gehörs den Menschen und dem Alltagsgeschehen."[121] While these points cannot be disputed, one should not forget that Schnitzler to the end of his life was interested in the events of the world around him. In *Der Gang zum Weiher*, he presents the rebellious activities of the young generation as an opposite to the peace-loving loyalty of the old statesman which, according to Rey, "demonstrieren Schnitzlers Bemühungen, sich für die Auseinandersetzung zwischen politischen Ideen offen zu halten."[122]

The idea of freedom formed an important aspect, for without freedom there cannot be individuality. But Schnitzler conveyed clearly his message that freedom in itself is no absolute value. It is connected to the question of responsibility and commitment, and the willingness of human nature to accept these premises. If the concept of freedom is misunderstood, it leads to selfishness and thus in the end to utter loneliness.[123]

Schnitzler's main concern in the drama, *Der Gang zum Weiher*, centered on the area of the I-Thou relationship, the all-important basis for the concept of the total human being. It is true, as Foltin points out, that the total human being is "not just the well defined, rational 'ego,' but also the rebellious, not conscious, subconscious, unconscious, irrational 'id'."[124] But this human being, as total in itself as it may be, only leads a balanced, fulfilled life in its relationship to others through sharing of love on different levels as the highest form of living; for living means giving in its various ways — to be of service to others. This purpose in life, this high call, is hard to achieve, but being on the road to this goal is better than not trying at all. Schnitzler's characters in *Der Gang zum Weiher* show the degrees of effort in this respect. Liptzin describes this struggle most appropriately in the following way:

> During our all too few years on earth, however, we make frantic efforts to escape from our absolute solitude. In work we find a drug that helps us to forget, but it is only during the intoxication of love that we are enabled really to break through the bars that separate individual existence. Schnitzler's men — cool, rational, ironic — may, at best, resign themselves to work and forgetfulness. His women, on the other hand, do, at times bridge the gulf between soul and soul; and in ecstatic abandon they do attain perfect communion with the All. His women are, on the whole, more courageous than his men. The latter hesitate, deliberate, weigh all possible risks, and seek to postpone their decisions. If forced to act, they try to minimize their responsibility and to avoid every possible consequence of their act. The women, on the contrary, answer the call of life heroically, brave all dangers readily, and lose themselves successfully in others. They, thus more easily, experience true love [...]. Western civilization for a long time emphasized male superiority, and thereby made man ever more self-centered and egoistic. While woman has retained her capacity to respond naturally, naively, instinctively, man has been handicapped by an overabundance of rationalization. Schnitzler's women want love, Schnitzler's men offer understanding.[125]

Schnitzler's interest in this complex area of the I-Thou-relationship continues in his last drama *Im Spiel der Sommerlüfte*. It is relatively unknown and appears to be merely concerned with the moods of its characters and their feelings about themselves and those with whom they interact. In the end, no drastic changes take place, no deaths occur, but great gains have been made in human understanding which was, after all, Schnitzler's own search in life. In his last drama, he turns further inward where life is truly lived.

CHAPTER IV

IM SPIEL DER SOMMERLÜFTE

Background of the play and statement of purpose

The first performance of Schnitzler's play *Im Spiel der Sommerlüfte* took place on December 21, 1929, at the Deutsches Volkstheater in Vienna.[1] First publication was in 1930 by S. Fischer Verlag, Berlin.[2] According to Schnitzler's diary notes, he completed this three-act drama between February and April of 1928.[3] His first ideas, however, date back to 1898, when he recorded: "Ein Stück 'Sommernacht' wird lebendig [. . .]. Im Kaffeehaus entwarf ich den Plan eines dreiaktigen Stückes 'Sommernachtstraum'."[4] More sketches and notes were added between 1911-1913; five years later a new sketch was written under the present title, *Im Spiel der Sommerlüfte*. The term "Spiel" points to the fluctuating atmospheric conditions of summer, which, as analysis will demonstrate, affect significantly not only the various moods of the characters in the play, but also turn some of these characters further inward where life is truly lived.

Hartmut Scheible measures the success of this drama merely in terms of respect paid to the author and calls it an "Achtungserfolg."[5] It is a play, he states without further elaboration, "[. . .] das alte Motive aufgreift, sie aber in einer Schwebe lässt, die sonst nur von Chekhov erreicht wurde [. . .]."[6] The present study reveals some of the reasons Schnitzler may have had for leaving these motifs in limbo. The conflicts between generations in the play remain without consequences and catastrophes, it is true. The fact that everything ends well in it, even secondary plot lines, can only be attributed to the protagonists' regaining reason and recovering their internal balance, which had been disturbed by a troublesome confusion of the senses or of the imagination, just as after a brief violent thunderstorm the sun begins to shine again. In this respect, Scheible's comparison of Schnitzler to Chekhov discloses a number of similarities. A detailed comparison with Chekhov's plays, however, exceeds the scope of this work.[7]

The analysis discusses essential problems of modern individuals who find themselves living in a complex society. It shows how this society threatens their feelings of human worth and self-respect and why they are pushed, at times, into passive patterns of living. The symbolism of the weather is examined, along with its relationship to emotional patterns such as jealousy, doubt, guilt, despair. The antinomies of life as expressed in the thoughts, emotions, and concerns of the characters are discussed as they are exposed in youth and age, in art and love, in love and hate, "Pflicht und Neigung."[8] The chapter closes with a study of comparative points as they can be found in the other late dramatic works (*Die Schwestern oder Casanova in Spa, Komödie der Verführung, Der Gang zum Weiher*), thus providing for detailed analysis of most aspects of the play. Each character is analyzed and also viewed in polar relationship to other persons in the play as well as comparative characters in works previously discussed.

Outline of the play

Vincenz Friedlein, a prominent sculptor in Vienna, his wife and former model Josefa, and their seventeen-year-old son Eduard occupy a summer house in Kirchau, a village in southern Austria, not far from Vienna, where the action takes place around 1900. In the morning, Vincenz generally leaves for the city to conduct his business. He returns late in the evenings and sometimes not until the next day. Thus, he gives the audience the impression of being liberal in his morals and unconventional in his manners. His appearance is that of a successful artist; he is cheerful and positive about his talent. The marriage is merely an arrangement of convenience. He enjoys all the pleasant features without giving of himself in return. He takes Josefa's loving devotion to husband and child for granted without realizing that she might feel neglected in her desires as a woman of only thirty-six years of age. They have invited their niece, Gusti Pflegner, to their country home to help her regain health and strength before taking up her first engagement as an actress in Innsbruck. Only eighteen years of age, Gusti is aware of her attractiveness and uses this gift flirtatiously. Vincenz looks at her with the eyes of a sculptor, always in search of new models; young Eduard becomes her ardent admirer while assisting her in the study of *Romeo and Juliet*. Dr. Faber, a Viennese physician, considers himself virtually engaged to her. Lieutenant Robert Holl, the twin brother of the village chaplain, Ferdinand Holl, is attracted to her acting and hopes to resume acquaintance in Innsbruck, where he is to be stationed. He has left a deep impression upon her and with that confession to herself, "Der hat mir aber besonders gut gefallen" (994), the first act closes.

Act II unfolds the life of each of these characters as it is lived on deeper levels, where hidden desires and longings are exposed and waiting for expression. Vincenz uses the arrival of the "Exzellenz" from the Kassel theater as an excuse to spend the night in Vienna. Josefa hears about it by telegram, when she is on her way to the railway station to pick up her husband and walk home with him. Eduard is disappointed about the afternoon because the botanic excursion with the Kaplan has been cancelled on account of the sudden visit of the latter's twin brother. He now seeks to interest Gusti to follow him on a hike to Fallenböckhütte, a place in the mountains, where he will be waiting for her. Gusti will hike with Eduard, but first she has to finish a letter to her friend, Dr. Felix Faber. This letter contains a sensitive message: she decided not to bind herself to him at this point. Her career and the prospect of meeting other men are more attractive and important to her. After mailing the letter, she follows Eduard into the mountains to avoid disappointing him. Throughout the play Eduard has been forcing himself upon Gusti on every occasion, and her presence under the same roof keeps him inflamed. The unstable weather which is mentioned throughout the drama affects the balance of nearly all the characters. Finally, the rain begins to fall, trapping these young people in a mountain cabin. The closeness intensifies their emotions "and, without making any serious effort at resistance, they yield to the temptation of the moment. Gusti is delighted by the freshness and naturalness of the boy in contrast to the premature seriousness of [. . .] the physician. For Eduard she signifies the first experience of manhood."[8]

The relation between the Kaplan and Josefa develops within the last part of Act II. It is characterized by restraint on physical levels. Of course, they are more mature than their younger counterparts, but on the other hand, they have allowed greater frustration and even resignation to build up within themselves. The sultriness of the evening moves them to be more at ease in disclosing their innermost feelings.

The Kaplan, who is linked by friendship to Eduard in their common interest in botany, but also in the young man's need for tutorial help, has always performed his priestly duties with exactness and devotion. However, various references in the play indicate that he had been promised a different destiny, for he is a man cultivated in all subjects and full of the most varied intellectual curiosities. He might have become, for instance, an officer like his twin brother, if his mother had not decided to send Ferdinand to the seminary from his fourteenth year. His officer brother is now bound to him by profound affection mixed with gratitude. The priest soon confides to Josefa that his brother, who has just paid him a visit, left behind a letter in which he announces his intention of fighting a duel. The text ends in these words: "Und Deiner Liebe werde ich es zu danken haben, Deiner Fürbitte, wenn ich frei von Sünden vor den höchsten Richter trete. Und so wage ich in unerschütterlichem Gottvertrauen, diesen Brief mit dem Wort zu enden: Auf Wiedersehen! Dein Robert" (1010).

This event and Josefa's words of comfort give rise between them to a free conversation that soon takes on the aspect of a confession in which each person admits doubt. Their discussion of faith brings both of them to the brink of a great temptation. A juxtaposition develops in which Josefa helps him to recognize challenges of everyday life, and the Kaplan leads her into higher, previously unsuspected regions where she can see in new perspective her role of wife and mother. This enables them to resist the temptation, and their reward is not long delayed.

In Act III, Robert Hall, the lieutenant, retires unharmed from the duel, only lightly wounding his adversary; the Kaplan finds his balance again and continues reading of the mass. Josefa regains the love of her husband; Eduard tries to forget in botany his first disappointment in love. Gusti decides to leave the next morning in preparation for her acting career. Felix, whom she left in uncertainty about her contract in Innsbruck and who heard about it through the newspaper, does not want to accept the end of their relationship. But Gusti reminds him: "Wir gehen ja beide nicht aus der Welt. Wir werden uns ja wiedersehen. Wir wollen ja Freunde sein, Freunde bleiben — Freunde werden" (1024-25). Disappointed, Felix resumes his hospital practice. Josefa continues her devotion to her husband who in turn may give more of himself than before. The action closes in the light of a beautiful summer morning, just as the characters emerge untroubled by last night's storm.

Review of criticism

In general one can observe that *Im Spiel der Sommerlüfte* has not received such extensive reviews and criticism as the other three late dramatic works. In February 1930, Robert Arnold reviewed the play with his usual negative attitude toward Schnitzler and his dramas. In the end, however, he concedes that the play in its Christian and worldly resignation is an appreciated complement to the erotic "Reigen."[9] A year later the play was performed in Giessen. It received the attention of Hans Thyriot, who finds it impossible to give a plot summary of the play, "das weniger ein Drama als eine dialogisierte Novelle ist und völlig von Umrissen, Andeutungen und verschwebenden Stimmungen lebt."[10] As a possible motto, he suggests the *Paracelsus* verses: "Es fliessen ineinander Traum und Wachen [. . .]," the favorite stand-by quote of many critics.[11]

In Scheible's view the respect paid to the author saved the play from being rejected. It has nothing new to offer so far as motifs are concerned; they have already surfaced in previous dramas. The only difference, according to Scheible, can be seen in the happy ending.[12] Nevertheless, this difference constitutes a significant change which must be recognized. It prompted Schnitzler in a similar situation to write the following lines in a letter to Rilke: "Aber Sie wissen ja; ich bin in das Kastl mit der Aufschrift 'Liebelei' hineingethan (sic); die Kritiker haben das nicht gern, wenn die Taferln gewechselt werden."[13]

In the view of Mme Derré, the author in this play "semble avoir voulu pour une fois encourager la maîtrise de soi et donner une leçon d'optimisme."[14] But she admits: "Si tout y finit bien, et même les intrigues secondaires, c'est moins [...] grâce a l'intervention de données suprarationelles que parce que les protagonistes redeviennent raisonnables, retrouvent leur équilibre interne un temps rompu, par un trouble emballement des sens ou de l'imagination [...]."[15] "Still," she maintains, "Schnitzler has made a pretense of this somewhat slender plot, for at the end of it nothing has happened to compound the serious debate" (between the priest and Josefa) [...].[16] She considers it false to see in the play anything other than a psychological study or to seek in it a profession of faith."[17] Although Schnitzler parted early with his profession as a physician, he maintained nevertheless throughout his life a certain interest in the progress achieved in the field of depth psychology and dream interpretation. Schnitzler's diaries reveal numerous entries in this regard.[18] It is this depth psychology which in Schnitzler's late dramatic works receives ever-increasing attention, thus reducing its content to a "slender plot," as Mme Derré has chosen to call it.

Körner, who is concerned with Schnitzler's "Spätwerk" in a lenghty article, does not even mention this play.[19] A. E. Zucker in his review of the drama states that it "deserves full recognition" and places it above *Die Schwestern* and *Komödie der Verführung*,[20] but he does not substantiate his argument. To Martin Swales, on the other hand, the drama is "a deeply flawed work," because "moral thinking is not intrinsically conducive to great literature."[21] Referring to the "threatening storm" which "passes and leaves the secure, simple order cleansed and refreshed," he considers the play "reminiscent of Stifter" in its thematic and structural progression.[22]

In Offermanns' view, *Komödie der Verführung* represents "das letzte bedeutende Stück, das Schnitzler vollendete — und das sicherlich beziehungsreichste."[23] He completely ignores even the existence of *Der Gang zum Weiher*, a significant play, which likewise combines Eros and war, a major point of discussion in Offermanns' study. The play *Im Spiel der Sommerlüfte* turns his audience to the inner realms of the soul, where life is really experienced. With this new focus on the total human being, it is a logical consequence that exterior events are less well illuminated.

In his study entitled "Das Lebensgefühl in Arthur Schnitzlers Dramen," Müller-Freienfels admits, "Schnitzler will nicht in einem völligen Nihilismus enden und den Menschen jede Hoffnung und Zuversicht nehmen."[24] He seems to lean too much on Blume's evaluation of Schnitzler's *Weltbild*, which the latter placed on the level of pessimism and nihilism. Körner's viewpoint serves as another guideline closely followed by Müller-Freienfels. An example is the following conclusion about the play: "Man darf jedoch nicht übersehen, dass dieses letzte Stück des Dichters Märchencharakter besitzt und dass der gute Ausgang nicht dem eigentlichen Lebensgefühl seines Schöpfers entspricht. Im Grunde bleibt Schnitzler bis zu seinem Lebensende der Skeptiker und Zweifler, der er immer war."[25] Without referring to textual evidence, it is difficult for the reader to follow Müller-Freienfels' argument in pinpointing the "Märchencharakter," particularly in this rather realistic life situation. Furthermore, who is to say with certainty that this last play was written in an effort to represent the actual "Lebensgefühl seines Schöpfers?"

Sol Liptzin separates the author from his characters. He deals with this drama in his chapter entitled "Dream and Reality" and observes that Schnitzler has two ways to return his characters from dangerous experiences: "[...] they may either awaken, as from a dream, and return to their accustomed ways, or they may be transformed in body and soul. After employing the latter ending in many serious works, Schnitzler chooses the former alternative for his drama 'Im Spiel der Sommerlüfte'."[26] During his summary of the play, Liptzin also analyzes each character in his particular predicament. However, not all characters appear to be in a dream. Josefa, for example, truly is engaged in soul searching which lifted her to a higher level of consciousness.

"Das Abenteuer," writes Reinhard Urbach, "[...] gewinnt im Spätwerk eine therapeutische Funktion [...] oder löst sich in eine fast schon selbstverständliche Form augenblicklichen Lebens und momentaner Gemeinsamkeit auf, jenseits von Vorurteilen und Problemen der stickigen Luft der Jahrhundertwende."[27] The relationship between Felix and Gusti would be an example of such "momentaner Gemeinsamkeit." While no details are given in the play as to the nature of Vincenz's overnight stays in Vienna, Josefa seems to feel intuitively when an extramarital adventure is involved. The therapeutic effect Urbach speaks about can be seen in the end of the play. Vincenz renews his interest in the marriage. He shows again greater affection toward his wife. Long-promised travels are discussed more seriously. He also wants to take her along to participate in the festivities on the occasion of his latest work of art which he completed recently. Urbach further points out: "Das unbedenkliche — und früher als leichtsinnig oder zerstörerisch und schuldhaft Empfundene — gewinnt die Dimension des Harmlosen und Verantwortungsfreien."[28] With regard to Schnitzler's last work, Urbach concludes: "Diese Einstellung stiftet noch Verwirrung, aber nicht mehr Zerstörung [...]."[29]

Mme Derré seems to think that Schnitzler gave one of the principal roles to the priest, not as a "profession of faith" but rather to demonstrate the ease with which the author is able to manage the religious values in a central dialog.[30] Her interpretation is certainly valid, provided that one recognizes this aspect as part of Schnitzler's larger frame of reference: his never ending quest for truth. In his aphorisms he wrote down many statements pertaining to religion, all of which seem to underline his conviction against any kind of dogmatism.[31]

Willa Schmidt, on the other hand, finds that Josefa and Gusti have the most important roles. "It is in the portrayal of these characters that is found one of the most noteworthy elements of the play, since the difference between the past and the new era in the making, so typical of Schnitzler's later works, is emphasized in *Im Spiel der Sommerlüfte* mainly by means of the two women."[32]

This brief review of criticism demonstrates the variety and discrepancy of views, a situation which usually occurs when only certain aspects of the play are discussed to the exclusion of other important parts. Let us now turn to an attempt at a comprehensive analysis, viewing the play as a totality.

Analysis of the drama

The title in view of Goethe's Faust: "Sind wir ein Spiel von jedem Druck der Luft?" — This verse from Goethe's *Faust*[33] was used by Schnitzler as motto for his last drama. It was a popular question to ask at that time of world-wide disarray, for it had application to all aspects of human existence.[34]

The scene in *Faust* in which this verse occurs is entitled "Abend" and shows Margarete's small but immaculately neat room which Faust soon enters. The function of this scene is to make vivid the basic antagonism between Margarete's simple purity of heart and the baseness of the threat to her peace. Neither Faust's heedless passion nor Mephistopheles' lewd sensuality is compatible with the cleanliness of this room and its occupant. The atmosphere of the room, therefore, translates into simplicity, serenity, and contentment which has its effect upon Faust. He recognizes the despicable nature of the intention which brought him there. His passion is, for the moment, sublimated in a romantic analysis of the objects around him, until he realizes the incongruity of his present endeavor with his former standard of conduct. Although his biological urge is strong, some change has come over him. The forthright impulse to animal indulgence has changed, with the disillusion of his emotions, into a dream of love.[35] Thus, his unrestrained nature that might have erupted like a storm and destroyed everything with its intensity is momentarily arrested, and a new, deeper aspect of Faust emerges in his quest for truth. But under the influence of Mephistopheles, events take their turn, and when Faust in the end returns to his nobler self, it is too late to alleviate the suffering which he has caused to Gretchen. Although Faust is dazed in the last scene of the drama, Gretchen's voice still reaches him; it is the voice of love which will not pass away from his memory.

The detail recalled from Goethe's *Faust* serves as an important point of reference to understand Schnitzler's interpretation of the verse "Sind wir ein Spiel von jedem Druck der Luft? " in his play. The atmospheric pressure Faust experienced in Gretchen's room influences his moods and emotions. In Schnitzler's play the self appears not dependent on moods but on weather conditions; thus, the rain after a sultry evening clears the air and returns every character to reason. The evening scene in *Faust,* on the other hand, is characterized by more "Streben," however inconsistent as this striving may be in Faust's yet confused understanding of his services to God.[36] It is not on the strength of "good deeds" but of his human striving that Faust is granted ultimate salvation. The real world of Faust's actions and meditations, of his physical experiences and spiritual endeavors, is surrounded by another and "higher" reality.[37] In Schnitzler's *Im Spiel der Sommerlüfte,* on the other hand, earthly lives are not interrupted from the realm of the transcendental. Urbach observes correctly that Schnitzler's style of the late period places emphasis upon "little causes and large effects which remain, however, without great consequences. And the causes disappear and are charged to the account of summertime."[38]

The games initiated in *Faust,* therefore, represent man's "journey" through life, as he is torn by two forces: the dictates of his nature and the demands of his reason, a duality which can be observed in Schnitzler's characters as well without the experience of their entire earth journey. In contrast to the game played by Faust, which had disastrous consequences for Margarete, her mother and brother, the games in Schnitzler's *Im Spiel der Sommerlüfte* have a happy ending. Some characters are more or less drawn into the game and, because of their passivity, they have no control over it. They wait and, because they do not use their will power, they are "ready to follow every lure which presents itself until a thunderstorm ends everything."[39]

Faust, on the other hand, exerts tremendous will power in his strivings. He needed to stay active and use his will power, for the negative force tried every moment to keep Faust at rest and in one place, in an effort to deliver him from life to destruction, thereby gaining control over his soul and winning the wager with Heaven. By comparison the games played in *Im Spiel der Sommerlüfte* are of less serious nature by far, but they likewise constitute matters of the soul.

Character analysis in light of triangularity: Different from Goethe's drama, Schnitzler's places his women characters in the foreground. The two women in their contrasting representations of "the past and the new era in the making," in Willa Schmidt's words, are also at opposite ends in their activity of playing the game in their relation with others. Gusti, who represents "the new era in the making" — relating to political and social change, is instrumental in setting the game in motion in her relationship with Eduard and Felix, whereas Josefa, who signifies "the past," is for the most part "Mitspieler" in her position as part of a triangle with Vincenz and the Kaplan.

a) *Gusti-Felix-Eduard.* Gusti's attractiveness has drawn both men for different reasons into her orbit. Felix is seriously interested in Gusti, but in his capacity as "Sekundararzt im Krankenhaus [...] mit einem Monatsgehalt von sechzig Gulden" he finds it impossible to start a family (988). His visits to Kirchau on weekends are "im Grunde nur eine Quälerei" (987), for it is no pleasure for him to spend the night away from Gusti in a guestroom at the nearby inn. Still, he is happy that he can see her early in the morning for a hike in the forest. In his possessive nature he suffers from feelings of jealousy. With "gerunzelter Stirne" (984) he shows displeasure toward Gusti as she lets Eduard drink the rest of her milk. What bothers him even more is the fact that Gusti practices her roles with Eduard. Felix considers this activity utterly unnecessary (986). When he finds out that Gusti might stay two or three weeks longer in the countryside, he wants to persuade her to return to Vienna earlier (986), since her health has already improved enough for the journey.

Quite concerned over the possibility of Gusti's engagement at the theater away from Vienna, he inquires whether she had received any more letters in that respect. "Liegen keine neuen Engagementsanträge vor? Deutschland, Amerika, Australien —? " (987). He would like to see her study another winter in Vienna, he says, so that she can ask for a larger honorarium the following year. This is a thin veiling of his own selfish interest in such a proposal, for it would keep her away from other possible suitors until his own promotion. Already we have seen him "verstimmt" (985) when Gusti asks the Kaplan whether his brother Lieutenant might visit him a longer time. Her decision to return to Vienna the next day, and from there in a few days to Innsbruck, may have something to do with the officer's transfer to Innsbruck and the possibility of meeting him there soon. In fact, Felix is suspicious of the Kaplan as well. He would bet that Josefa "mit dem Kaplan was hat" (988), admonishing Gusti at the same time by saying, "Du bist übrigens auch verliebt in ihn" (988). Gusti leaves that possibility open just to underline again her point made earlier: "keine Lust" (988) of getting married so soon.

The relation between Eduard and Gusti develops along different lines. In contrast to Felix, Eduard admires Gusti's talents as an actress. He is happy to provide Romeo's lines as prompter, especially since he has a chance in that role as Romeo to give Juliet a kiss, a moment for which he waited long, always trying to be near Gusti. She denies him that privilege because "auf den Proben wird nur markiert" (991). Eduard, too, is jealous at the thought that any strange man in Innsbruck might kiss her just because he is cast in the role of Romeo on stage. The name Innsbruck creates other associations in Eduard's mind as well. Jealously he asks Gusti: "Was sagt denn dein Doktor dazu, dass du nach Innsbruck gehst? " (990), thus revealing that he knows about Gusti's secret. In fact, Innsbruck arouses the desire in him of becoming an actor likewise. "Möchtest mich nicht mitnehmen nach Innsbruck? " (1004) is his candid question to Gusti. It would serve two purposes: First, he would be close to Gusti, as he really begins to like her very well; and second, he would not have to finish his school, especially since he does not like to learn Greek in the first place, and would have no need for it as an actor, anyway. "Der Vater hat auch keine Matura gemacht und ist ein berühmter Mann geworden und Professor dazu" (996), he reasons more confidently from the time his mother mentions at the beginning of Act II that Felix, the physician, is not betrothed to Gusti but is only an acquaintance (995). Many ideas and questions apparently fill his mind and distract him from his studies. Finally he closes his notebook and with the question, "Möchtest du vielleicht später mit mir spazierengehen? " (996), he addresses himself to Gusti, obviously in the hope of firming up his future plans with Gusti's help.

It is easy to open his heart to Gusti for still another reason. She looks upon him as an equal, thus placing him in the adult world. This is first indicated by her manner of address to him: "junger Herr," "junger Mann" (984, 1033). Although in Eduard's absence or in conversation with his parents, she picks up on "Bube," a term his parents like to use — not just out of habit. At one point in the drama, however, Gusti and Eduard have a quarrel over the word "Bube." In Gusti's eyes Eduard behaves like an adolescent when in a moment of jealousy he speaks his mind regarding Felix, whom he would prefer to kill because of the favored position with Gusti (1002). When he realizes his negative behavior, he begs forgiveness from Gusti and in a theatrical gesture throws himself on the floor crying — later laughing, truly playing a role (1002-1003). The serious point underlying this encounter is made by Eduard. He wants to erase the image of a child and be counted among the adults, especially since he is only one year younger than Gusti. So he tells her: "Ich versteh' überhaupt mehr, als gewisse Leute meinen," and further, "Ich bin kein Bub, Gusti" (1002-1003).

He has a more difficult time establishing himself as an adult among the members of his family than elsewhere. Both the Rainer-Mädeln, for example, address him without hesitation as "Herr Eduard," and Kathy, the servant at Friedleins, has breakfast "für den jungen Herrn" (979); later on she praises "Herrn Eduard" for his diligence in his study habits (995). The real initiation into manhood, however, results from his mountain experience with Gusti during the night of the rainstorm. The next morning, his heart is overflowing; he wants to share with everybody, but Felix, above all, needs to know about the tables that have turned — no more visits in Kirchau to see Gusti! Some more guidance is necessary on Gusti's part, for discretion is a man's first duty (1018); Eduard must learn this right from the beginning. When she sends him affectionately to sleep (1018), he does not know yet that she has decided to leave the next morning for Vienna.

Liptzin describes Gusti as being "delighted by the freshness and naturalness of the boy in contrast to the premature seriousness of her betrothed, the physician."[40] But the text does not reveal any such statement, nor is she betrothed to Felix, as has already been pointed out in the discussion. Stage directions only tell "nimmt plötzlich seinen Kopf zwischen beide Hände, sieht ihn zärtlich an [...]" (1018). She shows some emotions but is silent about the experience. Her conduct suggests a logical reason with regard to the advice she gave the young man: "Diskretion ist die erste Pflicht," a rule pertaining to both partners.

Indeed, she seems to have her emotions very well under control, especially with respect to farewells. The night spent with Eduard appeared to both of them a joyful experience, unhampered by feelings of parting. She uses a similar pattern in her relation with Felix. Knowing that he is already troubled by jealousy and the prospect of her engagement in Innsbruck, she withholds any further information in order to make their time spent together as harmonious and pleasant as possible. Finally, she reminds him: "Wir haben's doch immer gewusst, vom ersten Monat an, Felix. Du genau so gut wie ich, dass es so kommen wird [...]. Deswegen haben wir uns um nichts weniger gern gehabt und sind um nichts weniger glücklich gewesen. Vielleicht sogar mehr — als wenn wir an die Ewigkeit geglaubt hätten" (1024).

Müller-Freienfels, who is concerned in his study with the "Lebensgefühl" of Schnitzler's characters, summarizes relations of short duration as follows: "Gerade das Wissen um die Kurzfristigkeit der Verbindung kann manchmal auch noch den Genuss vertiefen und ihm den Charakter der Einmaligkeit verleihen."[41] These sudden farewells have, according to him, still another advantage: "Man vermeidet durch die zeitliche Begrenzung auch das allmähliche, qualvolle Absterben und Verfallen einer Liebesbeziehung, das Schnitzler's Personen noch mehr fürchten als das Ende selbst."[42]

It is, therefore, best to avoid the word "Abschied," as Gusti suggests to Felix: "Sag nicht Abschied. Durch so ein Wort macht man sich das Schwere, das man ja doch durchmachen muss, nur noch schwerer, als es sowieso schon ist" (1024). Bernhard Blume, who discusses this subject also, adds: "Sich schmerzlos zu verabschieden, wird also ihr Bemühen. Natürlich sind es die eigenen Schmerzen, die sie vermeiden möchten, nicht die des anderen, auch wenn sie das Gegenteil behaupten."[43] Schnitzler, of course, knew best the problems involved in love relationships. The following aphorism from *Buch der Sprüche und Bedenken* laments the discrepancy of commitment involved in any more or less long-term relationship: "Dass wir uns gebunden fühlen mit der steten Sehnsucht nach Freiheit — und dass wir zu binden versuchen, ohne die Überzeugung unseres Rechts dazu, das ist es, was jede Liebesbeziehung so problematisch macht."[44] The concept of freedom, however, cannot be viewed in isolation — other areas of human conduct enter into it, such as a sense of responsibility and commitment to oneself as well as others. Liptzin reads Schnitzler this way: "Freedom is, to Schnitzler, that ideal state in which a person understands himself and the world around him. No person can enter on the road to freedom so long as he lies to himself, nor so long as he feels conscience-stricken when others condemn those actions of his which he deems justified."[45] The key words are "to understand oneself," which is such a difficult task because one has to master honesty with oneself first. Schnitzler's characters are always shown in various stages of their own understanding, which therefore influences their concept of freedom accordingly. Gusti also values freedom most of all, and so she tells her aunt Josefa: "Und — was den Doktor anbelangt — du hast gestern schon recht gehabt [. . .] ich werde Schluss machen, noch ehe ich ins Engagement fahre. Wird g'scheiter sein" (1019). The real motive, however, is her desire to make the acquaintance of the Lieutenant in Innsbruck.

b) *Josefa-Vincenz-Kaplan*. Josefa's decisions, on the other hand, are not as easily made, for she is married and has responsibilities. For various reasons I call her "Mitspieler" in her triangular constellation with Vincenz and the Kaplan. To begin with, her husband's extensive absences from the family disrupt the flow of communication between the two partners considerably, and this in turn affects their affinity and reality. On the surface she appears to be a complacent wife and mother, devoted to her husband whenever he is home. In her devotion she is motivated by admiration of the artistic talent that brings him recognition and success. Her expression of love has lost spontaneity because her husband does not reciprocate; in fact, he pays her almost no attention. That has changed her, and when the play begins, Schnitzler gives the following description of her: "[. . .] etwa 36, sehr jugendlich [. . .] spricht und bewegt sich etwas müde, doch häufig und immer häufiger bricht durch ihr Wesen die Lebhaftigkeit ihres Temperaments" (976). Her sense of unfulfillment creates a great deal of frustration hidden behind a rather transparent facade. Her role as mother provides a partial outlet for pent-up emotions; she is interested in her son's activities, especially those which he undertakes with the Kaplan of the village. On occasion she participates in their excursions, the highlights of which are stimulating discussions with the Kaplan. This contrasts with the small talk that takes place with her husband about weather, Gusti's fling with the Doctor, and her theatrical engagement in Innsbruck. In the eyes of Gusti and probably of Vincenz as well, Josefa appears as a harmless, simple person; Felix is the only one who senses a deeper involvement between Josefa and the Kaplan:

Felix: Harmlos? Die? Ich — wette —
Gusti: Was denn?
Felix: Dass sie mit dem Kaplan was hat.
Gusti: Aber du bist ja verrückt.
Felix: Pass nur einmal auf, wie sie ihn anschaut [. . .] . (988)

The underlying reason, of course, goes back to Vincenz, who is so occupied with himself and his work that he has neither time nor courtesy to give her approval, encouragement and appreciation. Naturally, Josefa becomes insecure and turns against herself in judgment and self-condemnation, thus losing self-confidence. Twice stage directions describe her as tired: "[...] bewegt sich etwas müde" (976); "kommt langsam, etwas gedrückt durch die Gartentür" (1006).

At only thirty-six years of age, she feels herself old and unattractive. She probably interprets her husband's frequent solitary travels as rejection. "Berufsreisen — Geschäftsreisen sozusagen" (982), he explains to the Kaplan; however, he still hopes to go to Italy on a vacation trip with Josefa, but she shrugs her shoulder in a gesture of doubt and disbelief (982). Earlier, when Vincenz had spoken about his trip to Kassel for the unveiling of his newest piece of art and had turned to Josefa with these words: "Und du fährst mit — diesmal! — Wenn's dir Spass macht" (982), she only looked at him "befremdet" (982). Later in the play, this gesture translates into a question to her husband: "Liegt dir denn was dran, dass ich bei so was dabei bin?" (1027), which is another expression of her deeper feeling of inadequacy.

In a reminiscent mood she looks back to her youth, when she was engaged as a model for Vincenz. Now she is jealous of the girls which he may have used in his "Dionysoszug," his latest work, for they may be more beautiful than she was. Even her husband's protest does not erase her deep-seated suspicions to the contrary. "Also das kann ich beschwören, Josefa, ein schöneres Modell hab' ich nie wieder gefunden als —," and Josefa continues: " — als ich einmal gewesen bin" (980), indicating again how far into the past she places everything. Vincenz tells her: "Also, Josefa, auf die ältere Dame brauchst du dich wirklich noch nicht hinauszuspielen" (980), but his words lack the warmth which only comes from a loving heart and therefore draw a somewhat stubborn response from her. Previously, she has already reminded him not to call her "Madame," a term she probably associates with older age.

The reason for this irritation goes in part to Gusti, the cause of Josefa's jealousy. When Gusti tells Josefa how her mother was able to rent out the large room but kept "das gelbe Kabinett," jokingly adding that this was done in case she might be sent home from Innsbruck, Josefa replies spontaneously: "Sie werden dich schon nicht nach Hause schicken. Mit dem G'sichtl und mit der Figur! [...] Das ist immer die Hauptsache beim Theater" (997). Of course, she speaks from experience, because attractiveness and a good figure were important factors in her own short profession as a model. Once she married Vincenz, he did not use her as a model anymore, especially since their son was born a year later. One might surmise that her early marriage was necessitated by the pregnancy and that she has not reconciled within herself the changes in her life style.

When Gusti mentions that Felix will visit her regularly in Innsbruck, at least once a month, Josefa advises: "Es tut kein gut. In solchen Fällen gibt's nur ein Entweder — Oder. Sei froh, dass du hinaus in die Welt kommst mit deinen neunzehn Jahren, in die Freiheit und ins Leben ..." (998). In retrospect, Josefa actually regrets the development her career took, for Vincenz, too, might have visited her too often, thus ending her life as a single person and with it the prospect of freedom, as she sees it. Gusti, in a moment of ill humor, exclaims in reply to Josefa's advice: "Ich wollt', ich wär' lieber neunzig, und alles wär' vorbei" (998). In a passion, Josefa admonishes her, for Gusti does not know what it means "all over." Gusti deems Josefa ungrateful, especially since she has an attractive husband and a boy of eighteen. Josefa finds it necessary to register a correction about the boy's age; he is only seventeen. If this situation was not such a sore spot in Josefa's heart, she might have reacted differently by not placing so much importance upon it.

Josefa's somewhat subdued and disillusioned "happiness" in her marriage is another indication that she faces difficulties within herself. Her devotion to Vincenz and the child might be motivated by a sense of duty instead of her heart's desire. Therefore, she is more of a "Mitspieler" rather than wholeheartedly in it, letting circumstances rule her life instead of accepting the turn of events in the knowledge that she has primary responsibility in her life and affairs.

"Jeder muss seinen eigenen Weg gehen," points out William Rey, "Er muss aber auch die Verantwortung für seine Entscheidung auf sich nehmen. Das Wagnis der Freiheit bleibt keinem erspart. Nur wenige erkennen, dass der höchste Sinn der Freiheit die Bindung ist."[46] Both partners, therefore, have the same responsibility to work toward a happy marriage. Schnitzler, however, seems to demand more of his women characters because of their finer insight, of which his male characters without exception seem to be incapable. John Nelson Whiton, who studied the problem of marriage in Schnitzler's works, places Vincenz in the category of "the dull, complacent husband who provides his wife with status and material security, but not with love."[47] The kind of double standard which Vincenz has created in his marriage, as indicated by his frequent late returns home, is not conducive to a happy marriage, especially since it is clear that he reserves these evenings or overnight stays for extra-marital pleasures. Of course, these extra freedoms on the part of Vincenz are thinly veiled under the pretense of work that has to be accomplished, but Josefa intuitively knows the truth: "Nur ihr Kunstwerk interessiert diese Menschen," writes Müller-Freienfels, "und das lebendige Modell ist ihnen gleichgültig geworden, sobald es seine Aufgabe erfüllt hat."[48]

Vincenz is not vicious, however, as was his artistic counterpart Gysar in *Komödie der Verführung*; a certain amount of ignorance in understanding himself and others prevents him from recognizing Josefa's deeper desires as a woman. "Es kümmert sie auch nicht, ob dieses lebendige Modell dadurch, dass es von ihnen nur als Instrument und Mittel für ihre künstlerischen Zwecke gebraucht wurde, vielleicht selbst Schaden genommen hat," observes Müller-Freienfels.[49] "Der Weg zum Mitmenschen besteht nur für denjenigen, der keine Maske trägt, beständig und innerlich gefestigt ist," says Anna Stroka.[50] But Vincenz hides behind the image of a successful artist and Professor; he is not as steadfast and secure a person as he shows in outer ways. His frequent absence from home indicates that he needs constant reassurance as a man. His marriage is for him a matter of convenience more than anything else, and this places a twofold responsibility upon Josefa. Not only does she have the same responsibility in working toward a happy marriage as her husband does, but also an additional accountability toward the child.[51] Her sense of devotion and her unselfishness help her to shoulder these responsibilities remarkably well, even though occasional frustrations upset the balance. The paradox of "Selbsterfüllung in der Selbsthingabe," which Rey discovers in some of Schnitzler's women characters, applies in general to Josefa also, so that "die männliche Eroberungslust [...] ihren Gegenpol in der weiblichen Opferbereitschaft [findet]."[52]

Her moments of frustration on the one hand find a pleasant relief on the other hand in the challenging and inspiring dialog with the Kaplan, and the understanding and sensitivity he shows her toward the end of the discussion uplift her in consciousness. No physical enjoyment takes place between them, but they both had their weak moments, to be sure. Significantly enough, the long dialog between Josefa and the Kaplan is placed in the center of the drama, preceded by one of the more disappointing moments in Josefa's marital experience. She had intended to meet her husband at the railway station and looked forward to walking home with him. But she returns alone, having received a telegram on the way which informs her that Vincenz is staying in town, entertaining his guest from the Kassel theater. Seeing that she is somewhat depressed, Gusti tries to console her aunt: "Es ist ja nicht das erste Mal, dass der Onkel drin übernachtet." This prompts Josefa to say: "Nein. Es kommt sogar ziemlich oft vor. Aber manchmal muss man's im Gefühl haben ... Ob man einen allein lassen darf oder nicht" (1007). It appears that her feelings this time are mixed, and suspicious as well. Her churning emotions find a corresponding expression in the embroiled state of nature: the wind has increased, there is summer lightning on the horizon with a rolling of distant thunder, and people hurry by to get home before the rain begins. Among them are the Rainer-Mädeln (1007-1008).

Just at that moment the Kaplan is passing by the fence and, looking into the garden, he unintentionally hesitates. He is not looking for Eduard this time; instead his goal is the railway station, but Josefa invites him to seek shelter there until the rain has passed. Thus their encounter not only takes place in the middle of the drama, but also at the height of a storm and in the absence of most occupants of the house. Vincenz, Eduard and Gusti — all have left to experience their own pleasures. Josefa has a keen perception of the situation which at one point in the dialog she communicates to the priest this way: "[...] keine Mutter hat ihren Sohn, und keine Frau hat ihren Mann — so, wie sie ihn haben möchte. Wenn es gerade ruft und lockt von irgendwoher, so laufen sie ins Wetter, in die Nacht und ins Leben hinaus — und man bleibt allein" (1013). Indeed, her son has gone off with Gusti into the storm, her husband into the night — all three for the purpose of experiencing life differently. The combination of weather, night, and life has symbolic meaning which will be discussed later on. The fact remains that Josefa finds herself alone at a moment when she most needs the presence of some company. In contrast to her previous role as "Mitspieler," she now initiates the game with the priest. In keeping with her generally unselfish nature, she allows him to speak his mind first, but during the course of their conversation she is able to reflect upon her own concerns as well, not always accepting as advice or reassurance the cleric's convictions which at times seem to her to be out of touch with the reality of life.

An alarming letter from Robert Holl, informing his brother, the Kaplan, indirectly of a serious duel, gives rise to a philosophical discussion about guilt, temptation, inner struggle, self-conquest, doubt; it also brings these two people to a better understanding of themselves and of each other. The Kaplan resigns himself to an attitude of waiting and praying, although he is painfully aware that prayer in its miracle-working power cannot undo what has been done — the sin remains, in his way of thinking. Josefa is an understanding woman, knowing that there are many temptations for a young person. But the Kaplan in his stoic attitude insists that it is one's duty to fight temptation, for weakness in this regard is a sin as well. "Not everyone is probably created for such a struggle," replies Josefa, reminding the priest of God's concept of mercy for those who miss the mark (1011). Unaware that Josefa's words might be based on experiences of herself and her family, the Kaplan considers her a "Good woman" and expresses his gratitude for her empathy which comes from "the peace of her pure heart and the shelter of this home" (1011). This invites opposition from Josefa: "Wer ist denn überhaupt geborgen, wer in dieser Welt? Wem ist ein friedliches Herz geschenkt?" (1011). Again, the Kaplan's answer is remote from any real life situation: "Through inner struggle and self-conquest to peace and happiness" (1011). His words sound like a mindless slogan to Josefa, who had just raised the question as to whether or not everyone is equipped to handle such inner difficulties. In her mind, it takes more courage to accept happiness on the basis of life's polarities — joy and sorrow, good and bad, beauty and ugliness, but she is told that this kind of courage often looks more like sin because the happiness attained is followed by remorse (1012).

The argument is brought down to more concrete levels, when Josefa applies the priest's line of thought to the situation of his own brother. How can he be so sure about his brother's state of mind? Perhaps he cherishes the very same experiences that brought him into the present position so much that they are worth any remorse felt afterwards. Josefa's daring ideas are foreign to the Kaplan and perhaps a bit frightening, because he hides now behing the word "Absolution" (1012), mentioned in his brother's letter, giving it his own clerical interpretation. Actually, Robert expressed gratitude toward his priestly brother for everything he had done for him in the past, at the same time assuring him that every word, handshake and embrace will mean absolution to him, when they see each other tomorrow (1009-1010). In a sudden move, the Kaplan puts the spotlight back on Josefa, interpreting her behavior as adverse reactions to the letter that must have caused anxiety and perhaps even doubt. However, Josefa considers doubt as a part of her nature and emphasizes instead those rare moments in a person's life when the real truth from within is revealed, when a new perspective of life is gained (1012-1013).

In light of Josefa's profound realization about herself and her family, the priest's position on the various issues raised seems rather inflexible, merely touching the surface of Josefa's concerns. Even when she speaks about the lure which draws husband and son into the weather, the night, and life, his only consolation is that they will be back soon (1013). Josefa's reply: "Und werden beide nicht da sein" (1013) opens up a whole new vista of her psychological insight. She knows well that they will return, but for a while thereafter they are only physically present, while on mental and emotional levels they are still involved with the experiences gained from those nocturnal activities.

Finally, the priest changes his attitude and becomes "beinahe herzlich" (1013), only to miss the point again, as he interprets Josefa's words to be a kind of confession, consoling her that tomorrow her anxiety will have passed. He is perplexed by Josefa's quick response: "Ja, das wird sie gewiss. Und man wird sich wieder belügen, sich und die andern dazu" (1013). Josefa's ideal is a truthful life, and this kind of role-playing does not satisfy her any longer. Throughout the dialog she is searching for deeper answers beyond conventional religious views of guilt, temptation, inner struggle, and self-conquest, but every one of her concerns has been misinterpreted or superficially answered. Step by step she has drawn a tighter mental circle around the priest in the hope of hearing words of deeper sincerity. She is greatly puzzled, therefore, to hear the priest abruptly change the subject by pointing out that it is time for him to attend his duties elsewhere. She considers this latest move on his part nothing less than flight, and wonders whether he would leave if there had been a true confession on her part. She had wished to speak to him as a friend, for in her mind a priest is above all a human being, and as such a friend. Of course, he cannot deny his human nature, which does not give him any greater virtues or rights, but he does believe that his vocation exacts higher duties, and as a priest he sets himself apart. Certainly, one such "higher duty" might have called for a more distinct effort to understand Josefa's concerns, which were born out of a sudden realization of the discrepancies between ideal and real life situations, as well as states of consciousness.

There is still more disagreement in store for her which finally breaks the distance which the priest tries to maintain under all circumstances:

Kaplan: [...] Kommen Sie zur Besinnung, Frau Josefa. Versuchen Sie Ihre abirrenden Gedanken wieder auf den richtigen Weg zu leiten.
Josefa: Wissen das Hochwürden ganz bestimmt, welches der richtige Weg ist? Mein rechter Weg?
Kaplan: Der ist vorgezeichnet, wie nur je einer war, es ist der Weg einer Gattin, einer Mutter.
Josefa: *einfach* Ich bin auch eine Frau, Hochwürden, und ich bin nicht so sicher, ob ich meinen Weg als Frau so gehe und gegangen bin, wie Gott ihn mir vorgezeichnet hat (1014).

When the Kaplan tries to tell her that such thoughts have nothing to do with God, Josefa closes in on him. How does he know where thoughts come from; which thoughts reach us from above and which from below and which are within us? And what about our prayers? Is Heaven or Hell responding to them?

Josefa in Schnitzler's character portrayal demonstrates deeper insight than the priest, for she knows that everything in life is of rather complex nature. Just as in the beginning of their discussion, she now draws again upon his brother to demonstrate her point. As he prays for Robert and wants him to be saved because he is his brother, does he not at the same time invite death for the other person, who most likely is less guilty than the brother? The discussion about a "believing heart" (1015) finally helps the Kaplan realize that he himself has been a doubter all along, and that he had no right to judge Josefa for her doubts. Of course, the difference between these two characters lies in the degree of self-honesty. Josefa felt free to speak to the priest about her innermost concerns. This was perhaps easier for her to do than for the Kaplan, for she revered him, as was already apparent by her form of address. He, on the other hand, as one sworn to strict vows before the altar of the priesthood, wanted to uphold this priestly aura of strength and faith, thus forgetting that he still is a human being and as such troubled with certain weaknesses as well. He finally has the courage to reveal to Josefa that he is more than a doubter, because when he read the letter he felt rebellion, dissatisfaction with his calling as a priest, even jealousy toward his brother who experiences life in such diversity. He fears, therefore, that his prayers may have dissipated in space, for they were spoken without belief and conviction (1016).

There seems to be a lack of balance within the priest, for when he condemns himself for being worse than a doubter, he leaves out his feelings of love and concern for his brother. Josefa can see these connections very clearly, and when the Kaplan passes by the garden in Act III to meet the mailman, she knows intuitively that he will carry a good message to him. This time the priest is freer in his expression toward Josefa. He even tells her about last night's dream he had, which involved the two of them in reverse roles and how his earthly longing for her through confession changed at the end of the dream to clarity of thought, purpose, and action. Josefa does not consider it a sin "[. . .] dass wir einander — beinahe — verstanden hätten" (1021). The priest understands now that Josefa is stronger than he himself, but she corrects him "frommer, Hochwürden" (1021). It seems, however, that each has learned from the other and emerged as a stronger and more balanced personality in the end, ready "to return to their daily life with renewed appreciation for its values," points out Davis.[53] "Everything ends on a conciliatory note."[54]

Concerning the first part of the dialog, Müller-Freienfels' observations are correct: "Der Kaplan erscheint im Grunde unehrlich: er sucht sich in seine Kirchen und seine Dogmen zu flüchten, allen Fragen und Bedenken ängstlich auszuweichen und nach aussen hin einen festen Glauben vorzutäuschen, den er innerlich gar nicht besitzt."[55] A significant change, however, has occurred within the priest at the beginning of Act III as a result of the dream. Vicariously, he experienced with Josefa what Vincenz and Eduard that night looked for in the physical world. He also seems to be closer now to his God, strengthened in his faith, and more in tune with his inner nature.

Herbert Lederer's evaluation of the Kaplan is, that he does "not quite come up to the high ideals expected of [him]."[56] One must ask the question here: How valid are expectations? In general, the Kaplan is portrayed as a devoted "shepherd of the flock" at Kirchau. He sees poeple, comforts those near death like the Hofrat, and also has time for the interests of the younger generation, as seen in his relation to Eduard. Only in his encounter with Josefa does one find his human nature revealed in all its hidden aspects. He had repressed a broad scale of emotions, including the aspect of doubt, so that what might have appeared insincere within him was really a result of this long history of emotional repression.

Schnitzler addressed himself to this problem in connection with belief: "Auch Glaube und Zweifel sind nicht allzu häufig als Charakteranlage vorhanden. Gerade sie sind fliessende Seelenzustände [...] und häufig genug kommen sie sogar nur als Stimmungen vor. Wie könnte man sonst verstehen, dass auch gläubige Naturen nicht selten an ihrem Gott irre werden — und dass immer wieder Zweifler sich zu einem Glauben oder ganz allgemein zum Glauben bekehren."[57] Furthermore, since Schnitzler gives the Kaplan these words: "Ich bin Priester, Frau Josefa" (1014), it is clear that he wanted him to be a positive character on the left side of his triangular diagram as "Erfüller einer Sendung [...] einer göttlichen Aufgabe."[58]

Davis believes that the Kaplan's "doubts are dangerous to him, but he has the touch of mysticism essential to his calling."[59] This cannot be proven with certainty through textual evidence, unless the dream is considered as a "touch of mysticism." Indeed, priests should have a mystic inclination; "[...] doch fehlt es nicht an Priestern [...] die zweiflerisch oder skeptisch angelegt sind [...]," Schnitzler adds in his discussion.[60] This reflects more truly the role of the priest in his particular drama. Georgette Boner sees this polarity of doubt and belief, balanced by a new courageous attitude, in the context of Schnitzler's effort to eliminate impressionistic elements from his work.[61]

Polarities: Schnitzler uses this concept of courage to establish a synthesis for such polar opposites as doubt and belief. Referring to Boner's observation (footnote 61), the priest has the courage to express the "heroic belief" of the woman, and Josefa finds the courage to address herself to the "heroic doubt" of the man. This was only possible when both were willing to take off their masks, particularly in the case of the priest. Other polarities find a balance as well, which could be considered a synthesis along Boner's line of thinking. The Kaplan spoke of inner struggle and inner peace: "Niemandem bleiben innere Kämpfe ganz erspart. Aber ohne die wäre wohl auch der innere Friede nicht viel wert [...]. Erst Selbstüberwindung ist Friede, ist Glück" (1011). If this somewhat negative attitude of "self-conquest" could be seen in light of "self-mastery," it represents a much desired synthesis. Self-control through inner guidance creates a balanced person who can face the antinomies of life and still remain peaceful at heart. This would also include the polarities Josefa pointed out: "Freude und Leid — Gutes und Böses — Schönes und Hässliches auch" (1012). These, too, are "fliessende Seelenzustände," to use Schnitzler's expression, which can be controlled through knowing the self.

Related to this concept of self-mastery is the polarity of "Stadt und Land." The lure and complexity of the city, as opposed to the sheltered atmosphere and simplicity of the countryside, demand balance. Throughout the drama, there is movement between these two poles.[62] Every morning Vincenz leaves for the city to carry out his work, but instead of returning home in the evening, he often stays overnight to experience the night life of the city. Finally, when feelings are held in check, there is less urgency to be in the city. Vincenz at the end of the play tells Josefa to her surprise: "Dass du gerade jetzt auf die Idee kommst, in die Stadt zu ziehen, wo ich mir vorgenommen habe, einmal vierzehn Tage lang in Ruhe da heraussen auf dem Land zu verleben" (1030).

Regarding the urban motif, mention must be made not only of Vienna but of Innsbruck as well. Innsbruck is the city where Gusti found her first employment as a professional actress. In that respect, it corresponds to Vienna where Vincenz' art studio is located. What lures Gusti away from her countryside "spa" several weeks earlier than she had planned, is the expectation of excitement. She is motivated not only by her desire to stay away from Felix in Vienna, but by her need to gain distance from Eduard. Furthermore, the lieutenant's transfer to Innsbruck presents an opportunity for new adventure in her quest for freedom of expression.[63]

But in all fairness to Gusti, one must not forget her sincerity as an actress. Although she is on vacation, we observe her immersed in the role of Shakespeare's Juliet, which is her first assignment at the Innsbruck theater. She demonstrates energy and enthusiasm for her profession, and talent in addition, as indicated by the nature of her first role in Innsbruck. Even the mere practice of her lines earned heart-felt "bravos" from passersby such as the lieutenant (992). She also reveals a seriousness of purpose when she speaks of her work. In a discussion with Eduard, her ardent admirer, about her contract for the coming season in Innsbruck, she explains rather firmly: "Ich hab' was Gescheiteres und was Wichtigeres zu tun in Innsbruck, als Besuche von Herrn zu empfangen oder Schulbuben. Ich hab' zu arbeiten. Ich muss schau'n, dass ich vorwärts komm'. Ich muss Geld verdienen für mich und für die Mutter. Seine Pflicht hat man zu tun vor allem" (1006). Uwe Rosenbaum, who investigates "Die Gestalt des Schauspielers auf dem deutschen Theater," offers this comment: "Es ist das Verhältnis des bürgerlichen Mädchens, das den Beruf der Schauspielerin als einzig möglichen ergreift, um sich eine Lebensgrundlage zu sichern, weniger aus künstlerischen Gründen."[64] Whether or not Gusti had artistic reasons for her career as an actress is difficult to evaluate, because the information given in the drama is limited. But her family background seems to point to an artistic orientation. Gusti's aunt Josefa probably selected her brief career because she was attracted to artistic circles.[65]

The characteristics of the two women relating to polar opposites have already been discussed, but ultimately Josefa and Gusti achieve a synthesis through better understanding of each other's innermost nature. When Gusti returns with Eduard from the mountain, having spent the night together in the cabin, she is prepared to give Josefa all kinds of excuses: "[. . .] grad' noch im richtigen Moment bin ich in die Hütte gekommen. Sonst — ich glaub', es hätt' mich heruntergeschwemmt" (1019). But Josefa suggests smilingly: "Ich glaub', es ist besser, du redest nichts" (1019), which is a gesture of understanding. Later on, the embarrassment is Josefa's, because Gusti wants to know how she knew about the lieutenant's duel. Josefa is prepared for a lengthy reply, all in an effort to justify the priest's evening visit, when nobody else was in the house. But Gusti helps her out — even the tone of her voice and the words are the same as Josefa's: "Ich glaub' halt, es ist besser, du redest nichts" (1030). A further gesture seals the secret between them: "Dann nimmt Gusti Josefas Kopf in ihre Hände und küsst sie" (1030).

The harmony which exists now between the two women, in spite of age differences, is not apparent between Vincenz and his son Eduard. Unlike Josefa, Vincenz is never outwardly concerned about his own age, to judge by anything he says in the course of the play. His experiences in town seem to give him assurance that he is still attractive to women. At home, the fact of a seventeen-year-old son might remind him of his age, but he handles that on psychological levels. He does not recognize his son as an adult. First he laughs when the Rainer-Mädeln send a greeting to "Herrn Eduard," repeating this form of address to himself as if he were rather amused about it. Perhaps he has been away so much that he has not really had a chance to watch his son grow up. He is complaining to Josefa about it early in the drama: "Ich hab' überhaupt nichts von dem Buben da heraussen (978). Josefa and Gusti pick up on this term also, at one point adding "insult to injury," when they call Eduard "dummer Bub" (996). However, Josefa is keenly aware of Eduard's feeling in this respect and tries to convince her husband also: "Der ist kein Bub mehr. Das ist ein väterlicher Wahn. Ein junger Herr ist er, ein Jüngling. 'Ein schlanker

Jüngeling' hat gestern der Doktor gesagt. Hast du denn noch gar nicht bemerkt, wie die Weiber ihn anschau'n?' " (980).

As his mother, Josefa is deeply conscious of this stage in Eduard's life, for it signals to parents that the time has come to release their child to make his own life.[66] The Kaplan is the only one who never calls Eduard "Bube." But he uses the term, when he talks about his own childhood: "[. . .] wie wir noch Buben gewesen sind — Kinder —" (999), referring to his twin brother Robert also. The age of twelve, it seems, is the last year of childhood in the mind of the priest, for, as he entered his teens, serious considerations were given to his future career. His twin brother went to the Military Academy at the same time that the Kaplan entered the Seminary. With regard to Eduard, much emphasis is placed on his school work, for he seems to have failed his examinations or part of them once before. Now his parents are concerned that he pass "die Nachprüfung,"[67] and he is constantly reminded to take tutoring lessons from the priest rather than going on hiking tours with him (979). Whenever Eduard is interested in some aspect of the adult world, the magic word "Nachprüfung" resounds and pushes him back to the childhood level: "Schau lieber, dass du bei der Nachprüfung [. . .] nicht durchfliegst."[68] Thus, there is a correlation between "Bube" and "Nachprüfung," neither of which Eduard cares to hear about. Thereafter, the word "Bube" occurs in the drama only in passing, among the various characters, but hardly in the presence of Eduard.[69]

An exception can be observed in the relation between Gusti and Eduard, who wanted to establish himself as an equal adult (1003, 1005). At the end of the play Eduard is uncontrolled in his disappointment over her sudden decision to depart. She copes with his outburst by reminding him that he must show that he is a man. But to Josefa and Vincenz she admits: "Er ist ja doch noch ein Bub" and, asking his permission, she kisses him with these words: "Also denk manchmal an mich, junger Mann!" (1033).

Symbolism (weather, Dionysos, the mountains): The one term which is mentioned consistently by almost every character in the play is the weather.[70] It is already anchored in the title *Im Spiel der Sommerlüfte* and indeed involves many components: wind, thunder, lightning, rain, sunshine. Weather usually is related to the sensation of the characters. In the beginning of the drama, Vincenz justifies taking his overcoat along in spite of the warm weather: "Ich trau' dem Wetter nicht. Und wenn ich abends drin in der Stadt bleib' — " (977). That he does so is indicated by the telegram he sends later.

Gusti during her vacation in the countryside "ist förmlich aufgeblüht" (984), and Vincenz attributes this improvement either to the milk she drinks or to the good air. In the late afternoon of that day, Josefa knows "Es kommt ein Wetter," but Kathi does not think much will happen before the night (995). It is interesting to observe Schnitzler's method: he lets a simple girl utter some simple words that prove to have far-reaching consequences. Gusti finds the weather sultry and, just in case of rain, takes an umbrella along as she goes to the mailbox (1007, paralleling Vincenz' earlier provision for the coat, for she will need that umbrella as she follows Eduard into the mountains.

A dramatic turn in the weather occurs when the Kaplan visits Josefa. "Stärkeres Wetterleuchten" is accompanied by a "Windstoss" as he greets her; "Windstoss" again as she invites him in (1008). "The wind," points out J. E. Cirlot, "is air in its active and violent aspects, and is held to be a primary element by virtue of its connexion with the creative breath or exhalation."[71] Although no overt act takes place during the ensuing dialog between the priest and Josefa, their heightened mental activity certainly stirs up inner turmoil. This sheds light not only on traditionally accepted concepts but also on spiritual horizons, as "Wetterleuchten" does in nature. Cirlot points out that "Jung recalls that in Arabic (and paralleled by the Hebrew) the word *ruh* signifies both 'breath' and 'spirit'."[72] Spirit, of course, is recognizable by its luminous intensity, just as lightning for a split second releases large amounts of energy. Through the long process of dialog, Josefa and the priest are able to understand themselves better, as they turn to the spirit of truth.

Josefa, in the course of their discussion, speaks about her husband and son who run into the weather, into the night, and into life, leaving her alone (1013). The common symbolic denominator of this triangularity of concepts is creativity and light. Weather in this drama is synonymous with rain which "has a primary and obvious symbolism as a fertilizing agent, and is related to the general symbolism of life and water," according to Cirlot.[73] As with the water symbol, rain "signifies purification,"[74] a creative power at work. Purification involves a clearing process which seems to be active within Vincenz, Eduard, and Gusti. Their nocturnal experiences clear up false ideas and thought patterns to achieve clarity in their future actions. "Night is related to the passive principle, the feminine and unconscious," writes Cirlot.[75] The feminine principle in man is also the creative aspect within him, and the Greeks thought that night and darkness preceded the creation of all things. Night "is an anticipatory state in that, though not yet day, it is the promise of daylight."[76] It is symbolic of the principle of understanding in the mind. Thunder is also an active force, "a symbol of the supreme, creative power [...] at the same time, the flash of lightning is related to dawn and illumination."[77] The night, therefore, with its outbursts of illumination in nature, brought light into the mind and heart of each character who was away from his usual habitation.

A related symbol, perhaps less complex than weather, is that of Dionysos. Vincenz has just finished a large sculpture for the Kassel theater which he calls "Dionysoszug" (980). It represents "einen Fries für das neue Schauspielhaus in Kassel. Zwölfeinhalb Meter lang" (981). When asked by the Kaplan whether he created it in antique style, Vincenz replies: "[...] in ziemlich freier Auffassung" (981). This reply includes not only the physical aspect of the artwork, but also Vincenz' moral and ethical convictions regarding the relations between an artist and his various models. Dionysos is described by Cirlot as "an infernal deity, and a symbol of the uninhibited unleashing of desire, or of the lifting of any inhibitions of represssion."[78] Vincenz seems to answer all. In *Komödie der Worte* (1915), consisting of three one-act plays, Schnitzler devotes the third play to the Dionysian aspect. He calls this play *Das Bacchusfest*. What Felix the poet created in words, Vincenz the sculptor changed into visual form, allowing himself the freedom to experience every aspect of his creation. Felix explains to Guido the details of this custom in these words:

> Das Bacchusfest war [...] ein religiöser Brauch [...]. Er bestand darin, dass einmal in jedem Jahr, eine Nacht hindurch, zur Zeit der Weinlese [...] der Menschheit — in gewisser Hinsicht uneingeschränkte Freiheit gegönnt war [...]. Für diese eine Nacht waren alle Bande der Familie, alle Gebote der Sitte einfach aufgehoben. Männer, Frauen, junge Mädchen verliessen bei Sonnenuntergang das Haus, dessen Friede sie sonst umgab und behütete, und begaben sich in den heiligen Hain [...] um dort unter den schützenden Schleiern der Nacht das göttliche Fest zu feiern [...]. Bei Anbruch des Tags — war das Fest vorbei, und jeder Teilnehmer war verpflichtet zu vergessen, mit wem er für seinen Teil das göttliche Fest gefeiert hatte. Verpflichtet. Das gehörte mit zum religiösen Brauch — wie die Feier selbst [...]. Und wie die Sage berichtet, sollen die Festteilnehmer zuweilen etwas ermüdet, aber doch erfrischt, ja gewissermassen geläutert nach Hause wiedergekehrt sein" (DW II, 551).

Vincenz, too, returned home the next morning with no trace of fatigue, but rather refreshed in spirit as well. He bought the atlas for Eduard; he now has travelling plans for the family, and meets Josefa in her somewhat embarrassed behavior with an embrace and these rather symbolic words: "Es muss doch ziemlich arg gewittert haben da heraussen" (1031). The promise of a new, different life becomes apparent — a life that will be spent in closer sharing of interests.

When Eduard receives the atlas, he feels that this wonderful illustrated edition is not his alone to enjoy; he thinks immediately of the priest as well: "Und der Herr Kaplan wird auch eine Freud' haben" (1031). Indeed, a deep friendship connects these two men, a friendship that has taken them on many excursions into the mountains. As the drama ends, the Kaplan appears "im Touristenanzug" (1031), ready to hike with Eduard just as he had hiked with his brother a year ago for a whole week in Kärnten and around the Grossglockner (999). This time their goal is the Gaisental, where they hope to find some rare orchids that grow usually only in the Dolomites (998). When Eduard first appears in the drama, he has just returned from the Katzenstein in record time (978). He meets Gusti at the Fallenböckhütte which later gives them shelter for the night (1006, 1019), and even Josefa has been up there to testify to the beauty of the surroundings.

The mountains represent an exalted state of mind: the priest finds new inspiration and enthusiasm for his calling; Eduard seems drawn to the mountains whenever his book learning overwhelms him; Josefa joins her son and the Kaplan on their hikes, whenever she is disturbed by marital frustration. The mountains, therefore, can symbolize a state of spiritual realization and uplift, but in the case of Gusti and Eduard that is also a state of physical enjoyment. Deriving from the idea of height "are interpretations such as that of Teilhard, who equates the mountain with inner 'loftiness' of spirit, that is, transposing the notion of ascent to the realm of the spirit."[79] One also gains a clear view from the mountain top. The characters in the play see their lives more clearly, and have a better perspective, whenever they return from the mountains.

Comparison with other late dramatic works: The symbolism of the mountain can be compared with that of the tower in *Der Gang zum Weiher*. Both are symbols of ascent and denote also spiritual elevation. Yet, the tower experience in *Der Gang zum Weiher* did not achieve anything comparable to the mountain experience in *Im Spiel der Sommerlüfte*. All characters, except Vincenz who had never time to be in the mountains, enjoyed them, because they felt uplifted; whereas the guestroom in the tower only involved Sylvester and Konrad. It had an adverse effect upon Sylvester, who did not even spend a single night there. After burning his diary notes page by page, he still had not been able to lift himself into a new state of awareness by accepting the truth about himself at his present station in life. He felt uncomfortable with himself and, rather than facing himself in self-honesty this time, he ran away — as so often before — to avoid this promising lifting experience.

Konrad enjoyed the tower guestroom as he would have any other bedroom after his experience of sex with Leonilda. The memory of his encounter lingered on. In that respect he can be compared with Eduard who experiences his sexual initiation in the mountains. Another comparison between Konrad and Eduard involves the question of adolescence. Both young men wanted to be counted as adults. In contrast to Eduard, Konrad was only once called "Bube" when he was challenged by Sylvester to a duel (834). That was an issue of biological difference in age. Eduard never had strong feelings toward age, because unlike Konrad (cf. 805), he did not perceive a threat to his self-esteem from this direction.

The idea of the duel is present in all four dramas. In *Die Schwestern oder Casanova in Spa* and *Im Spiel der Sommerlüfte* it is actually carried out, but no serious difficulty arises; in fact, Casanova and his two opponents are prevented from fighting through the intervention of Teresa, the dancer (726). In *Komödie der Verführung*, it was established that Prince Arduin was rather duel-happy but never entered a fight; in *Der Gang zum Weiher*, the outbreak of war prevented the duel between Konrad and Sylvester, but Konrad had already indicated that their ages were incompatible (834). With regard to Schnitzler's position in this matter, Davis concludes that "if Schnitzler [...] were really concerned about this point, we should expect to find the same process of constant clarification of his attitude that we have found on other subjects."[80] No death is caused by any duel in the late dramatic works, and this represents a significant difference from Schnitzler's earlier dramatic writings. According to Davis, "Schnitzler in his late works uses the duel frequently as a tool to point out something important about a character, and as poetic justice."[81]

On the other hand, one could suspect that the issue of the duel may be rooted in Schnitzler's inability to accept the changes from Old Vienna to postwar Vienna. The duel is a holdover from the past which he retains to keep evergreen the precious memories of his own youth. In his book *Jugend in Wien* Schnitzler recalls vividly his feelings of younger years about the duel:

> Es war vom Duell die Rede, und wir alle, ohne uns gerade als prinzipielle Anhänger dieser Sitte zu fühlen, betonten aus unserem Studententum heraus und mehr noch als Einjährige-Freiwillige und künftige Reserveoffiziere unsere Bereitschaft, erforderlichenfalls ritterliche Satisfaktion zu geben [...]. Wir waren zwar alle weder Raufbolde noch besonders tüchtige Fechter, und keiner von uns lechzte daher nach einem Waffenhandel, aber ebensowenig hätte es einer versucht, sich einer studentischen Mensur oder selbst einem Duell zu entziehen, wenn es den geltenden Regeln nach als unausweichlich gegolten hätte."[82]

One can glean from this discussion that Schnitzler never believed in any procedure justifying the duel, but that he would not have retreated, had there been a serious necessity of fighting one. Schnitzler, therefore, did not change his position throughout his life. His stand had always been against this convention, but in the last analysis dueling is a matter of inner conscience. If one does not heed inner guidance, one will find himself no longer balanced, no longer centered, a condition which some characters in the various plays call "Schuld."

To Leonilda in *Der Gang zum Weiher* guilt is present only when one knowingly turns the wrong way (789). In this she moves away from conventional thought patterns, by which a person is made to feel humiliated by imputations of guilt made by someone else. Gusti, in *Im Spiel der Sommerlüfte,* continues in Leonilda's footsteps. When Felix tries to blame her for his anxiety, fear, and painful thoughts during her absence from Vienna, she defends herself: "An denen bin ich nicht schuld. Das ist nur deine unglückselige Natur. Wenn du mehr Vertrauen hättest — " (1024). Schnitzler indicates here through Gusti that the responsibility for one's emotional wellbeing rests within each person. Strong negative emotions such as hate, anger, fear, jealousy, guilt hamper a person's ability to master life's challenges successfully.

The priest, on the other hand, represents traditional theological thinking in the matter of guilt: he blames himself for Josefa's stirred-up emotions on account of the letter he has read to her: "[...] morgen wird Ihre unruhvolle Stimmung — an der ich leider auch mir einige Schuld zumessen muss —, morgen wird sie wieder vorbei sein" (1013). He does not comprehend that his visit to Josefa that evening was "mehr freundschaftlicher als amtlicher Natur" (981), just as the Hofrat needed to confide in a friend, when he called for the Kaplan.

In *Komödie der Verführung,* the question of guilt rests with Falkenir. He blames himself for the suicide of his first wife, which shapes his decision to withdraw from his marriage proposal to Aurelie. "[...] du wagst es nicht, glücklich zu sein — als hättest du irgendetwas zu sühnen —, was du doch nicht verschuldet" (871), she tells him, in order to remind him that he has a choice in life. Falkenir does not grasp this idea at all, for he accepts guilt. "Ist Vorhersicht nicht Schuld? " (871) is the question to which he finds no answer, and when he meets Aurelie again at the Danish coast, he has accepted additional guilt for her present state of abandon. "Wenn es hier etwas wie eine Schuld gibt, so liegt sie bei mir allein" (950).

An interesting polarity is created with the term "Rechenschaft oder Treue schuldig sein": Judith wants to enjoy irresponsibly without being accountable to anybody (865); Gysar lures Aurelie by reminding her of independence (894); Arduin asks Aurelie: "Bist du irgendeinem Menschen, wer es auch sei, Treue schuldig? " (947). In *Die Schwestern oder Casanova in Spa,* the term "Schuld" has likewise two connotations. On the one hand, Casanova is constantly concerned with his obligation of paying his debt[83] — on the other hand, the question arises as to whether the two women feel any guilt for their assignations with him (694, 699).

The theme of "Schuld," then, has been treated by Schnitzler in all four dramas, the lighter aspect of which is represented in *Die Schwestern oder Casanova in Spa.* The more conventional concept of feeling guilty for another person's actions is developed in *Komödie der Verführung.* The absence of "Schuld" is demonstrated in *Der Gang zum Weiher* through Leonilda, the emancipated woman, who determines for herself what course her life will take instead of feeling compelled to bow to a hypocritical social code. Her father likewise showed this conviction when the message reached him about Sylvester's drowning. He knows: "Sie trägt keine Schuld" (840), speaking of Leonilda. Each person rules his own moral actions and is responsible for them. The last drama, *Im Spiel der Sommerlüfte,* deals again with a juxtaposition between old and new ideas in this respect, thus connecting to the first drama and completing the circle. Schnitzler's contemporaneity rests on his assumption for his characters that no guilt attaches to any behavior so long as one accepts the responsibility for the consequences of one's decisions and actions.

There is another correspondence between the first and the last drama in terms of the women characters. Flaminia and Anina considered themselves sisters in that they both felt a strong attraction to Casanova, once they had physical contact with him. But the quarrel over Casanova brought out the worst within them and even their seeming harmony at the end of the play was not sincerely demonstrated. Josefa and Gusti, on the other hand, became sisters because of their states of mind. They understood each other's concerns on deeper levels, so that no significant disharmonies interrupted their life in the countryside. Gusti and Leonilda are mental sisters in their desire to remain unmarried for a while, and both offer friendship to their suitors. Neither Sylvester nor Felix, however, feels inclined to accept it (824, 1025).

Another combination justifies a brief comparison: Josefa and Aurelie. Both were models for artists, one for a sculptor and the other for a painter. Whereas Josefa was trained professionally for this work and enjoyed her brief career, Aurelie never had such ambitions for the profession and only yielded under pressure from Gysar. In consequence, her despair of soul confused her. Josefa married and has, apart from certain frustrations, lived a sheltered life in devotion to her husband and son. She is a mature woman who deepens her understanding of herself through a healthy quest for truth, even if it means doubting the validity of certain traditions and conventions. Aurelie, rejected as a marriage partner, is left without balance or discernment, in a state of mental disarray. She never reaches a state of healthy introspection.

The polarity of "Stadt und Land" in *Im Spiel der Sommerlüfte* finds a correspondence in all four dramas. The complexity of city life — its business atmosphere as well as the lure and excitement after working hours — related to one's personal code of conduct in Schnitzler's last drama. The movement between the two poles of "Stadt und Land" in

Der Gang zum Weiher has its cause in political maneuvers. The main reason for the entire drama's taking place in the countryside of castle Mayenau is the dismissal of the Freiherr as chancellor to the emperor six or seven years earlier. Whereas the main characters seem to have adjusted to this quiet, peaceful life, Dominik, the servant, is bored and nostalgically awaits the moment when he can be with his master in the stream of events again. Leonilda breaks the news of pending war by talking about the two messengers on horseback who stopped briefly in the village on their way to the emperor to deliver secret documents. Konrad, who carries a letter from his father to Mayenau, is moving on to the capital. Finally, Mayenau himself is on his way to the city — first, to catch his adversary and then, together with him to be on a peace mission to the emperor. After Mayenau is reinstated as chancellor, preparations begin for moving to Vienna to take up permanent residence at the court.

In *Komödie der Verführung* the movement is first between countries, as Arduin fulfills his diplomatic mission. Money speculations carried out by Westerhaus also take place between countries, as the various telephone calls are interpreted. Later, when most of the characters meet again away from Austrian city life in the simplicity of a Danish sea resort village, the declaration of war sends them into frantic preparations to meet the last train in Copenhagen to cross the border. The polarity of "Stadt und Land" in this drama involves its greatest complexity of the international political situation.

In *Die Schwestern oder Casanova in Spa,* it is the Belgian resort town of Spa which has become "unsafe" to some characters on account of Casanova's presence. Andrea, therefore, suggests at one point to Anina that they should leave this place so as to expose themselves no longer to the lure of the various pleasures which are there. The polarity of "Stadt und Land" shows a gradual increase of importance and urgency, as each drama unfolds from a personal realm to international politics, then local politics, to end up again on a note of personal conduct, thus completing a circle.

In summary: There is a coherence among the last four plays which in terms of their publication dates all appeared after the First World War. Of course, one must not forget that Schnitzler began collecting ideas for these dramas over a long period of time. Anna Stroka's observation about "Schnitzlers Tragikomödien" can also apply in part to these four weeks: "Mit diesen Werken hat Arthur Schnitzler ein ernstes Problem des Menschen seiner Epoche behandelt und gleichzeitig kritisch zu diesem Stellung genommen. Er deckte die feinsten Seelenregungen dieser Menschen auf, enthüllte ihre innere Leere, wollte mithin nicht nur entlarven, wollte seiner Zeit nicht nur einen Spiegel vorhalten, sondern auch warnen." [84]

The soul had always been an area of interest and concern to Schnitzler because of his own training in psychology. Each drama is concerned with the souls of its characters, but the most complete study takes place in *Der Gang zum Weiher.*[85] One of Schnitzler's aphorisms speaks of the immortality of the soul, a conviction seldom dwelled upon in his works: "Unsere Seele ist ewig, ja, aber nicht mehr in gleicher Weise die unsere. Das, was in uns Seele war, ist ewig, wie auch das, was in uns Körper war, ewig ist, wie überhaupt alles ewig ist, da innerhalb der Unendlichkeit nichts verloren gehen kann."[86] "That which in us was soul is eternal," says Schnitzler in a carefully worded way which places the soul on a cosmic scale, "das All" in Schnitzler's words. For Karl Joël the soul is the center of life,

> nicht weil sie zufällige Mitte [...] sondern weil sie Einheit des Lebens ist, und mehr, weil sie bildende Kraft des Lebens ist. Sie ist das eigentlich Lebende, der Leib das Gelebte, Durchlebte, ja das grosse Mittel des Lebens; denn die Seele lebt durch den Leib hindurch, in die Welt hinein. Der Leib ist die letzte Gliederung der Seele, ihre Instrumentierung auf die Welt hin, und die Seele waltet durch den Leib so unsichtbar wie der Dirigent unhörbar durch das Orchester."[87]

The soul, therefore, is the most important part of a human being. Within the soul antinomies are unified to a harmonious concert. As Joël says so eloquently:

> Die Seele ist Mann und Weib, Krieg und Frieden, Scheidung und Bindung, Spannung und Lösung, Lust und Leid. Sie ist wie das von ihr beherrschte Leben gerade der Ineinanderklang von Gegensätzen. Es ist das Wesen des Lebens, dass es nicht eindeutig ist, sondern Reibung und Ausgleich. Noch jeder hat gelogen, der das Leben auf einen Begriff zog. Optimismus und Pessimismus sind hier so parteiisch wie Monismus und Dualismus. Denn die Gegensätze bedingen sich." [88]

The soul, as the part of man that is forever searching, is a characteristic ingredient of Schnitzler's own career and his fascination with Goethe's *Faust*. He questioned himself in the same way Faust did: "Sind wir ein Spiel von jedem Druck der Luft?" Schnitzler's own answers would be based upon the antinomies of life, the polarities — as I called them throughout the study. The more man turns within for answers, the stronger mastery he gains over these opposites.

It is in light of this inner search that his last drama, *Im Spiel der Sommerlüfte,* gains in value and deserves more recognition than it has been accorded so far. Without violence, each character in the play emerged as a more complete person with deeper understanding of himself and the world around him, through the searching of his soul. Each character reaches a synthesis, so to speak. The answer to the question: "Sind wir ein Spiel von jedem Druck der Luft?" depends upon the strength of character to maintain its identity [89] and to govern the intensity of one's life experiences.

SUMMARY AND CONCLUSION

The preceding study of Schnitzler's late dramatic works uses the method of detailed analysis to show evidence that the author in his last four plays, *Die Schwestern oder Casanova in Spa, Komödie der Verführung, Der Gang zum Weiher,* and *Im Spiel der Sommerlüfte,* is a better dramatist than critics have been willing to admit in the past. The results of these thorough interpretations demonstrate the author's importance as a dramatist. The study reaffirms the generally accepted conclusion reached by critics: Schnitzler's late dramatic works are characterized by the complexity of theme and character portrayal. However, the contention that these dramas do not hold together because the various themes and characters are not developed in order of their priority has been challenged. The complexity in his late productions has added to rather than diminished Schnitzler's dramatic excellence as a humanist who concentrates his analytical powers on the one legitimate object of humanism: man in his multiple manifestations. The complexity, therefore, is Schnitzler's tool to sharpen the conflict which arises from human action and interaction. In each drama he deepens his insight into human nature and demonstrates a keen understanding of the timelessly contemporary dynamics that govern human conduct.

This study defines those dynamics in terms of polarity and triangularity and, admitting that existing scholarship recognizes these constellations as a principle of form in Schnitzler's character arrangement, demonstrates that they are also integral to the author's concepts of fidelity, responsibility, and freedom. Contrary to common assumption, recurring "Leitmotive" and "Leitgestalten" are deliberately employed to show the author's process of ethical and moral revaluation in his late dramatic works. Significant parallels exist in his theoretical writings ("Der Geist im Wort und der Geist in der Tat," 1927; and *Über Krieg und Frieden,* 1939), which in existing scholarship have not received sufficient attention. Each drama gives proof of Schnitzler's soul-searching activity in order to gain more maturity and understanding in his quest for truth and the deeper meaning of life. Dominant in all four dramas is his concern with the emancipation of women in matters of companionship, courtship, and marriage. Women are no longer reflected through the eyes of men as in the case of the *Anatol*-cycle; instead, they become characters of major importance, as can be seen in the titles of the dramas.

Die Schwestern oder Casanova in Spa (Chapter I) has been seen by critics as a drama which moves along old established lines of Schnitzler's trend of thought. However, the complexity of human nature is demonstrated in regard to the three women characters — Anina, Flaminia, and Teresa — who are portrayed in various degrees of independence. Schnitzler stresses the importance of free will and personal choice, which must be balanced by responsible conduct not only in matters of one's own life and affairs, but also with regard to society as a whole. Solutions in this drama, as well as in the other three, are achieved on psychological rather than moral grounds. The question of fidelity is resolved in terms of "Wiederkehr" on the basis of "forgive and forget." This is a new idea and, significantly enough, the concept is advanced by Casanova, the worst offender against fidelity. With the author's deeper insight in the later plays, "Wiederkehr" changes to "Heimkehr" bringing a new perception of "forgetting."

This drama is important in Schnitzler's artistic development because it demonstrates his willingness to revaluate earlier concepts of life styles and personality traits. He discusses the consequences as a result of selecting one over the other. Jealousy, responsibility, freedom, and fidelity are key issues throughout the play. They also provide the basis for further treatment in later plays.

In *Komödie der Verführung* (Chapter II) this range of theme is expanded to include such issues as social injustice, the duel, and the double standard. Schnitzler shows how perverted love affects the fiber of society, fine arts, politics, and the fate of the entire nation. The realm of man-woman relationships gains importance in this drama as the basis of increased psychological complexity. It is demonstrated that the concept of triangularity goes beyond the arrangement of characters to include ideas designed to expose the decadent social environment of pre-war Austria, including members of the nobility and the educated bourgeoisie as well. Schnitzler proves his tremendous skill as a dramatist by combining these diverse aspects of the play into the constellation of *Eros-Krieg-Märchen/ Imagination*. The problem of communication creates disaster in personal lives as well as in the life of the nation: it destroys a potentially happy marriage between Falkenir and Aurelie and plunges the nation into war because of corruption in banking circles and failures in diplomatic missions. As Schnitzler's characters pervert the ideals of love, art, and business, they eventually ruin themselves, and society as a whole falls apart. This study points out Schnitzler's keen awareness of the political maneuvers which took place in his time. His casually used term of "Kameltreiber" reveals the Berlin-Baghdad railway negotiations carried out on an international scope. The carefully designed setting of the play to take place between May and August prior to the outbreak of the First World War further underlines the author's own concern in this respect.

Schnitzler's concept of "Wiederkehr" is reexamined in this drama in favor of "Heimkehr." However, by adding psychological complexity to the main characters, the author demonstrates that "Heimkehr" does not provide a viable solution, because stronger emotions such as fear and guilt can never provide the peace and security related to "Heimkehr."

By adding surrealistic elements of water and vision to his next drama, *Der Gang zum Weiher* (Chapter III), it became evident that "Der Gang" related symbolically to Leonilda's future, which promises to open new and more complete experiences for her; whereas for Sylvester the path symbolizes the last stretch of road for the adventurer who returns from a frivolously wasted life. Mayenau and Konrad are shown as polar opposites in the political issue which involved loyalty to established rules of conduct as opposed to rebellion. This study shows how Schnitzler found a synthesis by stressing the concept of unity in diversity from the standpoint of the polar principle as it relates to the antinomies of life. They are expressed in attraction and repulsion, intimacy and detachment, realism and surrealism, youth and age, art and life, life and death, peace and war, love and hate, selflessness and egotism. The significance of the play lies in Schnitzler's accomplishment as a humanist. His characters face the antinomies of life on physical, mental, and spiritual levels; each one achieves balance and restores inner peace in a unique way.

This study demonstrates also that its surrealistic content is an important aspect of Schnitzler's versatility as a dramatist. He uses the symbols of water, vision, and the tower to focus on the mystical aspects of I-Thou relationships, thereby revealing his fascination with matters of intuition and the higher mind in general. The study reveals that this mystical content of the author's Weltanschauung has its roots in his *Buch der Sprüche und Bedenken* (1927). Existing scholarship with the exception of the contributions made by William Rey, Vincent LoCicero, and Harold Dickerson had neglected this "other side" of Schnitzler's creative talent. These states of consciousness are also important in the last drama which critics generally considered as having too meager a plot.

The discussion of *Im Spiel der Sommerlüfte* (Chapter IV), however, demonstrates how the various characters gain a greater awareness of life by turning further inward where life is truly lived. It also reveals the challenges people face at a time when they are no longer at home in the religious, social, moral, and existential certainties of past ages. Each character in the play emerges with a deeper insight into his role as a member of the human family. In their soul-searching they gain more maturity and understanding which help them to solve the problems in their lives.

Although Schnitzler did not formulate his question "Sind wir ein Spiel von jedem Druck der Luft? " until his very last play, it undoubtedly serves as a means to measure and evaluate his life's work. The answer to the question depends upon strength of character to maintain one's identity and integrity, which the author exercised courageously in spite of harsh criticism. It is in light of the persistence and courage with which Schnitzler defended his diversified Weltanschauung that his late dramatic works will continue to demonstrate his importance as a dramatist to future generations.

NOTES
INTRODUCTION

1. Bernard J. F. Lonergran, S. J., *Method in Theology* (New York: Herder and Herder, 1972), p. 209.
2. Richard Alewyn, "Nachwort," *Liebelei-Reigen* (Frankfurt/Main: Fischer Bücherei, 1960), p. 155.
3. *Ibid.*
4. Other excellent articles have been written in an effort to reevaluate Schnitzler's artistic accomplishment by critics such as Friedbert Aspetsberger, Frederick J. Beharriell, Herbert Cysarz, Harold D. Dickerson, Jr., Lore B. Foltin, Friedrich Wilhelm Kaufmann, Vincent LoCicero, and Wolfdietrich Rasch. They will be considered in the discussion of the late dramatic works.
5. Alewyn, p. 156. Cf. Ernst Lothar, "Tod und Renaissance," *Forum*, 9, No. 101 (1962), 213, quoting Wedekind: "Kein anderer verdient so wie er die Bezeichnung eines Meisters [...]. Heute, wo die literarische Falschmünzerei jener Tage aufgedeckt und abgetan ist, steht Arthur Schnitzler als der Dichter da, der Deutschland [...] die grösste Zahl vollendeter Werke geschenkt hat."
6. Alewyn, p. 156. Modern literary historians at times have tended to present Schnitzler in a one-sided view. In the judgment reached by Karl Holl, Schnitzler is reduced to a few trivial notations, bordering on incomprehension: "Passivität," "Verfallsstimmung," "nachdenklich-ironisches Dämmern," "reizbare Subjektivität," "völliger sittlicher Relativismus." (*Geschichte des deutschen Lustspiels*, Darmstadt: Wissenschaftliche Buchgesellschaft, 1964, pp. 316-317.)
   Not only Schnitzler, but also Hofmannsthal, Bahr, and Salten are in the estimation of Holl all representatives of the same milieu which is a world of grace and charm where all characters seem "etwas angefault mit ihren Liebeleien" (Holl, p. 316).
   "Aus Schnitzlers Werk sprach das Ende des Kulturbewusstseins," says Fritz Martini (*Deutsche Literaturgeschichte von den Anfängen bis zur Gegenwart*, 13th ed., Stuttgart: Alfred Kröner Verlag, 1965, p. 474) and jumps in his discussion from *Der Weg ins Freie* (1904) to *Fräulein Else* (1924) without mentioning Schnitzler's late dramatic works at all.
7. Reinhard Urbach, *Schnitzler Kommentar zu den erzählenden und dramatischen Schriften* (München: Winkler Verlag, 1974), p. 7. (Hereafter referred to as *Kommentar*.)
8. Arthur Schnitzler, *Gesammelte Werke. Die dramatischen Werke*. Zweiter Band (Frankfurt/Main: S. Fischer Verlag, 1962, 1972), pp. 651-1034. The bibliographical data concerning Schnitzler and the Schnitzler research is comprised in the volume by Richard H. Allen, *An Annotated Arthur Schitzler Bibliography. Editions and Criticism in German, French, and English 1879-1965* (Chapel Hill: The University of North Carolina Press, 1966). The information is kept current in the subsequently published bibliographies by Jeffrey B. Berlin, "Arthur Schnitzler: A Bibliography of Criticism, 1965-1971," *Modern Austrian Literature*, 4, No. 4 (1971), 7-20; "Arthur Schnitzler: A Bibliography," *Modern Austrian Literature*, 6, Nos. 1/2 (1973), 81-122; "Arthur Schnitzler Bibliography for 1973-1974," *Modern Austrian LIterature*, 7, Nos. 1/2 (1974), 174-191; "Arthur Schnitzler Bibliography for 1974-1975," *Modern Austrian Literature*, 8, Nos. 3/4 (1975), 248-265; "Arthur Schnitzler Bibliography for 1975-1976," *Modern Austrian Literature*, 9, No. 2 (1976), 63-72; "Arthur Schnitzler Bibliography for 1976-1977," *Modern Austrian Literature*, 10, Nos. 3/4 (1977), 335-339. The dates cited in this study are those listed in these works. Dates pertaining to the time a drama was first drafted or actually written, but not published until later, will be in accordance with information supplied by Gerhard Neumann and Jutta Müller in *Der Nachlass Arthur Schnitzlers. Verzeichnis des im Schnitzler-Archiv der Universität Freiburg i. Br. befindlichen Materials* (München: Wilhelm Fink Verlag, 1969). When necessary, reference will be made to Urbach's *Kommentar* to trace the genesis of a particular work.
9. Frederick J. Beharriell, "Arthur Schnitzler's Range of Theme," *Monatshefte*, 43, No. 7 (1951), 301-311. The intention of Beharriell's article was "to emphasize by means of 'Stichproben,' that he (Schnitzler) offers a great deal more" (p. 311). But the present study thoroughly examines the range of theme with regard to the late dramatic works which Beharriell only mentioned in passing (cf. pp. 306, 309). I also include the author's ethics and philosophy which Beharriell's view excluded from further consideration because of the "relativistic attitudes of the man for whom, as

10 Werfel said, 'auf Erden so wenig zu glauben übrig bleibt' " (p. 310, footnote 38).
10 Allen, p. 6.
11 Josef Körner, "Arthur Schnitzlers Spätwerk," *Preussische Jahrbücher,* 208 (April-Juni, 1927), 162. (Hereafter referred to as "Spätwerk.")
12 William H. Rey, "Arthur Schnitzler," *Deutsche Dichter der Moderne,* 3rd ed., ed. Benno von Wiese (Berlin: Erich Schmidt Verlag, 1975), p. 257.
13 Reinhard Urbach, *Arthur Schnitzler* (Velber b. Hannover: Friedrich Verlag, 1968), p. 25.
14 George Sylvester Viereck, *Glimpses of the Great* (New York: The Macaulay Company, 1930), p. 408. (Rpt. in *Modern Austrian Literature,* 5, Nos. 3/4 [1972], 7-17, under the title "The World of Arthur Schnitzler.")
15 Beharriell, 310.
16 Martin Swales, *Arthur Schnitzler. A Critical Study* (Oxford: University Press, 1971), p. 55.
17 William H. Rey, *Arthur Schnitzler. Die späte Prosa als Gipfel seines Schaffens* (Berlin: Erich Schmidt Verlag, 1968), p. 13.
18 Arthur Schnitzler, *Buch der Sprüche und Bedenken. Aphorismen und Fragmente* (Wien: Phaidon-Verlag, 1927).
19 Arthur Schnitzler, *Gesammelte Werke. Aphorismen und Betrachtungen.* Ed. Robert O. Weiss (Frankfurt/Main: S. Fischer Verlag, 1967), pp. 135-166.
20 Josef Körner, *Arthur Schnitzler. Gestalten und Probleme* (Zürich, Leipzig, Wien: Amalthea-Verlag, 1921), p. 18. (Hereafter referred to as *Gestalten und Probleme.*)
21 *Ibid.* According to DR II, 1040, *Paracelsus* appears to have been completed by 1897 and published in *Cosmopolis* 35 by November, 1898, which also coincides with Urbach, *Kommentar,* p. 64.

"Männlich," according to Körner, refers to a greater maturity on the part ot the author with respect to the problem of marriage. The characters he portrays move away from a mere erotic experience and aspire to a sense of true companionship.
22 *Ibid.,* p. 18.
23 Allen, p. 6.
24 Urbach, *Kommentar*, p. 22.
25 Schnitzler, *Buch der Sprüche und Bedenken,* p. 215.
26 Schnitzler-Nachlass, File 13 (1908). See also Robert O. Weiss, "Arthur Schnitzler's Notes on Journalistic Criticism," *Germanic Review,* 38, No. 3 (1963), 226-237.
27 Urbach, *Kommentar,* p. 7. Cf. William H. Rey, who states: "Der ganze Reichtum der dichterischen Welt Arthur Schnitzlers kann jedoch nur durch Analysen der einzelnen Werke erschlossen werden. Hier sind noch viele Aufgaben zu lösen." ("Beiträge zur amerikanischen Schnitzlerforschung," *German Quarterly,* 37, No. 3, 1964, 283.)
28 *Preussische Jahrbücher,* 208 (April-Juni, 1927), 53-83.
29 *Ibid.,* 53-54.
30 Sol Liptzin, "The Call of Death and the Lure of Love," *German Quarterly,* 5-6 (1932-33), 36.
31 Urbach, *Arthur Schnitzler,* p. 93.
32 "The Impact of Triangularity in Selected Prose Works by Arthur Schnitzler," Diss. University of California at Riverside, March 1977. (Hereafter referred to as "Impact of Triangularity.")
33 Urbach, *Arthur Schnitzler,* pp. 26-27: "[. . .] das Gestaltendrama, das den Menschen nachschaffen will in seiner Vielfalt und Wirklichkeit."
34 Rey, "Beiträge zur amerikanischen Schnitzlerforschung," *German Quarterly,* 37, No. 3 (1964), 283.
35 *Ibid.*
36 Heinz Politzer, "Arthur Schnitzler: The Poetry of Psychology," *Modern Language Notes,* 78, No. 4 (1963), 365.
37 *Ibid.*
38 M. W. Swales, "Arthur Schnitzler as a Moralist," *Modern Language Review,* 62, No. 3 (1967), 473-474.
39 Stockholm: Bermann Fischer Verlag, 1939.
40 *Neue Rundschau* (1932), 678-681.
41 Robert O. Weiss, "The Human Element in Schnitzler's Social Criticism," *Modern Austrian Literature,* 5, No. 1/2 (1972), 32.
42 *Ibid.*

⁴³ His diagram entitled "Der Geist im Wort und der Geist in der Tat" (*Aphorismen und Betrachtungen*, pp. 135-166) is also considered in so far as it relates to the characters in these plays.

⁴⁴ Willa Elizabeth Schmidt, "The Changing Role of Women in the Works of Arthur Schnitzler," Diss. University of Wisconsin, 1973, p. 314. Concerning the portrayal of women in Schnitzler's work, I have been unable to gain access to the dissertation which Barbara Gutt submitted to the Freie Universität in Berlin.

⁴⁵ Cf. Erhard Friedrichsmeyer, "Zum 'Augenblick' bei Schnitzler," *Germanisch-Romanische Monatsschrift*, 16, No. 1 (1966), 62.

⁴⁶ Herbert Lederer, "Arthur Schnitzler: A Chronicle of Loneliness," *German Quarterly*, 30, No. 1 (1957), 91.

⁴⁷ Cf. Lore Foltin, "The Meaning of Death in Schnitzler's Work," *Studies in Arthur Schnitzler*, eds. Herbert W. Reichert and Hermann Salinger (Chapel Hill: The University of North Carolina Press, 1963), pp. 34-44. Theodore Ziolkowsky, *Dimensions of the Modern Novel. German Texts and European Contexts* (Princeton, N. J.: Princeton University Press, 1969), pp. 215-257.

⁴⁸ William H. Rey, "Die geistige Welt Arthur Schnitzlers," *Wirkendes Wort*, 16, No. 3 (1966), 184. Cf. Frida Ilmer, "Schnitzler's Attitudes with Regard to the Transcendental," "[. . .] Instead of skepticism, therefore, we find in Schnitzler's utterances a reverent attitude which is so strong that it causes him to view the universe itself and all life in it as the greatest conceivable miracles." (*Germanic Review*, 10, No. 2, 1935, 120.) Cf. also less carefully drawn conclusions, for example, in the account of H. S. Reiss, "The Problem of Fate and of Religion in the Work of Arthur Schnitzler," *Modern Language Review*, 40 (1945), 306-307. Robert Kann, "Das Österreich Arthur Schnitzlers," *Forum*, 6, No. 71 (1959), 421.

CHAPTER I

¹ Arthur Schnitzler, *Gesammelte Werke. Die dramatischen Werke*. Zweiter Band (Frankfurt am Main: S. Fischer Verlag, 1962), pp. 651-737. All quotes from this second volume pertaining to the text will hereafter be referred to by page number only.

² Oskar Seidlin, ed., *Der Briefwechsel Arthur Schnitzler-Otto Brahm. Schriften der Gesellschaft für Theatergeschichte*, Band 57 (Berlin: Selbstverlag der Gesellschaft für Theatergeschichte, 1953), p. 61. (Hereafter referred to as *Schnitzler-Brahm-Briefwechsel*.)

³ Therese Nickl/Heinrich Schnitzler, eds., *Hugo von Hofmannsthal-Arthur Schnitzler. Briefwechsel* (Frankfurt am Main: S. Fischer Verlag, 1964), p. 286. (Hereafter referred to as *Hofmannsthal-Schnitzler-Briefwechsel*.) The letter to Hofmannsthal is dated October 1, 1919.

⁴ Arthur Schnitzler, *Gesammelte Werke. Die erzählenden Schriften*. Zweiter Band (Frankfurt am Main: S. Fischer Verlag, 1961), pp. 231-323. Reference to the prose works are indicated hereafter by ES I or ES II.

⁵ Urbach, *Kommentar*, pp. 128-29.

⁶ Kurt Bergel, ed., *Georg Brandes und Arthur Schnitzler. Ein Briefwechsel* (Bern: Francke Verlag, 1956), p. 134. (Hereafter referred to as *Brandes-Schnitzler-Briefwechsel*.) Letter S 49, dated January 30, 1922. Cf. Richard Alewyn's comments regarding the Memoiren: "In ihnen wird – wie immer es um die Zuverlässigkeit des einzelnen bestellt sei – eine Form der Existenz zu Ende gelebt, ohne die unser Bild von den Möglichkeiten des Menschseins ärmer wäre: das Abenteurertum." ("Casanova," *Neue Rundschau*, 1959, 102).

⁷ Cf. William H. Rey, "Schnitzler in neuer Sicht. Ein bedeutender Forschungsbericht aus Frankreich," *Modern Austrian Literature*, 1, No. 1 (1968), 34: "Erst wird man Schnitzlers Casanova (sei es der junge in *Die Schwestern* oder der alte in *Casanovas Heimfahrt*) nicht als historische Figur, sondern als höchst aktuelle und zugleich mythische Verkörperung des Abenteurertums in all seinem Glanz und seinem Elend sehen müssen."

Cf. Heinz Otto Burger, "Dasein heisst eine Rolle spielen," *Germanisch-Romanische Monatsschrift*, N. F. 11 (Oct., 1961), 373: "Vom Dichter erwartet man nicht, dass er historisch getreu schildere oder frei erfinde, sondern dass er die 'Muster der Lebensweisen' finde und wiedergebe."

Cf. Susanne M. Polsterer, "Die Darstellung der Frauen in Arthur Schnitzlers Dramen," Diss. Wien, 1949, Paragraph 2.27. (There are no page numbers used in the main body of the text. Therefore, one has to depend solely on the numbered paragraph divisions.

Cf. Urbach, *Kommentar*, pp. 129-30.

⁸ Körner, "Spätwerk," p. 57.

143

[9] Cf. Bernhard Blume, *Das Weltbild Arthur Schnitzlers* (Stuttgart: Buchdruckerei Knöller GmbH, 1936), p. 29: "Der glückliche Casanova erscheint in einem von Schnitzlers Nebenwerken, in dem Verslustspiel 'Die Schwestern oder Casanova in Spa'."

[9] Körner, *Gestalten und Probleme*, pp. 26, 81, 97, 111, 115.

[10] Letter dated January 4, 1913, quoted by Klaus Kilian, *Die Komödien Arthur Schnitzlers. Sozialer Rollenzwang und kritische Ethik* (Düsseldorf: Bertelsmann Universitätsverlag, 1972), p. 89.

[11] Cf. p. 134 of this monograph where Schnitzler places his concept of the soul on a cosmic scale as well.

[12] Viereck, p. 399.

Cf. Robert Roseeu, *Arthur Schnitzler*, p. 43: "Die Grösse des Schauspiels beruht eben nicht in der Führung der Handlung, vielmehr in der Schilderung der modernen Seele, in den weiten und grossen Lebensanschauungen, die daraus hervorleuchten." (Berlin: Wilhelm Borngräber Verlag Neues Leben, 1913.)

Cf. Theodor Reik, *Arthur Schnitzler als Psycholog*, p. 301: "Das eigentliche Produktive des dichterischen Schaffens bleibt eben im unbewussten Seelenleben." (Minden/Westf.: J. C. C. Bruns, n.d., Forword 1913.) This spiritual concept of the soul conceiving the ideas for the mind appears to be the latest conclusion which Schnitzler reached in his search as to the nature of creativity. Some years earlier in his aphorisms (1927) we hear the scientist speak: "Ebenso, wie nun eine solche Zelle alles in sich aufnimmt, was ihr zur Nahrung, zur Vollendung dienlich ist, so nimmt auch jener Stoff alles in sich auf, was aus des Dichters Erlebnissen, Erfahrungen, Gefühlen ihm nutzbar sein mag, verschmäht das Unverwertbare, stösst es aus und dehnt sich allmählich immer weiter, so dass er endlich den ganzen Inhalt der Dichterseele zu bilden, ja dass die Dichterseele selbst in den Stoff umgewandelt scheint." (Arthur Schnitzler, *Buch der Sprüche und Bedenken. Aphorismen und Fragmente,* Wien: Phaidon-Verlag, 1927), p. 191. (Hereafter referred to as *BdSp*.)

Schnitzler has frequently allowed us "glimpses" into the active mind of a dramatist: "Dramatiker sein, heisst an den freien Willen glauben, wie, nein als einen Gott. Denn was ist das Drama? Der Widerstand, der Kampf des Einen, des Willens des Einen mit dem Schicksal? Die Summe, das Quadrat, kurz irgendeine Zusammenfassung aller andren freien Willen plus den unabänderlichen Naturgesetzen." (Schnitzler, "Gedanken über die Kunst," *Neue Rundschau*, 43, 1932, 38). An unavoidable prerequisite for the drama is the presence of a distinct "Weltanschauung" and the acceptance of certain paramount ethical values (Schnitzler, *BdSp*, 181).

[13] Arthur Schnitzler, *Gesammelte Werke. Aphorismen und Betrachtungen*. Ed. Robert O. Weiss (Frankfurt am Main: S. Fischer Verlag, 1967), p. 287. (Hereafter referred to as *AuB*.)

[14] For further detail of plot see also Sol Liptzin, *Arthur Schnitzler* (New York: Prentice Hall, Inc., 1932), pp. 256-58; and Françoise Derré, *L'œuvre d'Arthur Schnitzler. Imagerie viennoise et problèmes humains* (Paris: Librairie Marcel Didier, 1966), pp. 294-95.

[15] Ernst L. Offermanns, *Arthur Schnitzler. Das Komödienwerk als Kritik des Impressionismus* (München: Wilhelm Fink Verlag, 1973), pp. 110-127.

[16] *Ibid.*, p. 127.

[17] *Ibid.*

[18] *Ibid.*, p. 110.

[19] Kilian, pp. 110-116. It was originally a 1969 dissertation at the Ruhr University of Bochum.

[20] *Ibid.*, pp. 132-33.

[21] *Ibid.*, p. 114.

[22] *Ibid.*, p. 111.

[23] Schnitzler, *AuB*, p. 142.

[24] Kilian, p. 113.

[25] Friedbert Aspetsberger, " 'Drei Akte in einem.' Zum Formtyp von Schnitzlers Dramen," *Zeitschrift für deutsche Philologie*, 85 (1966), 285-308.

[26] *Ibid.*, 291.

[27] *Ibid.*, 296.

[28] Derré, pp. 284-85.

[29] *Ibid.*, pp. 293-96.

[30] Richard Alewyn, "Casanova," 110-116.

[31] *Ibid.*, 103.

[32] Schmidt, p. l4.

[33] *Ibid*

[34] Cf. Schmidt, pp. 248-57; pp. 308-328.

[35] *Ibid.*, p. 243.

[36] *Ibid.*, p. 242.

37 Polsterer, Paragraph 1.3.
38 *Ibid.*, Paragraph 1.3.
   Cf. Rena R. Schlein in her more balanced view of Schnitzler: "Schnitzler's writings that have remained unparalleled represent a fusion of scientific insight, intuitive knowledge and perception, and artistic genius. This is the explanation of the renaissance his works are enjoying today. They will be read with joy by future generations, for, as all masterpieces, they are timeless." ("Arthur Schnitzler: Author-Scientist," *Modern Austrian Literature*, 1, No. 2, Summer 1968, 37.)
39 Heinrich (Henry) Schnitzler, " 'Gay Vienna' — Myth and Reality," *Journal of the History of Ideas*, 15, N. 1 (Jan., 1954), 94-118. Robert A. Kann, "The Image of the Austrian in Arthur Schnitzler's Writings," *Studies in Arthur Schnitzler. Univeristy of North Carolina Studies in the Germanic Languages and Literatures.* Eds. Herbert W. Reichert and Hermann Salinger (Chapel Hill: The University of North Carolina Press, 1963), 45-70. Schlein, 28-38.
40 Schmidt, p. 6.
41 Reik dissects female as well as male characters according to psychoanalytic theories. Körner stresses the sensual as well as the emotionally overbalanced nature of women in Schnitzler's works who generally are shown in a state of dependency upon men. (*Gestalten und Probleme*, p. 34.)
42 Georgette Boner, *Arthur Schnitzlers Frauengestalten* (Zürich: Wintherthur Buchdruck, 1930), p. 15. Boner's dissertation was originally submitted at the University of Basel under the same title.
43 *Ibid.*, p. 16.
44 *Ibid.*, p. 15.
45 Schnitzler, *AuB,* pp. 135-166.
46 Most other aspects of Boner's study have been mentioned in Schmidt's analysis and need not be repeated here. Cf. Schmidt, pp. 2-5. The drama *Die Schwestern oder Casanova in Spa* is mentioned in some other dissertations; however, only certain aspects were treated as they fitted the overall purpose of these writings. These dissertations include: Evan B. Davis, "Moral Problems in the Works of Arthur Schnitzler," Diss. University of Pennsylvania, 1950; Reinhart Müller-Freienfels, "Das Lebensgefühl in Arthur Schnitzlers Dramen," Diss. Frankfurt, 1954; John Nelson Whiton, "The Problem of Marriage in the Works of Arthur Schnitzler," Diss. University of Minnesota, 1967. These dissertations will be recognized in the course of this study.
47 Aspetsberger, 291.
48 Whiton points out that "Throughout Schnitzler's works, resorts serve as the locals for the concentration of erotic temptation, and as a symbol of the erotic. This is especiallly true in [. . .] *Die Schwestern,* [. . .] *Komödie der Verführung,*" p. 246.
49 Johannes Jahn, *Wörterbuch der Kunst* (Stuttgart: Alfred Kröner Verlag, 1966), p. 591.
50 Derré, p. 285.
51 Alewyn, "Casanova," 115.
52 Cf. William H. Rey, *Arthur Schnitzler. Die späte Prosa als Gipfel seines Schaffens,* p. 30: "In Schnitzlers Spätzeit wird die Auseinandersetzung mit dem Abenteurertum auf einer höheren Ebene fortgeführt [. . .]. Auf der Schwelle des Alters beschwört Schnitzler also noch einmal den Glanz und das Elend des Abenteurers und zeigt damit, wie bedeutungsvoll die schöpferische Auseinandersetzung mit dieser Gestalt für seine eigene Entwicklung gewesen ist." (Hereafter this work is referred to as *Späte Prosa.*)
53 Gero v. Wilpert, *Sachwörterbuch der Literatur* (Stuttgart: Alfred Kröner Verlag, 1964), p. 55.
54 Schnitzler, *BdSp.*, p. 70.
   Cf. William M. Johnston, *The Austrian Mind. An Intellectual and Social History 1848-1938* (Los Angeles: University of California Press, 1972), p. 165. Cf. Jon D. Green, "The Impact of Musical Theme and Structure on the Meaning and Dramatic Unity of Selected Works by Arthur Schnitzler," Diss. Syracuse University, 1972, p. 42: "Schnitzler's mind actually seems to have functioned through a keen awareness of polarities. The fact that his works, almost without exception, contain a central conflict created by competing polar forces (Schein-Sein, freedom-determination etc.) creates a dramatic setting not unlike musical conflict and resolution."
55 Alewyn, "Casanova," 105.
56 *Ibid.*, 108.
57 Rey, *Späte Prosa,* p. 31.
   Cf. Swales, *Arthur Schnitzler. A Critical Study* (Oxford: University Press, 1971), pp. 16-17: "The adventurer seeks erotic experience on the one hand, because it is the most intense form of physical experience, and yet, on the other, he refuses to be bound by it, because ultimately his spirit continues to reassert the insufficiency of each specific erotic experience. Each experience must be

known in its intensity and yet transcend each time." (Hereafter this work is referred to as *Critical Study*.)

[58] Schnitzler, *AuB*, p. 164.

[59] Schnitzler, *BdSp.*, p. 165.

[60] Bernhard Blume in his study certainly goes too far, when he equates the characteristics present in Casanova with the nature of the author himself: "Der utopische und in sich unmögliche Versuch, den Ablauf der Zeit aufzuhalten und sich in den Genuss des Augenblicks zu retten, wie ihn die Schnitzlersche Lieblingsfigur des 'Casanova' symbolisiert, gleichsam die materialistische Verfallsform des Don Juan, ist freilich ein notwendiger Versuch für den Menschen des Verfalls, und deshalb ein Grundzug von Schnitzlers Wesen." (p. 13)
See also Rey, *Späte Prosa*, p. 192. Cf. Heinz Politzer, "Diagnose und Dichtung," *Forum*, 9 (1962), 270. He shows a more sensitive view of the author: "Der Dichter Arthur Schnitzler war ein guter Arzt. Stück um Stück, Buch um Buch stellte er die tragikomische Verwirrung fest, die über die Menschheit hereingebrochen war. Er analysierte die Psyche einer dem Untergang bestimmten Gesellschaft, weil er den epidemischen Charakter der Neurosen fürchtete, die hier gebrütet wurden. Aber er war zu sehr eins mit den Gestalten, die er schuf, um sie, wie seine Nachfolger auf dem Gebiet der Tragikomödie — Jean Cocteau etwa, Tennessee Williams, Samuel Beckett — von oben her blosszustellen und einem über sich selbst erschrockenen Gelächter preiszugeben. An ihren Betten, welche Betten der Liebe und des Todes waren, verweilte er lange und litt. Er wusste um ihr Geheimnis, und da er es wusste, bewahrte er es."

[61] What Uwe Rosenbaum in this context says about the "Graf" can be related to the "Abenteurer" as well. He is also "einer jener im Gesamtwerk Schnitzlers immer wiederkehrenden 'Augenblicksmenschen,' unterliegt einer illusionistischen Vorstellung. Denn auch der Augenblick ist in den Zeitlauf mit einbezogen, er ist Zeit, partielle Zeit." ("Die Gestalt des Schauspielers auf dem deutschen Theater des 19. Jahrhunderts [...]," Diss. Köln, 1971, p. 190).

[62] Schnitzler, *AuB*, p. 290.

[63] Cf. Schnitzler, *BdSp.*, p. 64: "Ein Schicksal mag äusserlich abgetan sein, es bleibt immer noch Gegenwart, solange wir es nicht völlig verstanden haben. Erst wenn es geheimnislos für uns wurde, haben wir das Recht, es Vergangenheit zu nennen."

[64] Swales, *Critical Study*, p. 17.

[65] Schnitzler, *BdSp.*, p. 114.

[66] *Ibid.*, p. 118. Cf. also pp. 80, 97, 106 with regard to understanding and forgiving.

[67] Schnitzler, *Jugend in Wien. Eine Autobiographie* (Wien-München-Zürich: Verlag Fritz Molden, 2nd. ed., 1968), p. 28.
Cf. Gudar at the beginning of the play speaking about Casanova: "So wie er oft mit wahren Worten lügt" (656).

[68] Schnitzler, "Der Geist im Wort und der Geist in der Tat," *AuB*, p. 142.

[69] This last idea is a problem which Schnitzler examines again in more depth in his next drama, *Komödie der Verführung*. Falkenir's first wife committed suicide to prove her fidelity. Similarly, the idea of "Wiederkehr" receives Schnitzler's most detailed attention in the present drama. Prior to this play, it occurred briefly in *Der grüne Kakadu* (1899), where the actress Léocadie for seven years returned periodically to Henri who finally marries her. From that point on, however, Henri no longer tolerated the escapades of his wife and, in fact, killed her lover Von Cadignan in the dressing room of the theater. Nevertheless, this episode only fills a minor detail within the political context of this one-act play on the evening of the French Revolution. The play *Die Schwestern oder Casanova in Spa*, on the other hand, deals with the idea of "Wiederkehr" at greater length and also provides entirely different circumstances. *Der grüne Kakadu* shows life as a crossroad between reality and illusion, wakefulness and dream, as the various entertainers within the play perform their act.

[70] Schnitzler, *BdSp.*, p. 118.

[71] *Ibid.*, p. 117.

[72] This is a Dionysian idea which the one-act play *Bacchusfest* handles in detail; it occurs again in *Komödie der Verführung* and *Im Spiel der Sommerlüfte*.

[73] Schnitzler, *BdSp.*, p. 116.

[74] Cf. Alewyn, p. 110: "Es bestünde auch für ihn kein Grund, dieses Spiel nicht endlos zu wiederholen, gäbe es nicht eines: das Altern. Casanova hat ein für seine Zeit hohes Lebensalter erreicht; aber schon auf der Mitte seines Lebenswegs, mit fünfunddreissig Jahren, erklärt er, dass er sich alt werden fühle, und mit vierzig beginnt seine Spannkraft nachzulassen, und damit erlischt seine Magie. Er wird von Frauen betrogen und versetzt, er muss betteln, wo er sich zu bedienen gewohnt war." Cf. Kilian,

75 pp. 111-12. He worked out comparisons between the two stories.
75 Davis, p. 127.
76 Boner, p. 30.
77 *Ibid.*
78 *Ibid.*
79 Liptzin, *Arthur Schnitzler*, p. 174.
80 *Ibid.*
81 Körner, *Gestalten und Probleme,* p. 94.
82 *Ibid.*
83 The dissertation by Georgette Boner represents the first positive contribution in sharpening the focus upon Schnitzler's women figures.
84 Modified from the original quote which reads: "[. . .] die Bedeutung der Schnitzlerschen Gestalten liegt nicht in 'ihrem Wesen,' sondern in 'ihrem Schicksal' (Bergel, *Brandes-Schnitzler-Briefwechsel,* p. 68).
85 Liptzin, *Arthur Schnitzler,* p. 224.
86 *Ibid.*
87 Schnitzler, *BdSp.,* p. 26.
88 Cf. Christa Melchinger, *Illusion und Wirklichkeit im dramatischen Werk von Arthur Schnitzler* (Heidelberg: Carl Winter Universitätsverlag, 1968), p. 131. See also Rey, *Späte Prosa,* pp. 10-11. Richard Plant, on the other hand, gives a superficial evaluation of "Schnitzler as a juggler of psychological situations which he wheels around and around [. . .]" ("Notes on Schnitzler's Literary Technique," *Germanic Review,* 25 (February, 1950), 18.
89 Schnitzler, quoted by Viereck, p. 407.
90 Körner, "Spätwerk," 54-55.
91 *Ibid.,* 56-57.
92 Viereck, p. 400. See also Schnitzler in *BdSp.,* p. 56: "Ohne unseren Glauben an den freien Willen wäre die Erde nicht nur der Schauplatz der grauenhaftesten Unsinnigkeit, sondern auch der unerträglichsten Langweile. Verantwortungslosigkeit hebt jede ethische Forderung, kaum dass sie ins Bewusstsein trat, als wesenlos wieder auf: das Ich ohne das Gefühl der Verantwortung wäre überhaupt kein Ich mehr [. . .]." Cf. Herbert Lederer, "The Problem of Ethics in the Works of Arthur Schnitzler," Diss. Chicago, 1953, p. 159. Selma Köhler, "The Question of Moral Responsibility in the Dramatic Works of Arthur Schnitzler," *Journal of English and Germanic Philology,* 22 (1923), 410, denies that freedom of will and choice are possible. She calls it a "[. . .] delusion, however, contrasted with the more potent influences of environment, epoch, and heredity, and particularly is the power of choice a delusion when social conventions are brought to bear upon the individual." Cf. also her concluding remarks (411): "The question of individual responsibility," she says, "is replaced, in his estimation, by the vaster conception of man as a being subject to laws over which he has little or no control, those of physiological, biological, and social science." Her statement may have had more application in Schnitzler's early works, certainly not in his late dramatic works.
93 Viereck, p. 400.
94 Schnitzler, *BdSp.,* p. 65: "Selbstüberwindung, Erkenntnisdrang und Opfermut sind die einzigen wirklichen Tugenden unter allen, die man so zu nennen pflegt, denn nur in ihnen ist der Wille betätigt."
95 Urbach, *Arthur Schnitzler,* p. 27.
96 "Arthur Schnitzler" in: *Deutsche Dichter der Moderne. Ihr Leben und Werk,* ed. Benno v. Wiese, 3rd ed. (Berlin: Erich Schmidt Verlag, 1975), p. 243.
97 Boner, pp. 83, 89.
98 Swales, *Critical Study,* p. 23. For a discussion regarding "time," see p. 21.
99 Alewyn, "Casanova," 116.
100 Cf. Kilian, p. 110, who feels that Schnitzler needed to gain perspective of the political situation. Cf. Offermanns, p. 110: "Der impressionistische Abenteurer des Fin de Siècle wird in die kulturgeschichtlich verwandte Epoche des Rokoko projiziert und so der ungleich bedrängenderen aktuellen Wirklichkeit entrückt." Also see p. 125: "Das Lustspiel 'Die Schwestern' mag als der Versuch eines Gegenbildes zum 'grauenhaften Weltzustand' genommen werden."
101 Schnitzler, *BdSp.,* p. 168. In an interview with Viereck, the author expands his position this way: "I oppose Bolshevism, not for political reasons but because Bolshevism denies differentiation. Differentiation is a fundamental law of nature. If man were not differentiated, he would be a monstrosity standing outside the pale of nature. To negate personality is to repudiate culture. I am disgusted by men of letters who coquette with Bolshevism."

[102] Swales, pp. 28-29. Cf. Offermanns, p. 179.
[103] Max Krell recorded this conversation with Schnitzler. He is quoted by Urbach, *Schnitzler*, p. 17. Cf. Swales, *Critical Study*, p. 26. He states: "Yet there is more to Schnitzler than this stereotyped image. In a very real way he partakes of the total upheaval that his world is undergoing and he embodies not only the traditional and backward-looking but also the modern and forward-looking aspects of the 'Jahrhundertwende.' He does, therefore, claim our attention as a representative figure of an important age, and not just as a patron saint of one limited segment of that age [...]."
[104] Bergel, *Brandes-Schnitzler-Briefwechsel*, p. 126. B 44, dated June 13, 1920.
[105] Jakob Wassermann, "Erinnerungen an Arthur Schnitzler," *Neue Rundschau*, 1 (Januar, 1932), 13. Cf. Politzer, "Diagnose und Dichtung" (II) who has an answer to Wassermann's 'warum': "Aber die Grundspannungen, die Schnitzlers reifes Werk tragen, haben weit mehr mit der konkreten Wucht des Barock zu tun als mit der sublimen Eleganz des Rokoko." (*Forum*, 102, Juni 1962, 269.)
[106] Rey, *Späte Prosa*, p. 30. Cf. also Blume, *Weltbild*, p. 29: "Hier wird er fast mehr genannt als gestaltet, dient als Umriss, der vom Wissen des Zuschauers gefüllt werden muss, als die Zitierung eines berühmten Namens, die die Entwicklung eines Charakters erspart [...]." It is true that much has been learned about Casanova before he enters the stage in Act II, but this is the kind of information that comes to mind in any audience, whenever the name Casanova resounds. However, he most definitely is involved in the central conflict raging about fidelity and imposes his antisocial convictions rather strongly upon all characters involved.
[107] Rey, *Späte Prosa*, p. 30.
[108] Alewyn, "Casanova," 107-108.
[109] Bergel, *Brandes-Schnitzler-Briefwechsel*, p. 148, S 58.
[110] Rey, *Späte Prosa*, p. 14.
[111] Schmidt, p. 242.
[112] Cf. Chekhov, Pirandello, Maupassant, Beckett, Dürrenmatt, Frisch — to name a few writers.
[113] Hofmannsthal, *Gesammelte Werke in Einzelausgaben. Aufzeichnungen*, ed. Herbert Steiner (Frankfurt am Main: S. Fischer Verlag, 1959), p. 272.
[114] Rey, *Späte Prosa*, p. 48.
[115] *Ibid.*
[116] *Ibid.*, pp. 40-45.
[117] *Ibid.*, p. 191.
[118] See Swales, who seems to have similar objections in his "Kritik an 'Arthur Schnitzler. Die späte Prosa als Gipfel seines Schaffens' — Rey," *Modern Language Review*, 65, No. 1 (January, 1970), 224: "And yet, for all the virtues of this study, one has reservations about many of its conclusions. One wonders firstly if the late prose works are in fact the high-point of Schnitzler's artistic achievements. It could, for example, be argued that none of the stories analyzed approaches the mastery and subtlety of 'Leutnant Gustl' [...]. Indeed, one feels at times that Professor Rey tries too hard to demonstrate the maturity and richness of the late work; he seems, for instance, excessively determined to prove the moral worth of the various characters involved."
[119] Offermanns, p. 110.
[120] Kilian, p. 114.

CHAPTER II

[1] Arthur Schnitzler, *Gesammelte Werke. Die dramatischen Werke*. Zweiter Band (Frankfurt am Main: S. Fischer Verlag, 1962), pp. 845-974. All quotes from this second volume pertaining to the text will hereafter be referred to by page number following the quote.
[2] Robert F. Arnold, "Die Schwestern oder Casanova in Spa," *Das literarische Echo*, 22 (1920), Echo der Bühnen: Wien, 924-26.
[3] Robert F. Arnold, *Die Literatur*, 27 (1924), 173.
[4] *Ibid.*, p. 173: "Sonst fügt sich die 'Komödie der Verführung' ohne weiteres dem Lebenswerk Schnitzlers ein, aber ohne weiteres könnte sie auch fehlen und würde nicht vermisst [...]."
[5] *Ibid.*, p. 173. Arnold's critique had little influence upon the success of the play. According to Urbach (p. 127) it was performed twenty-eight times from 1924-1927.
[6] Liptzin, *Schnitzler*, pp. 233-43.
[7] Urbach, *Kommentar*, p. 195.

8 *Ibid.*
9 Urbach, *Schnitzler* p. 93.
10 *Ibid.*, p. 27.
11 Hartmut Scheible, *Schnitzler.* Rowohlts Monografien, Ed. Kurt Kusenberg (Reinbek bei Hamburg: Rowohlt Taschenbuch Verlag, 1976), pp. 115-16.
12 Offermanns, p. 128.
It is important to emphasize the word "Eros" instead of "erotisch" for its larger meaning, because Schnitzler has made this distinction himself. When he speaks about the secret of human relationships, he writes: "Das Geheimnis liegt einzig im Eros, nicht im Erotischen, der daher als der oberste und weiteste Begriff zu gelten hat." (Schnitzler, "Bemerkungen aus dem Nachlass," *Neue Rundschau*, 1962, 355.)
13 Körner, "Spätwerk," 53-54, 57.
14 Letter to Richard Charmatz, dated January 4, 1913, quoted by Kilian, p. 89. Cf. Körner, who says: "[. . .] dass dieser Dichter, und zwar vor allem als Dramatiker, nach gewissermassen naturwissenschaftlicher Methode verfährt, indem es ihm weniger um die Gestaltung einmaliger Menschenindividuen zu tun ist als um die Findung psychologischer Gesetze, die aus der Begrübelung typischer 'Fälle' sich ihm ergeben." ("Spätwerk," 65).
15 Offermanns relegates him to "eine zweite Schicht mittlerer Figuren" (p. 129), which is debatable. Not only is Ambros one of the three suitors Aurelie has promised to choose from at the night of Prinz Arduin's garden ball, but he also appears in the second act and plays an important part in the third act, as will be shown.
16 Cf. Max-Peter Kammeyer, "Die Dramaturgie von Tod und Liebe im Werk Arthur Schnitzlers," Diss. Wien (1960), pp. 70-71. In terms of time, he does not carefully read Schnitzler's stage directions and thus loses the significance of an entire aspect of the play in his interpretation. The whole play takes place within a period of three months, beginning with May 1, 1914 for Act I. Six weeks (not four!) elapse before the socond act occurs within one day in mid-June; and again six weeks (not two months!) pass, when in the third act most of the major characters meet in Gilleleije, a Danish sea resort, on August 1, 1914. The timing in this play is of crucial importance as it parallels significant developments on the political front. They will be analyzed later in the discussion.
One further comment is in order here with regard to the individual scenes in Act II. According to Kammeyer, the Aurelie-"Szene beansprucht ein Drittel des zweiten Aktes," when in reality only one fifth is devoted to Aurelie and approximately two fifths each to the scenes with Judith/Julia and Elisabeth/Seraphine. This is, of course, no coincidence. It has to do with the intensity of emotions on the one hand, and the importance of all three plots on the other.
Regarding the sea resort of Gilleleije, Georg Brandes in a letter to Schnitzler defines the location of the town for us by mentioning the "Nordküste von Seeland," Bergel, *Brandes-Schnitzler-Briefwechsel*, p. 140.
17 Cf. Bergel, *Brandes-Schnitzler-Briefwechsel*, p. 140.
18 Körner, "Spätwerk," 61. However, Körner overlooks Seraphine, the violinist who is such an independent woman. A child to her is more than just an offspring. It represents responsibility and connects her with the reality of life, an addition to being a channel for her love, which reduces marriage to a position of secondary importance.
19 *Ibid.*, 63.
20 *Ibid.*, 61.
21 *Ibid.*, 65.
22 Offermanns, p. 128. Cf. Swales, who in his critical study of Schnitzler does not concern himself with the late dramatic works of the author for three reasons: (1) "much of his literary output is second-rate in that it succumbs to the world which it seeks to portray and understand" (p. 285); (2) "[. . .] for all their maturity and dramatic importance, none of these works in my view comes anywhere near *Professor Bernhardi* or *Leutnant Gustl* in artistic quality" (p. 281); (3) "[. . .] the intense seriousness of purpose behind these works [. . .] seems to me in part to explain their artistic failure" (p. 281) because this seriousness "[. . .] one would hardly associate with Schnitzler, who has gone down in literary history as the wistful chronicler of the graciousness and charm of Old Austria" (p. 281). I regard these statements appearing toward the end of the book as an unfortunate mistake on the part of an otherwise sincere critic, because they are superficial in their evaluation of Schnitzler's seriousness as an author. Schnitzler never intended his plays to be categorized as "wistful chronicles [. . .] of Old Austria."

23 Offermanns, p. 128.
24 Derré, p. 449.
25 Melchinger, p. 62.
26 Kammeyer, p. 68. Cf. Bergel, *Brandes-Schnitzler-Briefwechsel*, p. 142: "Das Stück hat es ziemlich schwer und wird sich — wie es mit meinen meisten Stücken geht — von meinen allerersten abgesehen — nur allmälig durchsetzen." He wrote this letter two months after the first performance.
27 Kammeyer, pp. 68-69.
28 *Ibid.*, p. 70.
29 *Ibid.*
30 Liptzin, *Schnitzler*, p. 243.
31 *Ibid.*, pp. 233-40.
32 *Ibid.*, pp. 226-27.
33 Schmidt, pp. 316-326.
34 Davis, p. 129.
35 *Ibid.*, pp. 184-189. Whenever necessary, references will be made to this letter.
36 Kilian, p. 20.
37 Schnitzler, *AuB*, p. 250.
38 The possibility of a coincidental title must be ruled out, if we keep in mind how meticulous Schnitzler was in each aspect of his writing, including the selection of titles.
39 Ernst Bux, Wilhelm Schöne, Hans Lamer, Paul Kroh, *Wörterbuch der Antike*, 7th ed. (Stuttgart: Alfred Kröner Verlag, 1966), p. 302.
40 *Ibid.*, p. 363.
41 The same variations of meaning exist in the English language. Yet, the most common title of the play in translation is "Comedy of Seduction." "Seduction," however, is only one aspect of the plot; others involve "enticement" as well as "temptation." In working with the verbs "entice, seduce, tempt," I found the synonym for all three definitions listed as "to lure" which "implies an irresistible and, often, baleful attraction." (Webster's New Collegiate Dictionary based on Webster's New International Dictionary, 2nd ed., Springfield, Mass.: G. & G. Merriam Co., 1959, p. 501.)
42 Urbach, *Schnitzler*, p. 93.
43 In Scene 1 of Act II Aurelie is attended by three men, one after the other: Gysar, Arduin, Max. In Scene 2 of Act II Judith meets Westerhaus, Ambros, Max. In Scene 3 of Act II Seraphine takes care of her father, Ambros, and Max.
44 Cf. footnote 12 above.
The term "Eros" is used here in its etymological definition based on Greek érōs = love, love desire, god of love as in Greek mythology. The name "Eros" is also the basis for Greek erōtikós = sensual love. (Der Grosse Duden in 9 Bänden. Etymologie, vol. 7, p. 143.) See also Duden, *Fremdwörterbuch*, vol. 5, p. 198: "Eros, gr.-lat. nach dem griech. Gott der Liebe: durch Liebe geweckter schöpferischer Urtrieb." Offermanns uses the same interrelationship of the terms "Eros" and "Erotik" in his discussion of the drama. (Cf. Chapter VIII, entitled "Eros und Geschichte — Die zerbrechende Idylle: 'Komödie der Verführung,'" pp. 129, 165f.)
45 Urbach, *Schnitzler*, p. 93.
46 Cf. pp. 890, 897, 910, 928, 929, 973.
47 Körner, "Spätwerk," 63.
48 A series of circumstances may have led to this uneasiness. By the pond Max ominously found a piece of jewelry which his father had made for Aurelie's mother. It was the last piece his father had produced prior to his death in a duel with Aurelie's father. Max had a part in the preparation of the jewelry, for he had designed it and his father worked from these drawings. Now Max becomes acquainted with the daughter of the Merkensteins under sensitive circumstances. Falkenir does not help to clear the atmosphere; in fact, his two comments add to the tension: "Wenn du abergläubisch wärest, Aurelie, so dürftest du die Kette niemals mehr anlegen oder müsstest sie gleich hier in den Teich werfen" (873). Aurelie, as yet fully anchored in the reality of life, does not believe that curses or blessings adhere to things or people. Besides, there is a meeting of minds between Max and Aurelie as she helps him complete the sentence: "[...] als für eine Frau zu sterben, die er geliebt hat" (873). To neutralize the heavy vibrations surrounding the word "blood revenge," Aurelie assures Max: "Ich empfinde kein Grauen vor diesem Schmuck. Und ich werde mich jederzeit freuen, Herr von Reisenberg, Ihnen zu begegnen" (873), which is further negotiated by a dance she grants Max, to comply with Falkenir's wish. However, at the end of Act I, Aurelie is no longer the positive person, centered in her own being. The experience with Falkenir, which led to the cancellation of the

marriage, has produced a state of shock. As she loses self-assurance, she also has doubts about the jewelry. Following Falkenir's earlier advice, she throws the jewelry into the pond. Max's question, "Also doch abergläubisch, Gräfin?" (889), symbolizes other thoughts crossing his mind. He realizes Aurelie needs help at this moment. Their conversation, however, is as ominous as the story about the jewelry. Each of her words contributes more to dark prophecy:

Aurelie:	Schönes Fest...
Max:	... ein märchenhaftes Fest.
Aurelie:	Wie mögen wohl die Märchen ausgehen, die nicht mit Hochzeit enden?
Max:	Sie enden alle mit Hochzeit... Und es gibt Abenteuer zu bestehen auf dem Weg.
Aurelie:	Gefährliche Abenteuer.
Max:	Auch harmlose. Und fröhliche. Am Ende aber unfehlbar kommt die Hochzeit.
Aurelie:	Oder der Tod.
Max:	Ein Märchentod (889).

Max walks with her from the park to her car to bid her farewell, but Aurelie invites him to "eine Spazierfahrt ins Freie" which starts her on the road of adventure.

[49] Müller-Freienfels (p. 87) writes in this regard: "Diese Menschen, deren ganzes Dasein auf das unmittelbare Jetzt und Hier eingestellt ist, die nichts Vergangenes fortführen und nichts Zukünftiges planen wollen, die immer nur für den gegenwärtigen Moment und aus diesem heraus zu leben bemüht sind, richten sich stets ganz nach ihrer jeweiligen Stimmung oder Laune. Auch in deren Wesen liegt das Flüchtige, das zeitlich Begrenzte, das Unmittelbare, auch ihnen fehlen Kontinuität und Dauer."

[50] Cf. Carl E. Schorske, "Politics and the Psyche in fin de siècle Vienna: Schnitzler and Hofmannsthal," *American Historical Review* (1962), 932-35 especially.

[51] Offermanns, p. 139.

[52] *Ibid.*

[53] Cf. Offermanns, p. 169.

[54] *Ibid.*, p. 129.

[55] *Ibid.*, p. 169.

[56] Schnitzler through Ambros points out here ever so gently a psychological as well as spiritual truth: Thoughts are things; thought forms are energy manifesting in words, and words are powerful because they give suggestion to our subconscious mind in the way a computer is programmed. Therefore, the results will be what has been programmed into our subconscious mind. Many times, we may not like the output. Likewise, Judith may not like her life as a "cocotte."
In his book *Jugend in Wien*, p. 275, Schnitzler talks about the name Judith and how she became patterned after Fräulein Nelly.

[57] Offermanns, p. 139.

[58] *Ibid.*

[59] Hartmut Scheible in his Schnitzler monograph (p. 115) reads the drama along similar lines, when he says: "[...] die Komödie der Verführung [...] ist zentriert um Valutenänderungen, die es dem begabten wie korrupten Bankpräsidenten Westerhaus als einzigem gestatten, den Ausbruch der Katastrophe exakt vorherzusagen, ohne dass er indessen den eigenen Ruin abwenden könnte [...]." However, the subject of "Valutenänderungen" and catastrophe of war form only one angle of the triangular constellation discussed in this analysis of the entire play.

[60] William L. Langer, ed., *Encyclopedia of World History* (Boston: Houghton Mifflin Co., rev. ed., 1958), p. 761.

[61] Offermanns, p. 143. Furthermore, there is no evidence in the drama that Westerhaus was an erotic adventurer, especially since Judith's love for him remained unrequited. The fact that Westerhaus did not wear a domino on the night of the festivities, as most other male characters did, is one more proof that he had not planned adventurous activities under the disguise of a domino.

[62] Cf. Barbara W. Tuchman, *The Guns of August* (New York, N.Y.: Dell Publishing Co., Inc., 1962), esp. pp. 91-187.

[63] Langer, pp. 715, 761-63.

[64] André Jolles, *Einfache Formen* (Tübingen: Max Niemeyer Verlag, rpt. 1968), pp. 218-46. Cf. Herbert Seidel in *Kleines Literarisches Lexikon*, vol. 3, Sammlung Dalp (Bern: A. Francke AG Verlag, 1966), pp. 247-49. Also Gero von Wilpert, *Sachwörterbuch der Literatur*, 4th ed. (Stuttgart: Alfred Kröner Verlag, 1964), pp. 408-11.

[65] Jolles, p. 240.
[66] *Ibid.*
[67] *Ibid.*, pp. 241-42.
[68] Cf. pp. 852, 855, 868, 874, 884, 885, 889, 919, 933, 937, 938, 942, 943, 947, 960, 962, 965.
[69] Jolles, p. 244.
[70] *Ibid.*
[71] Cf. pp. 883, 894, 895, 937, 947, 950.
[72] Cf. pp. 868, 874, 884, 885, 889, 919, 933, 938, 942, 943, 947, 960, 965. (See footnote 68).
[73] Melchinger, p. 64.
[74] Offermanns, p. 149.
[75] Schnitzler, *BdSp.*, p. 118.
[76] Cf. Reik, p. 111.
[77] Arthur Schnitzler, "Bemerkungen aus dem Nachlass," *Neue Rundschau* (1962), 348.
[78] Schnitzler, *BdSp.*, p. 83.
[79] Cf. Gerhart Baumann, *Arthur Schnitzler. Die Welt von Gestern eines Dichters von Morgen* (Frankfurt am Main, Bonn: Athenäum Verlag, 1965), p. 21: "Schnitzler weiss um das Verbindende in den Bewusstseinszuständen wie um die Kräfte des kollektiven Unbewussten. Die Bedeutung der Möglichkeiten ermisst er in ganzem Umfang; er durchschaut die Fiktionen und Erfindungen; das Lockende und Bedrohende in ihnen bleibt ihm bewusst wie die 'Komödie der Verführung' zeigt: das Unbegreifbare und dennoch Gegenwärtige der Möglichkeiten."
The ethical challenge is proclaimed: not to hold possibilities for the future less important than facts from the present; and not to judge human beings by their outer accomplishments or failures, but to understand their inner nature.
[80] Cf. Adolf D. Klarmann, "Arthur Schnitzler und wir": "Wir haben es hier letzten Endes mit einem weiteren Aspekt des österreichischen Barockerbes zu tun, nämlich wieder mit einer Art Bewährungsprobe, diesmal der Bewährungsprobe der Liebe, die ein Mann allerdings nur in seltenen Fällen besteht." (*Modern Austrian Literature*, 1, No. 2, 1968, 14.) Falkenir, however, is such a rare case.
[81] Hofmannsthal, *Gedichte und Lyrische Dramen*, ed. Herbert Steiner (Frankfurt am Main: S. Fischer Verlag, 1965), p. 179.
[82] Schnitzler, *BdSp.*, p. 229. Cf. auch Schnitzler, *AuB*, pp. 39, 47. Cf. Baumann, p. 21.
[83] Schnitzler, *AuB*, p. 102.
[84] Andreas Török, "Der Liebestod bei Arthur Schnitzler: Eine Entlehnung von Richard Wagner," *Modern Austrian Literature*, 4, No. 1 (1971), 57.
[85] *Ibid.*, 57-58 with reference to Melchinger, p. 65; Whiton, pp. 180-81; Rey, "Arthur Schnitzler" in *Deutsche Dichter der Moderne*, p. 264.
[86] Török, 58.
[87] *Ibid.*, 58-59.
[88] Richard Wagner, *Der fliegende Holländer*, Illustriertes Textheft No. 8 20 164-66 (Berlin: VEB Deutsche Schallplatten.)
When considering the importance of the oath in the Wagner-Schnitzler comparison, other operas come to mind as well. An oath is required in the marriage arrangement between Lohengrin and Elsa. (*Lohengrin*, Library of Congress Catalog Card No. R63-1388, Nos. 121-25 in the Angel International Series.) When she asks Lohengrin: "Den Namen sag' mir an! . . . Woher die Fahrt? . . . Wie deine Art?" (Act III, Scene 2), Lohengrin has to return to the fortress of Monsalvat, to the Holy Grail. The water symbolism here reflects tranquility when compared to *Der fliegende Holländer*. Tannhäuser, who loves Elisabeth and can only marry her if he wins the singers' contest, forgets his oath of reticence given to Venus in her mountain abode and is cursed away from the Wartburg, his only redemption being a pilgrimage to Rome. However, Schnitzler's romantic tendency is only one aspect of the play to which belongs the "Märchen" idea as well. His concern for political and social issues is predominant.
[89] Blume, p. 44.
[90] Urbach, *Kommentar*, p. 37.
[91] *Ibid.*
[92] Derré, p. 360.
[93] *Ibid.*, p. 378.
[94] Körner, "Spätwerk," 58.
[95] Cf. LoCicero, 16. See also Körner, *Gestalten und Probleme*, p. 94.
[96] Schnitzler, *BdSp.*, p. 98.

⁹⁷ Cf. Müller-Freienfels, pp. 58-59.
⁹⁸ In this respect, a comparison with Senta is possible. She also lived by the sea like Gilda and her mother, and found it easy to follow the Holländer when his ship plowed through the water.
⁹⁹ Offermanns, p. 197.
¹⁰⁰ Cf. Urbach, *Kommentar*, p. 37.
¹⁰¹ Polsterer, see "Einzelanalyse über Aurelie" in the appendix.
¹⁰² Körner, "Spätwerk," 62. Furthermore, to compare her dual personality on the surface with the Jewish "Tagschreiber Fliederbusch" (61) is truly an unfortunate error, because Aurelie is of more complex nature in her struggle for identity. Whereas for Aurelie the relativity of values in pre-war Austrian society becomes a reason for suffering, longing, and flight into the world of illusions, Fliederbusch displays a new merry indifference to this world of decaying norms, using the political and social changes pragmatically to his own advantage.
¹⁰³ LoCicero, 16.
¹⁰⁴ Schnitzler, "Bemerkungen aus dem Nachlass," *Neue Rundschau* (1962), 353: "Wer im Stich lässt, verleugnet; er muss es tun, um zu entschuldigen, dass er im Stich liess. Wer verleumdet, verleugnet: denn nur durch Verleumdung vermag er sein Verleugnen zu rechtfertigen. Und wer verleumdet, der hat auch schon verraten."
Cf. also Schnitzler, *BdSp*., p. 77: "Mancher pflegt den Abfall von einem Freund, einer Geliebten, einer übernommenen Pflicht mit dem Gebot der Treue gegen sich selbst zu entschuldigen – was oft genug nichts anderes bedeutet, als die bequemste und feigste Art der Selbsttäuschung. Denn wie wenige kennen die Gesetze ihrer eigenen Entwicklung so genau, dass sie entscheiden könnten, ob sie mit solcher Treulosigkeit gegen einen Menschen oder eine Sache nicht zugleich die schlimmste gegen sich selbst begangen haben?"
¹⁰⁵ Schnitzler, *BdSp*., p. 86.
¹⁰⁶ Arthur Henkel and Albrecht Schöne, *Emblemata. Handbuch zur Sinnbildkunst des XVI. und XVII. Jahrhunderts* (Stuttgart: J. B. Metzlersche Verlagsbuchhandlung, 1967), p. 101.
¹⁰⁷ *Webster's New Collegiate Dictionary*, p. 501. Seduce = leading astray from rectitude, propriety or duty by overcoming one's scruples.
¹⁰⁸ *Ibid.*
¹⁰⁹ Cf. Körner, "Spätwerk," 63: "Und dieser unwiderstehliche Max pflückt die drei Jungfrauenblüten eine nach der anderen. Aber beileibe nicht, weil er ein dämonischer Verführer ist, dem alle Frauen zufallen müssen. Sein Teil ist ein im Grunde klägliches Glück. Er wird genommen, er nimmt nicht; er darf diese Mädchen geniessen, aber er besitzt sie nicht."
¹¹⁰ Cf. Melchinger, p. 85 with reference to "das Spielbewusstsein der Frau."
¹¹¹ Schnitzler, *BdSp.*, pp. 84-85.
¹¹² Müller-Freienfels, p. 36.
¹¹³ Cf. Schnitzler, *BdSp*., p. 87.
¹¹⁴ Körner, "Spätwerk," 56.
¹¹⁵ Herbert Lederer, "The Problem of Ethics in the Works of Arthur Schnitzler," Diss. Chicago (1953), p. 151.
¹¹⁶ Stockholm: Bermann-Fischer Verlag, 1939.
¹¹⁷ "Aus dem Nachlass von Arthur Schnitzler," *Neue Rundschau* (1932), 678-81.
¹¹⁸ Schnitzler defended himself strongly: "Was soll mir das Geschwätz? Ich habe mich in meinem Leben nicht um die Politik gekümmert! Was hilft's dir, mein Freund? Sie kümmert sich um dich in jedem Augenblick deines Lebens" (*BdSp*., p. 47).
¹¹⁹ Schnitzler, "Aufzeichnungen aus der Kriegszeit," *Neue Rundschau* (1932), 679.
¹²⁰ *Ibid.*, previously published in *Über Krieg und Frieden*, pp. 14-15.
¹²¹ Schnitzler, *BdSp.*, pp. 165-66. The subsequent page deals with the injustices as a result of war.
¹²² Hofmannsthal, *Aufzeichnungen*, p. 306.
¹²³ Schnitzler, letter of November 3, 1924, to Jakob Wassermann, printed in "Briefe," *Neue Rundschau*, 68 (1957), 98-99.
¹²⁴ Schnitzler, letter of July 11, 1927, to Körner, printed in Davis, p. 186. Cf. Kammeyer, p. 68. He agrees with Körner ("Spätwerk," 54). Cf. Blume, who maintains that "die Grenzscheide einer neuen Zeit war für ihn unüberschreitbar; er blieb, wo er immer gewesen war, in den Bezirken des Verfalls" (p. 4).
¹²⁵ Schnitzler, *BdSp.*, pp. 212-13.
¹²⁶ Offermanns, p. 178.
¹²⁷ LoCicero, 17.
¹²⁸ *Ibid.*, 18.

CHAPTER III

1. Urbach, *Kommentar*, p. 195.
2. Bergel, *Brandes-Schnitzler-Briefwechsel*, pp. 142-143. Letter dated December 14, 1924.
3. Arthur Schnitzler, *Gesammelte Werke. Die dramatischen Werke*, Zweiter Band (Frankfurt am Main: S. Fischer Verlag, 1962), pp. 739-843. All quotes from this second volume pertaining to the text will herafter be referred to by page number following the quote.
4. Cf. DW II, 1038; also Urbach, *Kommentar*, p. 195.
5. Urbach, *Schnitzler*, p. 127.
6. Körner, "Spätwerk," 82.
7. Harold D. Dickerson, Jr., "Water and Vision as Mystical Elements in Schnitzler's 'Der Gang zum Weiher'," *Modern Austrian Literature*, 4, No. 3 (1971), 24.
8. Körner, "Spätwerk," 70.
9. *Ibid.*, 83.
10. Liptzin, *Schnitzler*, p. 260.
11. Derré, p. 452.
12. *Ibid.*
13. Swales, *Critical Study*, p. 45.
14. Davis, p. 142.
15. Swales, *Critical Study*, pp. 45-46.
16. Dickerson, 24-36.
17. *Ibid.*, 25. Cf. Davis, p. 138: "This pool is mysterious and symbolically treated."
18. Juan Eduardo Cirlot, *A Dictionary of Symbols*, transl. Jack Sage (New York: Philosophical Library, 1962), p. 345.
19. *Ibid.*
20. "Natürlich ein Phallussymbol," determines Körner, "Spätwerk," 69 (footnote). Anselma does not go that far. She relates "ungefüger Block" to "Opferstein," which places its existence back in ancient times, prior to Christianity. Mayenau does not share his sister's view. For him it is a stone like a thousand others, standing at that particular spot by mere chance (DW II, 748).
21. Urbach, *Kommentar*, p. 37.
22. Liptzin, *Schnitzler*, p. 10.
23. Arnold Whittick, *Symbols — Signs and Their Meaning and Uses in Design* (London: Leonard Hill, 1971), p. 348: "Cleansing by water appears to have been a purification rite with many religions before Christianity, as it was with the Jews. In Christianity the symbolism of water has survived chiefly in the rite of baptism. Its significance appears to cover purification, regeneration or rebirth."
24. Lore B. Foltin, "The Meaning of Death in Schnitzler's Work," *Studies in Arthur Schnitzler*, eds. Herbert W. Reichert and Hermann Salinger (Chapel Hill: The University of North Carolina Press, 1963), p. 39.
25. Dickerson, 30. "Mystic awareness" is neither apparent to the senses nor obvious to the intelligence; it is spiritual insight, intuition. Cf. LoCicero, 18.
26. It is important to pay attention to the name symbolism related to Ungnad, which means "without mercy." He is treated with compassion by Mayenau, Sylvester and everyone he comes in contact with, but Ungnad does not have compassion for himself nor for others. He is ill adjusted and therefore incapable of overcoming.
27. The idea of separation in connection with water symbolism has also been mentioned by Whittick (p. 348), who points out that "water has also been considered symbolically with the significance of separation, because rivers and seas are natural barriers."
28. Kammeyer, pp. 104-05.
29. Cf. pp. 99f. of this study for a more detailed discussion of this important concept in Schnitzler's late dramatic work.
30. Rey, "Schnitzler," p. 253.
31. Richard Specht, *Arthur Schnitzler. Der Dichter und sein Werk. Eine Studie* (Berlin: S. Fischer Verlag, 1922), p. 153.
32. Seidlin, *Schnitzler-Brahm-Briefwechsel*, p. 28.
33. Cf. Herta Singer, "Zeit und Gesellschaft im Werk Arthur Schnitzlers," Diss. Wien (1948), p. 22.

34 Rey, "Schnitzler," p. 256.
35 Herbert Cysarz, "Das Imaginäre in der Dichtung Arthur Schnitzlers," *Journal of the International Arthur Schnitzler Research Association*, NS. 1, III (1968), 8.
36 Baumann, *Schnitzler*, p. 30.
37 Körner, *Gestalten und Probleme*, p. 171. "Okkultismen" relates to surrealism in the terminology used by Imboden.
Cf. Specht, *Schnitzler*, p. 152.
38 Schnitzler, *AuB*, p. 73.
39 Michael Imboden, *Die surreale Komponente im erzählenden Werk Arthur Schnitzlers* (Bern, Frankfurt am Main: Verlag Herbert Lang & Cie AG, 1971).
40 Maurice Nadeau, *Geschichte des Surrealismus*, deutsche Übersetzung von Karl Heinz Laier, rde. Bd. 240/41 (Reinbek b. Hamburg, 1965), 8. Quoted by Imboden, p. 9.
41 Imboden, p. 9.
42 *Ibid.*, p. 11.
43 Dickerson, 30.
44 *Ibid.*
45 Cirlot, p. 95.
46 Imboden, p. 19.
47 Cirlot, p. 95.
48 *Ibid.*, p. 326.
49 Arthur Schnitzler, "Bemerkungen aus dem Nachlass," *Neue Rundschau*, 3 (1962), 351.
50 Schnitzler, *AuB*, p. 278.
51 *Ibid.*
52 *Ibid.*
53 Whittick, p. 329.
54 Derré, p. 372.
55 Davis, p. 141.
56 Körner, "Spätwerk," 70.
57 *Ibid.*
58 Schnitzler, letter to Körner, dated July 11, 1927, quoted by Davis, p. 185.
59 *Ibid.*
60 *Ibid.*, p. 187.
61 Sol Liptzin, "The Genesis of Schnitzler's 'Der einsame Weg'," *The Journal of English-Germanic Philology*, 30 (1931), 392-93.
62 Schnitzler, letter to Körner, quoted by Davis, p. 187.
63 Derré, p. 452.
64 Swales, *Critical Study*, p. 53.
65 Franz Grillparzer, *Ein Bruderzwist in Habsburg* in *Sämtliche Werke*. Historisch-kritische Gesamtausgabe, Part 1, vol. 6, ed. August Sauer (Wien: Verlag von Anton Schroll & Co., 1927), 182-83.
66 Rey, "Schnitzler," p. 251.
67 Schnitzler, *BdSp*, p. 139.
68 Cf. Swales, *Critical Study*, p. 45.
69 We recall that Flaminia already used the term "Geck" to refer to Casanova (DW II, 666), and Andrea uses the same word for him (p. 670).
70 Bergel, *Brandes-Schnitzler-Briefwechsel*, p. 143.
71 *Ibid.*
72 Wassermann, "Erinnerungen," 12.
73 *Ibid.*
74 Freud to Schnitzler, letter dated May 14, 1912, *Neue Rundschau*, 1 (1955), 96.
75 *Ibid.*, 95.
76 Schnitzler, *BdSp.*, p. 66.
77 Friedrich Wilhelm Kaufmann, "Zur Frage der Wertung in Schnitzlers Werk," *PMLA*, 48 (March 1933), 215.
78 Körner, "Spätwerk," 56.
79 Rey, "Schnitzler," p. 254.
80 Lederer, p. 76.
81 Swales, *Critical Study*, pp. 45-46.
82 Liptzin, *Schnitzler*, p. 244.

83 Swales, *Critical Study*, p. 46.
84 Schnitzler, *BdSp.* p. 86.
85 Cf. also Foltin, 42.
86 Polsterer, Section 3.3. She continues that "[...] die diversen süssen Mädels aus verschiedenen Herren Länder dagegen Namen tragen wie Annie, Anita, Annina, Annette, Ninette [...]. Auch wissen wir ja aus verschiedenen Aussprüchen seiner Figuren, dass der Dichter sich wohl über die Bedeutung der Namen und ihrer Verbreitung Gedanken machte."
87 Schmidt, p. 310.
88 *Ibid.*, p. 316.
89 Liptzin, *Schnitzler*, p. 269.
90 Boner, p. 38. Cf. also Schmidt, p. 314.
91 Polsterer, Section 3.31 entitled "Semasiologische Deutung."
92 Wolfdietrich Rasch, "Tanz als Lebenssymbol im Drama um 1900," in: *Zur deutschen Literatur seit der Jahrhundertwende* (Stuttgart: J. B. Metzlersche Verlagsbuchhandlung, 1967), p. 64.
93 *Ibid.*
94 *Ibid.*, p. 77.
95 *Ibid.*
96 Körner, "Spätwerk," 62.
97 Schmidt, p. 314.
98 Liptzin, *Schnitzler*, p. 32. Cf. also p. 4.
99 Otto P. Schinnerer, "The Literary Apprenticeship of Arthur Schnitzler," *Germanic Review*, 1 (1930), 67.
100 Körner, "Spätwerk," 71.
101 Cf. pp. 777, 778, 784, 785, 796.
102 Cirlot, p. 328.
103 Quoted by Davis, pp. 186, 189.
104 Rey, "Schnitzler," p. 253. In Judeo-Christian theology, this is called the "Brotherhood of Man."
105 *Ibid.*, p. 252.
106 *Ibid.*, pp. 252-53.
107 Cf. pp. 860, 864, 878, 971.
108 Lilac in Schnitzler's work dates back to *Liebelei* (1896).
109 Alfred Apsler, "A Sociological View of Arthur Schnitzler," *Germanic Review*, 18 (1943), 105.
110 Davis, pp. 145-46.
111 Cf. pp. 755, 766, 767, 769, 770, 771, 772, 773, 782, 788, 789, 791, 792, 825.
112 Müller-Freienfels, p. 97.
113 *Ibid.*, p. 101.
114 Blume, p. 34.
115 *Ibid.*
116 Schnitzler's later prose work entitled *Casanovas Heimfahrt* (1918) catches up with the old adventurer and pursues him into death.
117 Schnitzler, "Gedanken über Kunst. Aus dem Nachlass," *Neue Rundschau*, 43 (1932), 37.
118 Schnitzler, letter to Körner, quoted by Davis, dated July 11, 1927.
119 Imboden, p. 125.
120 LoCicero, 18.
121 Imboden, pp. 124-25.
122 Rey, Schnitzler. *Späte Prosa*, p. 18. Cf. Kammeyer's statement (p. 127 footnote 93) regarding Schnitzler and the first World War which shows a rather hasty assessment: "Die geistige Auseinandersetzung mit dem ersten Weltkrieg hat Schnitzler aus seinem dramatischen Schaffen ausgeschlossen; es existieren jedoch essayistische Aufzeichnungen aus seinem Nachlass [...]."
123 Cf. Rey, "Schnitzler," p. 262.
124 Foltin, 36.
125 Liptzin, *Schnitzler*, pp. 47-48. Cf. also Boner, p. 8: "Es sucht nach dem internen Gleichgewicht des Menschen, nach dem geistigen Jenseits der materiellen Aktionen und Gegenaktionen."

CHAPTER IV

1. Arthur Schnitzler, *Gesammelte Werke. Die dramatischen Werke*, Zweiter Band (Frankfurt am Main: S. Fischer Verlag, 1962), pp. 975-1034, 1042. All quotes from this second volume pertaining to the text will hereafter be referred to by page number following the quote.
2. Urbach, *Kommentar*, p. 197.
3. Arthur Schnitzler, *Tagebücher*, Mappe 126-127. Cf. Gerhard Neumann und Jutta Müller, *Der Nachlass Arthur Schnitzlers* (München: Wilhelm Fink Verlag, 1969), p. 64.
4. Arthur Schnitzler, quoted by Urbach, *Kommentar*, pp. 196-97.
5. Hartmut Scheible, *Arthur Schnitzler in Selbstzeugnissen*. Rowohlts Monographien, Ed. Kurt Kusenberg (Reinbek bei Hamburg: Rowohlt Taschenbuch Verlag GmbH, 1976), p. 127.
6. *Ibid*. With regard to Chekhov, Scheible reminds his readers that Schnitzler himself entered a note in his diary on February 10, 1929: "Die Russen könnten es spielen."
7. Cf. Gerhart Baumann,"Arthur Schnitzler: Die Tagebücher. Vergangene Gegenwart — Gegenwärtige Vergangenheit," *Modern Austrian Literature*, 10, Nos. 3/4 (1977), 159.
8. Liptzin, *Schnitzler*, p. 253.
9. Robert F. Arnold, *Die Literatur* 32, V (1930), 290: "Mag die betreffende Erörterung sich auch etwas lang gestalten, sie liegt auf so hoher Ebene, dass wir ihrer nicht entraten möchten und den erotischen Reigen gerne durch christliche und durch weltliche Resignation ergänzt sehen. Überraschungen freilich hat das anmutige Spiel nicht zu bieten, es wäre denn die, dass die Hand seines Schöpfers noch immer mit alter Leichtigkeit und Sicherheit gestaltet und lenkt."
10. Hans Thyriot, *Die Literatur* 33, IX (1931), 514.
11. *Ibid*.
12. Scheible, p. 127.
13. Schnitzler's letter dated July 4, 901 [sic], published in *Wort und Wahrheit*, 13 (1958), 288.
14. Derré, p. 408. Cf. also A. E. Zucker, "Criticism to 'Im Spiel der Sommerlüfte'," *Germanic Review*, 6 (1931), 92. He underlines "the hidden depth of the souls of (Schnitzler's) characters" which allow for an optimistic conclusion of the play.
15. Derré, p. 408.
16. *Ibid*., pp. 408-409.
17. *Ibid*., p. 409.
18. Cf. also Baumann, "Tagebücher," 157.
19. Körner, "Spätwerk," 53-83; 153-163.
20. Zucker, 93.
21. Swales, *Critical Study*, p. 75.
22. *Ibid*.
23. Offermanns, p. 128.
24. Müller-Freienfels, p. 191.
25. *Ibid*., p. 192.
26. Liptzin, *Schnitzler*, p. 251.
27. Urbach, *Kommentar*, p. 38.
28. *Ibid*.
29. *Ibid*.
30. Derré, p. 409.
31. Cf. Schnitzler, *AuB*, pp. 51, 84, 85, 254-266.
32. Schmidt, p. 255.
33. Johann Wolfgang von Goethe, *Goethes Werke. Hamburger Ausgabe in 14 Bänden, Dramatische Dichtungen*, Dramen I, Band 3, 8th ed., ed. Erich Trunz (Hamburg: Christian Wegner Verlag, 1967), Vers 2724, p. 88.
34. According to Urbach, Richard Beer-Hofmann also worked with this motto for his *Novellen* (*Kommentar*, p. 197).
35. *Faust I*, Vers 2723, p. 88.
36. *Ibid*., Vers 308, p. 17.
37. At the end of Part I, when Gretchen is dismissed by Mephistopheles with a rude "Sie ist gerichtet!", this other reality appears in the "Stimme von oben: Ist gerettet!" (Part I, 4611), thereby indicating that the supernatural, "heavenly" world may at any time assert its judgment in the empirical world of human affairs.

[38] Urbach, *Schnitzler*, p. 94.
[39] *Ibid.*
[40] Liptzin, *Schnitzler*, p. 253.
[41] Müller-Freienfels, p. 81.
[42] *Ibid.*
[43] Blume, p. 32.
[44] Schnitzler, *BdSp.*, p. 117.
[45] Liptzin, *Schnitzler*, p. 211.
[46] Rey, *Späte Prosa*, p. 17.
[47] Whiton, p. 141.
[48] Müller-Freienfels, p. 139.
[49] *Ibid.*
[50] Anna Stroka, "Arthur Schnitzlers Tragikomödien," *Acta Universitatis Wratislaviensis*, No. 128, *Germanica Wratislaviensia*, XIV (1971), 66.
[51] Cf. also Davis, p. 185.
[52] Rey, *Späte Prosa*, p. 17.
[53] Davis, p. 153.
[54] *Ibid.*, p. 152.
[55] Müller-Freienfels, p. 190.
[56] Lederer, "The Problem of Ethics," p. 195.
[57] Schnitzler, "Ein Zwischenkapitel über Begebungen und Seelenzustände," in *AuB*, p. 158.
[58] Schnitzler, "Der Geist im Wort," in *AuB*, p. 142; cf. also p. 146.
[59] Davis, p. 153.
[60] Schnitzler, "Der Geist im Wort," *AuB*, p. 142.
[61] Boner, p. 25: "Die Müdigkeit des Impressionismus wird durch einen neuen stosskräftigen Mut überwunden. Schnitzler hat diesem Mut durch das unerbittliche Zu-Ende-Denken des 'Reigens' einen Grundstein gesetzt und ihm eine Spitze gemeisselt durch das Gespräch in 'Im Spiel der Sommerlüfte,' in dem die menschliche Maskierung es mit sich bringt, dass der Kaplan den heroischen Glauben der Frau und Josefa den heroischen Zweifel des Mannes ausspricht. Der Weg ist weit vom frühen Impressionismus bis zu diesem Dialog, in dem der Mut sich zum verzweifelten Wort steigert: 'Auch Schwäche ist Schuld, Schwäche ganz besonders'."
[62] The train or necessity to reach it in time is mentioned many times: Cf. pp. 978, 983, 984, 985, 995, 997, 1000, 1001, 1007, 1008, 1011, 1027.
[63] The name "Innsbruck" is mentioned most frequently by Gusti herself, but almost as often by Eduard and Felix and the rest of the family. Cf. pp. 978, 985, 990, 993, 994, 997, 1004, 1005, 1006, 1022, 1023, 1026, 1027, 1032.
[64] Uwe Rosenbaum, "Die Gestalten des Schauspielers auf dem deutschen Theater des 19. Jahrhunderts mit der besonderen Berücksichtigung der dramatischen Werke von Hermann Bahr, Arthur Schnitzler und Heinrich Mann," Diss. Köln (1971), p. 84.
[65] Rosenbaum concludes: "Die Flucht aus der Wirklichkeit in die Welt des Theaters ist die Flucht vor der Lüge, vor dem Schein in neue Lüge, neuen Schein" (p. 219) which does not apply to Schnitzler's last drama, either. Gusti is serious about her career. Perhaps she is able to reverse the opinion commonly held about the theater. Rosenbaum summarizes one such opinion as follows: "Der schlechte Schauspieler, der Komödiant, der Gaukler ist zum 'Symbol' der Zeit geworden" (p. 219).
[66] Schnitzler had dealt with this theme on previous occasions, last in *Das weite Land* (1910), where the center of dramatic interest gradually shifted to the new theme, namely, the conflict of generations: age giving way to youth. Cf. Liptzin, p. 172: "Mrs. Meinhold-Aigner has no [...] illusions. She has frankly capitulated to the younger generation, and she does not feel obliged to maintain even a semblance of authority over her Otto. She reminds Genia that sons, also, grow up to be men." Cf. Singer, p. 139.
[67] Cf. pp. 979, 990, 995, 996, 1006, 1028, 1032.
[68] Cf. pp. 990, 995, 1006, 1028.
[69] Cf. pp. 998, 1000, 1007, 1008, 1028.
[70] Cf. pp. 976, 977, 981, 982, 984, 995, 996, 1004, 1006, 1007, 1008, 1011, 1013, 1017, 1018, 1028, 1031, 1032, 1034.
[71] Cirlot, p. 353.
[72] *Ibid.*
[73] *Ibid.*, p. 259.

74 *Ibid.*
75 *Ibid.*, p. 218.
76 *Ibid.*
77 *Ibid.*, p. 324.
78 *Ibid.*, p. 78. Cf. also *Wörterbuch der Antike* 7th ed. (Stuttgart: Alfred Kröner Verlag, 1966), p. 124: "Gott des Weines und des drängenden Lebens in der Natur, deren zeugende Kraft in ihm Gestalt gewinnt."
79 Cirlot, p. 208.
80 Davis, p. 174.
81 *Ibid.*, p. 175.
82 Schnitzler, *Jugend in Wien*, p. 155.
83 Cf. pp. 690, 721, 732.
84 Stroka, 73.
85 Cf. pp. 745, 746, 751, 759, 761, 773, 775, 777, 778, 788, 794, 803, 810, 817, 827, 828.
86 Schnitzler, *AuB*, p. 257.
87 Karl Joël, *Seele und Welt. Versuch einer organischen Auffassung* (Jena: Eugen Diederichs, 1912), p. 123.
88 *Ibid.*, p. 121.
89 Cf. Richard Alewyn, with regard to Hofmannsthal: "Der junge Hofmannsthal schon ist tief bewegt von der Erfahrung, dass die Seele keinen Grund hat und keine Grenze. Wir sind 'nicht mehr als ein Taubenschlag,' ein 'Spiel von jedem Druck der Luft,' wie die jungen Wiener gerne aus dem 'Faust' zitieren. Es ist diese Beschaffenheit, die es ihnen schwer macht, gegenüber dem unendlichen Andrang der Dinge die Identität der Person zu behaupten, es ist aber gerade auch diese Beschaffenheit, die Hofmannsthal zum Dichter macht. Denn sie erlaubt ihm jenes mystische Kommunizieren mit dem Kern aller Dinge, das diesen ermöglicht, aus dem Dichter mit seiner Stimme zu sprechen." (*Über Hugo von Hofmannsthal,* 2nd ed. (Göttingen: Vandenhoeck & Ruprecht, 1958/1960, p. 8).

SELECTED BIBLIOGRAPHY

1) Primary Literature

Schnitzler, Arthur. *Buch der Sprüche und Bedenken. Aphorismen und Fragmente.* Wien: Phaidon-Verlag, 1927.

—————. *Gesammelte Werke. Aphorismen und Betrachtungen.* Ed. Robert O. Weiss. Frankfurt am Main: S. Fischer Verlag, 1967.

—————. *Gesammelte Werke. Die dramatischen Werke.* 2 vols. Frankfurt am Main: S. Fischer Verlag, 1962.

—————. *Gesammelte Werke. Die erzählenden Schriften.* 2 vols. Frankfurt am Main: S. Fischer Verlag, 1961.

—————. *Entworfenes und Verworfenes. Aus dem Nachlass.* Ed. Reinhard Urbach. Frankfurt am Main: S. Fischer Verlag, 1977.

—————. *Jugend in Wien. Eine Autobiographie.* Eds. Therese Nickl and Heinrich Schnitzler. Wien-München-Zürich: Verlag Fritz Molden, 1968.

—————. *Über Krieg und Frieden.* Stockholm: Bermann-Fischer Verlag, 1939.

—————. "Aufzeichnungen aus der Kriegszeit. Aus dem Nachlass von Arthur Schnitzler." *Neue Rundschau,* 43 (1932), 678-681.

—————. "Bemerkungen. Aus dem Nachlass." *Neue Rundschau*, 73, Nos. 2/3 (1962), 347-357.

—————. "Gedanken über Kunst. Aus dem Nachlass." *Neue Rundschau*, 43 (1932), 37-39.

—————. "Kritisches. Aus dem Nachlass." *Neue Rundschau*, 73, Nos. 2/3 (1962), 203-228.

2) Correspondence

Schnitzler, Arthur and Otto Brahm. *Der Briefwechsel Arthur Schnitzler-Otto Brahm. Schriften der Gesellschaft für Theatergeschichte* 57. Ed. Oskar Seidlin. Berlin: Selbstverlag der Gesellschaft für Theatergeschichte, 1953.

———————— and Georg Brandes.	*Georg Brandes und Arthur Schnitzler. Ein Briefwechsel.* Ed. Kurt Bergel. Bern: Francke Verlag, 1956.
———————— and Sigmund Freud.	"Briefe an Arthur Schnitzler," *Neue Rundschau*, 66, No. 1 (1955), 95-106.
———————— and Dr. Hans Henning.	"Briefe," *Neue Rundschau*, 68 (1957), 88-101.
———————— and Hugo von Hofmannsthal.	*Hugo von Hofmannsthal-Arthur Schnitzler. Briefwechsel.* Eds. Therese Nickl and Heinrich Schnitzler. Frankfurt am Main: S. Fischer Verlag, 1964.
———————— and Josef Körner.	"Briefe an Josef Körner," Ed. Reinhard Urbach, *Literatur und Kritik*, 12 (1967), 79-87.
———————— and Rainer Maria Rilke.	"Rainer Maria Rilke und Arthur Schnitzler. Ihr Briefwechsel. Mit Anmerkungen versehen und veröffentlicht von Heinrich Schnitzler," *Wort und Wahrheit*, 13 (1958), 283-298.
———————— and Jakob Wassermann.	"Briefe," *Neue Rundschau*, 68 (1957), 88-101.

3) *Bibliographical Material*

Allen, Richard H.	*An Annotated Arthur Schnitzler Bibliography. Editions and Criticism in German, French, and English 1879-1965.* Chapel Hill: The University of North Carolina Press, 1966.
Berlin, Jeffrey B.	"Arthur Schnitzler: A Bibliography of Criticism, 1965-1971," *Modern Austrian Literature*, 4, No. 4 (1971), 7-20.
————————.	"Arthur Schnitzler: A Bibliography," *Modern Austrian Literature*, 6, Nos. 1/2 (1973), 81-122.
————————.	"Arthur Schnitzler Bibliography for 1973-1974," *Modern Austrian Literature*, 7, Nos. 1/2 (1974), 174-191.
————————.	"Arthur Schnitzler Bibliography for 1974-1975," *Modern Austrian Literature*, 8, Nos. 3/4 (1975), 248-265.
————————.	"Arthur Schnitzler Bibliography for 1975-1976," *Modern Austrian Literature*, 9, No. 2 (1976), 63-72.
————————.	"Arthur Schnitzler Bibliography for 1976-1977," *Modern Austrian Literature*, 10, Nos. 3/4 (1977), 335-339.
Neumann, Gerhard and Jutta Müller.	*Der Nachlass Arthur Schnitzlers. Verzeichnis des im Schnitzler-Archiv der Universität Freiburg i. Br. befindlichen Materials.*

Mit einem Vorwort von Gerhart Baumann und einem Anhang von Heinrich Schnitzler. Verzeichnis des in Wien vorhandenen Nachlassmaterials. München: Wilhelm Fink Verlag, 1969.

4) Secondary Literature

Alewyn, Richard. "Casanova," *Neue Rundschau* (1959), 100-116.

―――――. "Nachwort," *Liebelei-Reigen*. Frankfurt am Main: Fischer Bücherei, 1960, 155-160.

―――――. *Über Hugo von Hofmannsthal*. Göttingen: Vandenhoeck & Ruprecht, 1958; 1960.

Apsler, Alfred. "A Sociological View of Arthur Schnitzler," *Germanic Review*, 18, No. 2 (1943), 90-106.

Arnold, Robert F. " 'Komödie der Verführung.' In Drei Akten. Von Arthur Schnitzler. (Uraufführung im Burgtheater am 11. Oktober 1924)," *Die Literatur*, 27 (1924), 173.

―――――. " 'Im Spiel der Sommerlüfte.' In drei Aufzügen. Von Arthur Schnitzler. (Uraufführung im Deutschen Volkstheater am 21. Dezember 1929)," *Die Literatur*, 32 (1930), 290.

Aspetsberger, Friedbert. " 'Drei Akte in einem.' Zum Formtyp von Schnitzlers Dramen," *Zeitschrift für deutsche Philologie*, 85, No. 2 (1966), 285-308.

Baumann, Gerhart. *Arthur Schnitzler. Die Welt von Gestern eines Dichters von Morgen*. Frankfurt am Main-Bonn: Athenäum Verlag, 1965.

―――――. "Arthur Schnitzler: Die Tagebücher. Vergangene Gegenwart – Gegenwärtige Vergangenheit," *Modern Austrian Literature*, 10, Nos. 3/4 (1977), 143-162.

Beharriell, Frederick J. "Arthur Schnitzler's Range of Theme," *Monatshefte*, 43, No. 7 (1951), 301-311.

Blume, Bernhard. *Das Weltbild Arthur Schnitzlers*. Stuttgart: Buchdruckerei Knöller GmbH., 1936.

Boner, Georgette. *Arthur Schnitzlers Frauengestalten*. Diss. Universität Basel. Zürich: Winterthur Buchdruck, 1930.

Burger, Heinz Otto. "Dasein heisst eine Rolle spielen," *Germanisch-Romanische Monatsschrift*, N.F. 11, No. 4 (1961), 365-379.

Bux, Ernst und Wilhelm Schöne. *Wörterbuch der Antike*, 7th ed. Stuttgart: Alfred Kröner Verlag, 1966.

Cirlot, Juan Eduardo.	*A Dictionary of Symbols.* Transl. Jack Sage. New York: Philosophical Library, 1962.
Cysarz, Herbert.	"Alt-Österreichs letzte Dichtung (1890-1914). Strukturen und Typen," *Preussische Jahrbücher,* 214 (1928), 32-51.
------------.	"Das Imaginäre in der Dichtung Arthur Schnitzlers," *Wissenschaft und Weltbild,* 13 (1960), 102-112. (Rpt. in: *Journal of the International Arthur Schnitzler Research Association,* N.S. 1, iii, 1968, 7-17.)
Davis, Evan B.	"Moral Problems in the Works of Arthur Schnitzler," Diss. University of Pennsylvania, 1950.
DeLay, Brigitte Anne.	"The Impact of Triangularity in Selected Prose Works by Arthur Schnitzler," Diss. University of California Riverside, 1977.
Derré, Françoise.	*L'œuvre d'Arthur Schnitzler. Imagerie viennoise et problèmes humains.* Paris: Librairie Marcel Didier, 1966.
Dickerson, Harold D. Jr.	"Water and Vision as Mystical Elements in Schnitzler's 'Der Gang zum Weiher'," *Modern Austrian Literature,* 4, No. 3 (1971), 24-36.
Foltin, Lore.	"The Meaning of Death in Schnitzler's Work," in: *Studies in Arthur Schnitzler.* Eds. Herbert W. Reichert and Hermann Salinger. Chapel Hill: The University of North Carolina Press, 1963, pp. 35-44.
Friedrichsmeyer, Erhard.	"Der Augenblick bei Schnitzler," *Germanisch-Romanische Monatsschrift,* 16, No. 1 (1966), 52-64.
Goethe, Johann Wolfgang von.	*Goethes Werke. Hamburger Ausgabe in 14 Bänden. Dramatische Dichtungen III.* Ed. Erich Trunz. Hamburg: Christian Wegner Verlag, 1967.
Green, Jon D.	"The Impact of Musical Theme and Structure on the Meaning and Dramatic Unity of Selected Works by Arthur Schnitzler," Diss. Syracuse University, 1972.
Grillparzer, Franz.	*Sämtliche Werke. Historisch-kritische Gesamtausgabe.* Part 1, vol. 6. Ed. August Sauer. Wien: Verlag von Anton Schroll & Co., 1927.
Haida, Peter.	"Arthur Schnitzler," in: *Komödie um 1900. Wandlungen des Gattungsschemas von Hauptmann bis Sternheim.* München: Wilhelm Fink Verlag, 1973, pp. 75-91.
Hausner, Harry H.	"Die Beziehungen zwischen Arthur Schnitzler und Sigmund Freud," *Modern Austrian Literature,* 3, No. 2 (1970), 48-61.

Henkel, Arthur und Albrecht Schöne. *Emblemata. Handbuch zur Sinnbildkunst des XVI. und XVII. Jahrhunderts.* Stuttgart: J. B. Metzlersche Verlagsbuchhandlung, 1967.

Hofmannsthal, Hugo von. *Gesammelte Werke in Einzelausgaben. Aufzeichnungen.* Ed. Herbert Steiner. Frankfurt am Main: S. Fischer Verlag, 1959.

Holl, Karl. *Geschichte des deutschen Lustspiels.* Darmstadt: Wissenschaftliche Buchgesellschaft, 1964.

Holzinger, Alfred. "Sittenbild oder Weltdeutung — Das Werk Arthur Schnitzlers," *Wort in der Zeit,* 7, No. 10 (1961), 33-36.

Hutschneider, Josef. "Arthur Schnitzler als Aphoristiker. Bemerkungen zu seinem *Buch der Sprüche und Bedenken,*" *Journal of the International Arthur Schnitzler Research Association,* 4, No. 2 (1965), 4-19.

Ilmer, Frida. "Schnitzler's Attitudes with Regard to the Transcendental," *Germanic Review,* 10, No. 2 (1935), 114-125.

Imboden, Michael. *Die surreale Komponente im erzählenden Werk Arthur Schnitzlers.* Bern-Frankfurt am Main: Verlag Herbert Lang & Cie. AG, 1971.

Jahn, Johannes. *Wörterbuch der Kunst.* Stuttgart: Alfred Kröner Verlag, 1966.

Joël, Karl. *Seele und Welt. Versuch einer organischen Auffassung.* Jena: Eugen Diederichs, 1912.

Johnston, William M. *The Austrian Mind. An Intellectual and Social History 1848-1938.* Los Angeles: University of California Press, 1972.

Jolles, André. *Einfache Formen.* Tübingen: Max Niemeyer Verlag, 1968.

Kammeyer, Max-Peter. "Die Dramaturgie von Tod und Liebe im Werk Arthur Schnitzlers, Diss. Wien, 1960.

Kann, Robert A. "The Image of the Austrian in Arthur Schnitzler's Writings," in: *Studies in Arthur Schnitzler.* Eds. Herbert W. Reichert and Hermann Salinger. Chapel Hill: The University of North Carolina Press, 1963, pp. 45-70.

————. "Das Österreich Arthur Schnitzlers," *Forum,* 6, No. 71 (1959), 421-423.

Kapp, Julius. *Arthur Schnitzler.* Leipzig: Xenien-Verlag, 1912.

Kaufmann, Friedrich Wilhelm. "Zur Frage der Wertung in Schnitzlers Werk," *PLMA,* 48 (1933), 209-219.

Kilian, Klaus.	*Die Komödien Arthur Schnitzlers. Sozialer Rollenzwang und kritische Ethik.* Düsseldorf: Bertelsmann Universitätsverlag, 1972.
Klarmann, Adolf D.	"Arthur Schnitzler und der Existentialismus," *Journal of the International Arthur Schnitzler Research Association,* 2, No. 2 (1963), 35-37.
————.	"Arthur Schnitzler und wir," *Modern Austrian Literature,* 1, No. 2 (1968), 9-27.
Köhler, Selma.	"The Question of Moral Responsibility in the Dramatic Works of Arthur Schnitzler," *Journal of English and Germanic Philology,* 22 (1923), 376-411.
Körner, Josef.	*Arthur Schnitzlers Gestalten und Probleme.* Zürich-Leipzig-Wien: Amalthea-Verlag, 1921.
————.	"Arthur Schnitzlers Spätwerk," *Preussische Jahrbücher,* 208, No. 1 (1927), 53-83; 208, No. 2 (1927), 153-163.
Langer, William L., ed.	*An Encyclopedia of World History.* Boston: Houghton Mifflin Co., 1958.
Lederer, Herbert.	"Arthur Schnitzler: A Chronicle of Loneliness," *German Quarterly,* 30, No. 1 (1957), 82-94.
————.	"The Problem of Ethics in the Works of Arthur Schnitzler," Diss. Chicago, 1953.
————.	"Arthur Schnitzler's Topology. An Excursion into Philosophy," *PLMA,* 78 (1963), 394-406.
Liptzin, Solomon.	*Arthur Schnitzler.* New York: Prentice-Hall, Inc., 1932.
————.	"The Call of Death and the Lure of Love. A Study in Schnitzler," *German Quarterly,* 5-6 (1932-33), 21-36.
————.	"Genesis of Schnitzler's 'Das weite Land'," *PMLA,* 46 (1931), 860-866.
————.	"The Genesis of Schnitzler's 'Der einsame Weg'," *Journal of English and Germanic Philology,* 30 (1931), 392-404.
LoCicero Vincent.	"A Study of the Persona in Selected Works of Arthur Schnitzler," *Modern Austrian Literature,* 2, No. 4 (1969), 7-29.
Lonergran, S. J., Bernard, J. F.	*Method in Theology.* New York: Herder and Herder, 1972.

Lopatta, Rudolf.	"Der Einfluss des 1. Weltkriegs auf die österreichische Dramatik," Diss. Wien, 1951.
Lothar, Ernst.	"Tod und Renaissance," *Forum,* 9 (1962), 213-216.
Lucka, Emil.	"Arthur Schnitzler als Charakterologe," *Die Literatur,* 29, No. 8 (1927), 455-457.
Martini, Fritz.	*Deutsche Literaturgeschichte von den Anfängen bis zur Gegenwart.* Stuttgart: Alfred Kröner Verlag, 1965.
Melchinger, Christa.	*Illusion und Wirklichkeit im dramatischen Werk von Arthur Schnitzler.* Heidelberg: Carl Winter Universitätsverlag, 1968.
Müller-Freienfels, Reinhart.	"Das Lebensgefühl in Arthur Schnitzlers Dramen," Diss. Frankfurt, 1954.
Offermanns, Ernst L.	*Arthur Schnitzler. Das Komödienwerk als Kritik des Impressionismus.* München: Wilhelm Fink Verlag, 1973.
Perl, Walter H.	"Arthur Schnitzler und das Theater von heute," *Journal of the International Arthur Schnitzler Research Association,* 2, No. 3 (1963), 28-31.
Plant, Richard.	"Notes on Arthur Schnitzler's Literary Technique," *Germanic Review,* 25, No. 1 (1950), 13-25.
Politzer, Heinz.	"Arthur Schnitzler: The Poet of Psychology," *Modern Language Notes,* 78 (1963), 353-372.
————.	"Diagnose und Dichtung," *Forum,* 9, No. 101 (1962), 217-219; No. 102 (1962), 266-270.
Polsterer, Susanne M.	"Die Darstellung der Frauen in Arthur Schnitzlers Dramen," Diss. Wien, 1949.
Rasch, Wolfdietrich.	"Aspekte der deutschen Literatur um 1900," in: *Zur deutschen Literatur seit der Jahrhundertwende.* Stuttgart: J. B. Metzlersche Verlagsbuchhandlung, 1967, pp. 1-48.
————.	"Tanz als Lebenssymbol im Drama um 1900," In: *Zur deutschen Literatur seit der Jahrhundertwende.* Stuttgart: J. B. Metzlersche Verlagsbuchhandlung, 1967, pp. 58-77.
Rehm, Walther.	*Der Dichter und die neue Einsamkeit. Aufsätze zur Literatur um 1900.* Göttingen: Vandenhoeck & Ruprecht, 1969.
Reichert, Herbert W.	"Nietzsche and Schnitzler," in: *Studies in Arthur Schnitzler.* Eds. Herbert W. Reichert and Hermann Salinger. Chapel Hill: The University of North Carolina Press, 1963, pp. 95-108.

Reik, Theodor.	*Arthur Schnitzler als Psycholog.* Minden/Westf.: J. C. C. Bruns, 1913.
Reiss, H. S.	"The Problem of Fate and Religion in the Work of Arthur Schnitzler," *Modern Language Review,* 40, No. 4 (1945), 300-308.
Rey, William H.	*Arthur Schnitzler. Die späte Prosa als Gipfel seines Schaffens.* Berlin: Erich Schmidt Verlag, 1968.
————.	"Beiträge zur amerikanischen Schnitzlerforschung," *German Quarterly,* 37, No. 3 (1964), 282-288.
————.	"Arthur Schnitzler," in: *Deutsche Dichter der Moderne. Ihr Leben und Werk.* Ed. Benno von Wiese. Berlin: Erich Schmidt Verlag, 1975, pp. 247-269.
————.	"Die geistige Welt Arthur Schnitzlers," *Wirkendes Wort,* 16, No. 3 (1966), 180-194.
————.	"Schnitzler in neuer Sicht. Ein bedeutender Forschungsbeitrag aus Frankreich," *Modern Austrian Literature,* 1, No. 1 (1968), 31-39.
Roseeu, Robert.	*Arthur Schnitzler.* Berlin: Wilhelm Borngräber Verlag Neues Leben, 1913.
Rosenbaum, Uwe.	"Die Gestalt des Schauspielers auf dem deutschen Theater des 19. Jahrhunderts mit der besonderen Berücksichtigung der dramatischen Werke von Hermann Bahr, Arthur Schnitzler und Heinrich Mann," Diss. Köln, 1971.
Salkind, Alexander.	*Arthur Schnitzler. Eine kritische Studie über seine hervorragendsten Werke.* Berlin-Leipzig: Modernes Verlagsbüro Curt Wigand, 1907.
Scheible, Hartmut.	*Arthur Schnitzler in Selbstzeugnissen und Bilddokumenten.* Rowohlt Monographien. Ed. Kurt Kusenberg. Reinbek b. Hamburg: Rowohlt Taschenbuch Verlag, 1976.
Schinnerer, Otto P.	"The Literary Apprenticeship of Arthur Schnitzler," *Germanic Review,* 5 (1930), 58-82.
Schlein, Rena R.	"Arthur Schnitzler: Author-Scientist," *Modern Austrian Literature,* 1, No. 2 (1968), 28-38.
Schmidt, Willa Elizabeth.	"The Changing Role of Women in the Works of Arthur Schnitzler," Diss. University of Wisconsin, 1973.

Schnitzler, Heinrich.	" 'Gay Vienna' — Myth and Reality," *Journal of the History of Ideas,* 15, No. 1 (1954), 94-118.
Schnitzler, Olga.	*Spiegelbild der Freundschaft. Erinnerungen an Arthur Schnitzler.* Salzburg: Residenz Verlag, 1962.
Schorske, Carl E.	"Politics and the Psyche in Fin de Siècle Vienna: Schnitzler and Hofmannsthal," *American Historical Review,* 56 (1961), 930-946.
Singer, Herta.	"Zeit und Gesellschaft im Werk Arthur Schnitzlers," Diss. Wien, 1948.
Specht, Richard.	*Arthur Schnitzler. Der Dichter und sein Werk. Eine Studie.* Berlin: S. Fischer Verlag, 1922.
Stroka, Anna.	"Arthur Schnitzlers Tragikomödien," *Acta Universitatis Wratislaviensis* No. 128, *Germanica Wratislaviensia,* 14 (1971), 55-73.
Swales, Martin.	*Arthur Schnitzler. A Critical Study.* Oxford: University Press, 1971.
————.	"Arthur Schnitzler as a Moralist," *Modern Language Review,* 62 (1967), 462-475.
Szondi, Peter.	*Theorie des modernen Dramas.* Frankfurt am Main: Suhrkamp Verlag, 1959.
Thyriot, Hans.	" 'Im Spiel der Sommerlüfte.' Von Arthur Schnitzler. (Uraufführung im Stadttheater am 4. April 1931)," *Die Literatur,* 33 (1931), 514.
Török, Andreas.	"Der Liebestod bei Arthur Schnitzler: Eine Entlehnung von Richard Wagner," *Modern Austrian Literature,* 4, No. 1 (1971), 57-59.
Tuchman, Barbara W.	*The Guns of August.* New York: Dell Publishing Co., Inc., 1962.
Urbach, Reinhard.	*Arthur Schnitzler.* Velber b. Hannover: Friedrich Verlag, 1968.
————.	*Schnitzler Kommentar zu den erzählenden Schriften und dramatischen Werken.* München: Winkler Verlag, 1974.
Viereck, George Sylvester.	*Glimpses of the Great.* New York: The Macaulay Company, 1930.
————.	"The World of Arthur Schnitzler," *Modern Austrian Literature,* 5, No. 3/4 (1972), 7-17.

Wagner, Richard.	*Der fliegende Holländer.* Illustrated text No. 8 20 164-166. Berlin: VEB Deutsche Schallplatten.
——————.	*Lohengrin.* Nos. 121-125 in the Angel International Series.
——————.	*Tannhäuser und der Sängerkrieg auf der Wartburg.* Text No. UR 211. Kearny, N. J.: Urania Records Corp., US 5211.

Webster's New Collegiate Dictionary, based on *Webster's New International Dictionary*, 2nd ed., 1959.

Weiss, Robert O.	"Arthur Schnitzler's Literary and Philosophical Development," *Journal of the International Arthur Schnitzler Research Association*, 2, No. 1 (1963), 4-20.
——————.	"Arthur Schnitzler's Notes on Journalistic Criticism," *Germanic Review*, 38, No. 3 (1963), 226-237.
——————.	"The Human Element in Arthur Schnitzler's Social Criticism," *Modern Austrian Literature*, 5, Nos. 1/2 (1972), 30-44.
Werfel, Franz.	"Arthur Schnitzler zu seinem 60. Geburtstag," *Neue Rundschau*, 33 (1922), 488-513.
Wheelwright, Philip.	*Metaphor and Reality.* Bloomington: Indiana University Press, 1962.
Whiton, John Nelson.	"The Problem of Marriage in the Works of Arthur Schnitzler," Diss. University of Minnesota, 1967.
Whittick, Arnold.	*Symbols — Signs and Their Meaning and Uses in Design.* London: Leonard Hill, 1971.
Wilpert, Gero von.	*Sachwörterbuch der Literatur.* Stuttgart: Alfred Kröner Verlag, 1964.
Ziolkowski, Theodore.	"The Metaphysics of Death," in: *Dimensions of the Modern Novel. German Texts and European Contexts.* New Jersey: Princeton University Press, 1969, pp. 215-257.
Zucker, A. E.	"Arthur Schnitzler, 'Im Spiel der Sommerlüfte'," *Germanic Review*, 6, No. 1 (1931), 91-93.

INDEX

Alewyn, Richard: 9, 18, 20, 22, 40, 42, 141, 143 ff., 159.
Allen, Richard H.: 11, 141, 142.
Apsler, Alfred: 107, 156.
Arnold, Robert F.: 45, 115, 148, 157.
Aspetsberger, Friedbert: 18, 141, 144, 145.
Bahr, Hermann: 141.
Baumann, Gerhart: 9, 91, 152, 155, 157.
Beckett, Samuel: 148.
Beer-Hofmann, Richard: 11, 157.
Beharriel, Frederick J.: 10, 11, 141, 142.
Berend, Alice: 101.
Bergel, Kurt: 15, 41 f., 83, 101, 143, 147 ff., 154 ff.
Berlin, Jeffrey B.: 141.
Blume, Bernhard: 72, 108, 116, 121, 144, 146, 148, 152 f., 156, 158.
Boner, Georgette: 19 f., 37, 40, 104, 127, 145, 147, 156, 158.
Brandes, Georg: 15, 41 f., 83, 101, 147 ff., 154 f.
Burger, Heinz Otto: 143.
Bux/Schöne/Lamer/Kroh: 150, 159.
Charmatz, Richard: 15, 144, 149.
Chekhov, Anton Pavlovich: 113, 148, 157.
Cirlot, Juan Eduardo: 87, 93, 95, 106, 129 ff., 154 ff., 158 f.
Cysarz, Herbert: 91, 141, 155.
Davis, Evan B.: 37, 50, 97, 107, 123, 126 f., 132, 145, 147, 150, 153 ff., 158 f.
DeLay, Brigitte Anne: 12 f., 142.
Derré, Françoise: 9, 18 ff., 49, 72, 86, 97, 99, 115 ff., 144 f., 152, 154 f., 157.
Dickerson, Jr., Harold D.: 86, 90, 92, 138, 141, 154 f.
Dürrenmatt, Friedrich: 148.
Foltin, Lore B.: 110, 141 143, 154, 156.
Freud, Sigmund: 102, 155.
Friedrichsmeyer, Erhard: 143.
Frisch, Max: 148.
Goethe, Johann Wolfgang von: 117 f., 135, 157.
Green, Jon D.: 145.
Grillparzer, Franz: 86, 99, 155.
Grimm, Jakob und Wilhelm: 67.
Der Grosse Duden, vols. 5, 7: 150.

Gutt, Barbara: 143.
Henkel/Schöne: 76, 153.
Hofmannsthal, Hugo von: 11, 42, 71, 80, 90, 141, 143, 148, 153, 159.
Holl, Karl: 141.
Ilmer, Frida: 143.
Imboden, Michael: 9, 91, 93, 110, 155 f.
Jahn, Johannes: 20, 145.
Jöel, Karl: 134 f., 159.
Johnston, William M.: 145.
Jolles, André: 65, 151 f.
Kammeyer, Max-Peter: 49 f., 90, 149 f., 153 f., 156.
Kann, Robert: 19, 143, 145.
Kaufmann, Friedrich Wilhelm: 102, 141, 155.
Kilian, Klaus: 9, 17 f., 43, 50, 144, 146 ff.
Klarmann, Adolf D.: 152.
Köhler, Selma: 147.
Körner, Joseph: 10 ff., 15, 19, 37 ff., 46, 48 ff., 53, 73, 75, 78, 80, 83 ff., 91, 98 f., 102, 105 f., 110, 116, 142 ff., 147, 149 f., 152 ff.
Krell, Max: 148.
Langer, William L.: 151.
Lederer, Herbert: 79, 103, 126, 143, 147, 153, 155, 158.
Liptzin, Sol: 12, 37 f., 45, 50, 86, 89, 99, 103 ff., 111, 116, 120 f., 142, 144, 147 f., 150, 154 ff.
LoCicero, Vincent: 75, 80, 110, 138, 141, 152 f., 156.
Lonergran, S.J., Bernard J. F.: 9, 141.
Lothar, Ernst: 141.
Martini, Fritz: 141.
Maupassant, Guy de: 148.
Melchinger, Christa: 49, 68, 147, 150, 152 f.
Mozart, Wolfgang Amadeus: 57.
Müller-Freienfels, Reinhart: 77, 108, 116, 120, 123, 126, 145, 151, 153, 156 ff.
Musil, Robert: 49.
Nadeau, Maurice: 91, 155.
Neumann/ Müller: 141, 157.
Offermanns, Ernst L.: 9, 17 f., 43, 46, 49, 59, 63, 69, 74, 80, 116, 144, 147 ff., 157. 157.
Pirandello, Luigi: 148.
Plant, Richard: 147.
Politzer, Heinz: 13, 142, 146, 148.
Polsterer, Susanne M.: 19, 103 f., 143, 145, 153, 156.
Rasch, Wolfdietrich: 104, 141, 156.
Reichert, Herbert W.: 9.
Reik, Theodor: 144 f., 152.

Reiss, H. S.: 143.
Rey, William H.: 9 ff., 13 f., 19, 23, 39, 41 ff., 90, 100, 102, 106 f., 110, 123, 138, 142 f., 145 ff., 152, 154 ff., 158.
Rilke, Rainer Maria: 115.
Roseeu, Robert: 144.
Rosenbaum, Uwe: 128, 146, 158.
Salten, Felix: 11, 141.
Scheible, Hartmut: 9, 46, 113, 115, 149, 151, 157.
Schiller, Friedrich von: 65.
Schinnerer, Otto P.: 105, 156.
Schlein, Rena R.: 19, 145.
Schmidt, Willa Elizabeth: 18 f., 42, 50, 103, 105, 117 f., 143 ff., 148, 150, 156 f.
Schnitzler, Heinrich (Henry): 19, 145.
Schorske, Carl E.: 151.
Seidel, Herbert: 151.
Seidlin, Oskar: 90, 143, 154.
Singer, Herta: 154, 158.
Specht, Richard: 90, 154 f.
Stroka, Anna: 123, 134, 159.
Swales, Martin: 9, 11, 13, 29, 40 f., 43, 86, 99, 100, 103, 116, 142, 145 ff., 154 ff.
Thyriot, Hans: 115, 157.
Török, Andreas: 72, 152.
Tuchmann, Barbara W.: 151.
Urbach, Reinhart: 9 ff., 15, 39, 45 f., 52 f., 72, 88, 117 f., 141 ff., 147 ff., 152 ff., 157 f.
Viereck, George Sylvester: 11, 16, 38 f., 142, 144, 147.
Wagner, Richard: 152 f.
Wassermann, Jakob: 41, 80, 101 f., 148, 153, 155.
Webster's New Collegiate Dictionary: 150, 153.
Weiss, Robert O.: 9, 14, 142.
Werfel, Franz: 142.
Whiton, John Nelson: 123, 145, 152, 158.
Whittock, Arnold: 89 f., 97, 154 f.
Wilpert, Gero von: 145, 151.
Ziolkowsky, Theodore: 143.
Zucker, A. E.: 116, 157.

INDEX OF REFERENCES TO WORKS BY SCHNITZLER
(Quotations of Letters Appear in the Previous Index under the Name of the Recipient)

Anatol: 13, 137.
Aphorismen und Betrachtungen: 23 f., 51, 59, 64, 72, 96, 127, 144 ff., 150, 152, 155, 157, 159.
"Aufzeichnungen aus der Kriegszeit. Aus dem Nachlass von Arthur Schnitzler.": 13, 79, 142, 153.
"Bemerkungen. Aus dem Nachlass.": 149, 152 f., 155.
Buch der Sprüche und Bedenken. Aphorismen und Fragmente: 11 f., 23, 35 f., 38 f., 69 f., 73, 76, 78, 80, 100, 102 f., 121, 138, 142, 144 ff., 152 f., 155 f., 158.
Casanovas Heimfahrt: 15, 37, 42, 156.
Der einsame Weg: 11.
Fink und Fliederbusch: 153.
Fräulein Else: 80.
Der Gang zum Weiher: 9, 13 f., 81, *83-111*, 113, 116, 131 ff., 137 f., 159.
"Gedanken über Kunst. Aus dem Nachlass.": 144, 156.
"Der Geist im Wort und der Geist in der Tat. Vorläufige Bemerkungen zu zwei Diagrammen.": 11, 14, 18, 20, 23, 34, 59, 127, 137, 143 f.
Der grüne Kakadu: 146.
Die Hirtenflöte: 45, 50, 73.
Im Spiel der Sommerlüfte: 9, 13 f., 105, 108, 111, *113-135*, 137 f., 146.
Jugend in Wien. Eine Autobiographie: 33, 132, 146, 151, 159.
Komödie der Verführung: 9, 13, 17, 38, 43, *45-81*, 83, 101, 104 ff., 113, 116, 123, 131 ff., 137 f., 145 f., 152, 156.
Komödie der Worte: 11, 130, 146.
Liebelei: 11, 156.
Paracelsus: 115, 142.
Professor Bernhardi: 11, 149.
Tagebücher: 157.
Die Schwestern oder Casanova in Spa: 9, 13, *15-43*, 45 f., 52 f., 70 ff., 78 f., 84, 105, 107, 109, 113, 116, 131, 133 f., 137, 146.
Sterben: 12.
Über Krieg und Frieden : 14, 79, 137, 142.
Der Weg ins Freie: 13.
Das weite Land: 13, 45, 158.
Zwischenspiel: 73.